SF

D1341830

LV 32128495
Liverpool Libraries

Match of My Life

FA CUP FINALS
1953 - 1969

KNOW THE SCORE BOOKS PUBLICATIONS

CULT HEROES	Author	ISBN
CHELSEA	Leo Moynihan	1-905449-00-3
MANCHESTER CITY	David Clayton	978-1-905449-05-7
NEWCASTLE	Dylan Younger	1-905449-03-8
SOUTHAMPTON	Jeremy Wilson	1-905449-01-1
WEST BROM	Simon Wright	1-905449-02-X

MATCH OF MY LIFE	Editor	ISBN
ENGLAND WORLD CUP	Massarella & Moynihan	1-905449-52-6
EUROPEAN CUP FINALS	Ben Lyttleton	1-905449-57-7
FA CUP FINALS 1953-1969	David Saffer	978-1-905449-53-8
FULHAM	Michael Heatley	1-905449-51-8
LEEDS	David Saffer	1-905449-54-2
LIVERPOOL	Leo Moynihan	1-905449-50-X
SHEFFIELD UNITED	Nick Johnson	1-905449-62-3
STOKE CITY	Simon Lowe	978-1-905449-55-2
SUNDERLAND	Rob Mason	1-905449-60-7
SPURS	Allen & Massarella	978-1-905449-58-3
WOLVES	Simon Lowe	1-905449-56-9

HARRY HARRIS	Author	ISBN
WORLD CUP DIARY	Harry Harris	1-905449-90-9
HOLD THE BACK PAGE	Harry Harris	1-905449-91-7

AUTOBIOGRAPHY	Author	ISBN
TACKLES LIKE A FERRET (England Cover)	Paul Parker	1-905449-47-X
TACKLES LIKE A FERRET (Manchester United Cover)	Paul Parker	1-905449-46-1

FOOTBALL FICTION	Author	ISBN
BURKSEY The Autobiography of a Football God	Peter Morfoot	1-905449-49-6

CRICKET	Author	ISBN
MOML: THE ASHES	Pilger & Wightman	1-905449-63-1

FORTHCOMING PUBLICATIONS IN 2007

CULT HEROES	Author	ISBN
CARLISLE UNITED	Mark Harrison	978-1-905449-09-7
CELTIC	David Potter	978-1-905449-08-8
NOTTINGHAM FOREST	David McVay	978-1-905449-06-4
RANGERS	Paul Smith	978-1-905449-07-1

MATCH OF MY LIFE	Editor	ISBN
ASTON VILLA	Neil Moxley	978-1-905449-65-1
BOLTON WANDERERS	David Saffer	978-1-905449-64-4
DERBY COUNTY	Johnson & Matthews	978-1-905449-68-2
MANCHESTER UNITED	Brian Hughes	978-1-905449-59-0

GENERAL FOOTBALL	Author	ISBN
CHAMPIONS LEAGUE YEARBOOK	Harry Harris	978-1-905449-93-4
OUTCASTS The Lands FIFA Forgot	Steve Menary	978-1-905449-31-6
PARISH TO PLANET A History of Football	Dr Eric Midwinter	978-1-905449-30-9
MY PREMIERSHIP DIARY Reading's Season in the Premiership	Marcus Hahnemann	978-1-905449-33-0

CRICKET	Author	ISBN
GROVEL! The 1976 West IndiesTour of England	David Tossell	978-1-905449-43-9
MY AUTOBIOGRAPHY	Shaun Udal	978-1-905449-42-2
WASTED?	Paul Smith	978-1-905449-45-3
LEAGUE CRICKET YEARBOOK North West edition	Andy Searle	978-1-905449-70-5
LEAGUE CRICKET YEARBOOK North East edition	Andy Searle	978-1-905449-71-2
LEAGUE CRICKET YEARBOOK Midlands edition	Andy Searle	978-1-905449-72-9

Match of My Life

FA CUP FINALS 1953 - 1969

Editor: David Saffer
Series Editor: Simon Lowe

www.knowthescorebooks.com

First published in the United Kingdom
by Know The Score Books Limited, 2007
Copyright David Saffer, 2007

This book is copyright under the Berne convention.

No part of this book may be reproduced, sold or utilised in any form or transmitted in any form or by any means, electronic or mechanical, including photocopying, recording or by any information storage and retrieval system, without prior permission in writing from the Publisher.

© and ® Know The Score Books Limited. All rights reserved. 2007

The right of David Saffer to be identified as the author of this work has been asserted by him in accordance with sections 77 and 78 of the Copyright, Designs and Patents Act, 1988.

Know The Score Books Limited
118 Alcester Road
Studley
Warwickshire
B80 7NT
01527 454482
info@knowthescorebooks.com

www.knowthescorebooks.com

A CIP catalogue record is available for this book from the British Library
ISBN: 978-1-905449-53-8

Jacket and book design by Lisa David

Printed and bound in Great Britain
By Cromwell Press, Trowbridge, Wiltshire

Mixed Sources
Product group from well-managed
forests and other controlled sources
www.fsc.org Cert no. TT-TOC-2082
© 1996 Forest Stewardship Council
FSC

Photographs in this book are reproduced by kind permission of:
Colorsport, EMPICS

Front cover:
Top left: Spurs' double winning team of 1961 show off the FA Cup.
Bottom left: Stanley Matthews is chaired from the field having prompted
Blackpool's incredible comeback to win the 1953 'Matthews Final'.
Bottom right: Bobby Moore celebrates with the FA Cup after West
Ham's win in 1964.

Rear cover:
Top left: Captain Brian Labone collects the 1966 FA Cup from Her
Majesty The Queen after Everton's incredible comeback victory against
Sheffield Wednesday.
Top right: The programme from the legendary 1953 'Matthews Final'.
Bottom: From left, Maurice Setters, captain Noel Cantwell and Paddy
Crerand celebrate Manchester United's victory in the 1963 final.

Editor's Acknowledgements

Thanks go to all the players who took part in this exciting project and enjoyed rolling back the years to remember their glorious Wembley moments. Also to Nottingham Forest FC, Miranda at West Ham United FC, Neil Rioch, chairman of Aston Villa Former Players Association, Simon and Glynis Wright, Laraine Astle, Dave Woodhall, Adrian Goldberg, Louis Massarella, Matt Allen, Leo Moynihan, Peter Creed, Roger Martin and, of course, to my publisher Simon Lowe.

David Saffer
April 2007

Chapters on Spurs' 1961, 1962 and 1967 FA Cup wins have previously been published in part in 'Match Of My Life - Spurs', while the chapter on Wolves' 1960 triumph was previously published in part in 'Match Of My Life - Wolves', and the chapter on Liverpool's 1965 FA Cup victory was previously published in part in 'Match Of My Life - Liverpool'.

Contents

Introduction

The FA Cup is the oldest and most prestigious knockout competition in the world. Of the 126 finals thus far, 73 took place at the old Wembley Stadium. The 'Twin Towers' were truly twinned with so many seminal moments of the tournament's history, and even though Cardiff's Millennium Stadium has hosted spectacular occasions from 2001 to 2006, it does not have Wembley's iconic attraction.

In May 2007, the new Wembley Stadium stages its first FA Cup final and to celebrate, *Match of My Life - FA Cup Finals 1953-1969* tells the story of what it means to a footballer to win the Cup at the competition's spiritual home and fulfill the classic boyhood dream.

This volume relives a truly golden era in the game. It was a time when every football team boasted star players and numerous top sides shared the two major domestic trophies. For every football fan, the FA Cup final was a magical occasion; the occasion of the year. It was live on television, a rarity at the time. In addition, the build up started from mid-morning on both terrestrial channels, BBC and ITV, and every conceivable angle about the two teams was analysed. There was Cup Final Mastermind, cameras at the team hotels, on the team buses and in the dressing rooms of the victors afterwards. It made compulsive viewing.

The first FA Cup final took place on 16 March 1872 when the Wanderers defeated Royal Engineers at Kennington Oval. From 1923, the final was resident at Wembley and, during the coming three decades, legends came to the fore in their pursuit of winning the trophy; the 'White Horse', the Arsenal goalkeeping jersey, the Zeppelin final, Jack Tinn's lucky spats, the Wolves 'Monkey Glands' scandal, the bursting ball of 1946 and those three legendary victories for Newcastle in the 1950s.

It is at this point we begin to tell the tale of what it is like to win the Cup, because on 2 May 1953, Blackpool, inspired by Stanley Matthews, roared back from a 3-1 deficit to claim a famous 4-3 victory with a last-minute Bill Perry goal. Not only was this an incredible comeback, but the entire nation, Bolton fans excepting, were willing Stan to finally win an FA Cup medal. Perhaps most importantly for the development of the Cup final as the most important football match in any year, that match was the first for which television sets were available to the mass audience of the British working class. Football was, after all, their game and men like Matthews gave them cause to dream. For that is what the FA Cup is about as much as anything else; dreams.

Since the 'Matthews final', there have been many more iconic Cup final moments. Who could ever forget Bert Trautmann's bravery for Manchester City in 1956, Tottenham Hotspur's 'double' triumph in 1961 - the first for 64 years, Everton's sensational comeback in 1966, Sunderland's shock win in 1973, Norman Whiteside's stunning winner for ten-man Manchester United in 1985, Wimbledon's unlikely victory in 1988, Arsenal's last-gasp triumph in 1993, Roberto Di Matteo's wonder-strike for Chelsea in 1997 and Steven Gerrard's late equaliser for Liverpool in 2006. All are part of FA Cup folklore.

Five decades ago, playing in a Wembley cup final was rare, as only the League Cup (from 1967) and FA Cup offered an opportunity outside England home internationals. Many of the finest players to grace the game never walked the hallowed turf of Wembley, so playing in a final; especially the FA Cup final, was a top priority. Fewer still won. Tom Finney, Bobby Robson, George Best and Johnny Haynes all failed to lift the Cup. Frank McLintock famously won just one of his six final appearances, Matthews himself, one from three.

All that conferred mythical and mystical status upon almost every aspect of the stadium from lucky changing rooms, to the tunnel end, the colour of coat worn by the guest of honour to the ability of the pitch to weary the legs of even the stoutest man, the singing of *Abide With Me* and that old quiz question about what is always taken to Wembley and never used. In short, Wembley is the FA Cup final. The two became synonymous over the period described in this book and the memories that the players provide of some incredible finals, controversy, heartache and glory show why both they and millions of fans fell in love with the Wembley Cup final.

This then is the backdrop to *Match of My Life - FA Cup Finals 1953-1969*. Meeting and interviewing 16 giants of the game has been a truly amazing journey and I am indebted to all the players who contributed. Packed with anecdotes, the interviews would not have been possible without statistical information to jog memories, so I am indebted to my good friend and fellow football author Phil Goldstone for unlimited use of his vast football book library.

Brian Labone passed away in April 2006, less than a fortnight after being interviewed for this book. Like all football followers, I felt deeply saddened by Brian's death. I was privileged to meet him and will not forget the laughs we shared during his recollections of how Everton enjoyed FA Cup glory in 1966. For Brian, lifting the shining trophy was the moment of his life. He was Everton through and through and the passion of that moment meant everything to him.

So 54 years to the day from the 'Matthews final', as the final returns to the new Wembley, settle back and reminisce about the times when Bill Perry, Jimmy Dugdale, Vic Keeble, Bert Trautmann, Peter McParland, Tommy Banks, Chic Thomson, Norman Deeley, Dave Mackay, Bill Foulkes, John Bond, Ian Callaghan, Brian Labone, Pat Jennings, Tony Brown and Neil Young ruled the roost and won the FA Cup.

David Saffer
April 2007

Dedication

This book is dedicated to Sir Stanley Matthews.

Wembley's inspiration.

BILL PERRY 1953
LEFT-WING 1949–1965

BORN   10 September 1930, Johannesburg
SIGNED   November 1949 from Johannesburg
BLACKPOOL CAREER   436 appearances, 129 goals
HONOURS   1 FA Cup, 3 full England caps, Football League representative
LEFT   Transferred to Southport, June 1962

A legendary stalwart during Blackpool's greatest era; twice Bill Perry helped the Seasiders reach Wembley during a golden period of three finals in six years. A goal-maker rather than goal-getter, Perry carved his name into Cup final folklore when he scored the winning goal in the 1953 final, a match now renowned the world over as the 'Matthews Final'. The popular South African converted Stan Matthews' last minute cross to complete the most remarkable comeback in FA Cup final history, after his side had been 3-1 down, 22 minutes from time.

Blackpool 4 v Bolton Wanderers 3

FA Cup final
Saturday 2 May 1953

Wembley Stadium
Attendance 100,000
Gate Receipts £49,900

The greatest comeback of Cup final history sees Stan Mortensen score a hat-trick and Bill Perry the last minute winner, but still lose out on the naming rights to the incomparable Stanley Matthews

Teams

Joe Smith	**Managers**	Bill Ridding
George Farm	1	Stan Hanson
Eddie Shimwell	2	John Ball
Tom Garrett	3	Ralph Banks
Ewan Fenton	4	John Wheeler
Harry Johnston (capt.)	5	Malcolm Barrass
Cyril Robinson	6	Eric Bell
Stanley Matthews	7	Doug Holden
Ernie Taylor	8	Willie Moir (capt.)
Stan Mortensen	9	Nat Lofthouse
Jackie Mudie	10	Harold Hassall
Bill Perry	11	Bobby Langton
Mortensen 35, 68, 89 Perry 90	**Scorers**	Lofthouse 2, Moir 40 Bell 55

Referee: B Griffiths

THE WHOLE THING FELT like a whirlwind. One minute we were down and out, 3-1 behind with barely any time left to play. The next we were level again and pressing back a Bolton team smitten by injuries and reeling from the storm of attacks we'd subjected them to. It was incredible. Everyone was rapt in the moment as Stan Matthews sped away down our right flank yet again. My legs carried me forwards almost by instinct and when Stan sent the ball across it found me, 12 yards out in the centre of goal. Wembley was offering me an appointment with destiny.

During my football career, I represented England and played for one of the top teams during the 1950s. Blackpool may have fallen on hard times in recent decades, but in the golden age of football, they competed against the top First Division sides and reached three FA Cup finals. I played in two finals, the latter 1953, which gripped the nation because many believed it was the last that would offer the great Stanley Matthews a chance to win a cup winners medal. Blackpool had lost in 1948 and 1951, so hopefully it was going to be third time lucky for Stan and the Seasiders.

My journey to Blackpool started in Johannesburg, South Africa, a country better known for its rugby players than soccer players. Today, that is no longer the case, but in the 1940s when I was growing up, the Springboks were the best-known sporting icons.

I played rugby union at junior school in Johannesburg and as a loose forward proved quite useful before attending Queens Junior High School. Queens didn't play rugby union, so I took up soccer. I was 14 and naturally right-footed, but the only position vacant was outside-left. I was terrified of the sports master, so knew I would have to get my left leg going to cross the ball and keep my place in the side. I practiced all the time by kicking a tennis ball against a wall and must have done enough because I represented the U14 and U15 sides on a regular basis. My constant practicing did me a favour because when I joined Johannesburg Rangers after I left school at 16, I was competent both on the left and right wing.

All sides were amateur in those days, so I began an apprenticeship at a car parts factory whilst playing and waited for my opportunity. It quickly came when the regular outside left was injured and I never looked back. For around three years, I played in Rangers' U16 and U18 sides and represented Transvaal Province against Cape Province in the Currie Cup.

During the summer of 1948, Charlton Athletic manager Jimmy Seed approached me to consider trying my luck in England. Our football season ran opposite to the English football season, so Jimmy regularly scouted in South Africa looking for talent. It was a great opportunity for players because all we wanted as a guarantee was our return fare if we did not make the grade. It was like a working holiday.

I didn't know a lot about English football apart from the FA Cup. Everyone looked forward to cup final day in South Africa. Nobody had a television, so we used to listen to the match commentary on radio. The first final that I recall was Charlton Athletic against Derby County in 1946, a match in which ironically Jimmy won a cup winners medal as a player. I was only 18, so discussed the options with my parents, but I also took advice from Rangers coach Billy Butler, who'd played in the first cup final at Wembley in 1923 for Bolton Wanderers. Billy often told us what it was like to play at Wembley with the crowd and atmosphere, so the competition was something special to me from an early age.

Billy told me not to rush into a decision. If I was thinking about joining Charlton, other teams might be better suited. Billy told me it would be easier to play in a good team than a bad team. He knew Blackpool manager Joe Smith, who captained Bolton in their win over West Ham, and asked if Joe would take me on. Joe agreed. Charlton were not a bad team, but Stan Matthews was at Blackpool and everyone knew what a great player he was. My fate was sealed.

Blackpool had lost to Manchester United in the 1948 final, so I was aware of the club, and, of course, I knew all about Stan's reputation. Eventually, in October 1949, I boarded an ocean-liner at Cape Town and arrived at Southampton two weeks later. It was my first time outside South Africa. After a trial, Blackpool offered me a one-year contract on the understanding that if I didn't make it, I had my return ticket paid. I was determined to succeed.

Stan Matthews was a factor in me coming over, but he wasn't the main reason. I had a contract based on my own ability and Blackpool was a good place to be as I would be beside the seaside. In the 1950s there were no package holidays abroad, families travelled to British seaside resorts, so Blackpool was packed during the summer season. The town was buzzing.

I recall at the time in England that there was still rationing of sweets and meat, but clothes were not restricted. My salary was £12 a week; we got £2 bonus if we won and £1 if we drew. Blackpool was a team packed with international players. Over the years, supporters have often asked me what our team would be worth today. It is impossible to speculate. How could you put a value on the likes of Stan Matthews and Stan Mortenson, skipper Harry Johnson, Ernie Taylor and Jackie Mudie? Our team was packed with star names and we always entertained.

Crowds at football matches were massive. There was no swearing like today and no segregation, everyone mingled. The atmosphere was fantastic; there was tremendous banter between the players and supporters and there was no better time to be a professional footballer.

George Farm was a very good goalkeeper. He was brave, but rather unorthodox when catching a ball because it looked as if it may slip between his arms, but it rarely did. George was strong, but not a great dead ball kicker, so Eddie Shimwell took a lot of the goal-kicks. Eddie played right back and was a strong tackler. He was tough and preferred to slide tackle rather than shoulder charge. Left-back Tommy Garrett complemented Eddie at full-back. Tommy was skilful and preferred to play his way out of trouble rather than hoof the ball clear.

Centre-half Eric Hayward was underrated, but strong in the air and a solid tackler. Captain Harry Johnston played half-back and was the rock in defence. Harry was a very good skipper, forceful but very fair. He played hard and expected every one else to do the same thing. Harry led by example. Ewan Fenton broke into the side at half back, was a shrewd passer of the ball and joined the attack at every opportunity.

Ernie Taylor may have been only five foot four inches tall, but he was a very good ball player, as accurate as David Beckham in his heyday in his passes. Although he played inside-right, many of my goals for Blackpool came from Ernie's passes. Hughie Kelly was a sturdy wing-half and superb passer of the ball and complementing him was Allan Brown, who scored crucial goals from midfield. Jackie Mudie would soon break into the side and prove a good striker.

Stan Mortenson led the attack. Morty had a tremendous shot, a bullet header, was quick and scored fantastic goals. I think he scored more with his head than his feet. Stan was an old-fashioned type centre-forward and led the line brilliantly. Morty was as good as any centre-forward in the First Division and was also the biggest character in the dressing room. He was a bit of a comedian, always cracking jokes about the place and kept everybody in good spirits. Morty was also the most superstitions amongst us, coming last on to the field.

Then, of course, we had Stan Matthews, and what a player. When you played alongside someone like Stan, you really appreciated his skill. I played with him week in and week out, both in training and in matches, and he was absolute magic. Stan had a fantastic body swerve and superb balance, his timing was brilliant. The first five yards is the most important when you are a winger and that was true for Stan. In those first five yards, that is when he got away from his full-back. Once Stan was past, he was never caught.

As a person, Stan was quiet, modest and trained on his own. Not that he didn't want to mix with the other players, it was just his manner. He used to get butterflies before every match, loved the tension and got worked up before he went out. Stan used to say, "if I don't get butterflies before a match I am not right for the game". Blackpool was the most popular away team for crowds and that was mainly due to Stan playing. They said that Matthews would put 10,000 on any gate and if he didn't play fans would get upset. Managers quipped to Joe Smith that if Matthews wasn't fit he should include him in the team anyway to make sure the crowds came, then they'd announce before the match he was unwell.

I picked up the nickname 'Champagne Perry' from a reporter with the *Blackpool Gazette*. Speed was my asset on the left wing. I was faster than Stan was and played more of a direct game. Stan would get on the ball and then work his way slowly up the wing, tormenting his marker, whereas I was looking for a lot of through balls from the inside-forwards and wing halves. I had pace and strength and must have made an impression on Joe because inside three months I had forced my way into the first team. The number 11 must also have been lucky for me because I played just 11 games in the third team before being promoted to the reserves, then again 11 games in the reserves before being promoted to the first team, and, of course, I played in the number 11 shirt.

Joe's strength as manager was that he bought players into the team to suit certain positions. We were not coached as such and mainly did circuit training to keep fit. Some clubs had grounds nearby to train on, so they didn't cut up the pitch, we didn't. At Blackpool, we played a full-scale practice match every Tuesday. The pitch would cut up during a season and there would only be grass in the four corners by the end of the campaign. We also played with the old heavy ball unlike today's that move about. It would be interesting to see how keepers coped with Morty ripping a shot at them!

There was never a great rousing team talk by Joe, we hardly saw the manager from one Saturday to the next. Joe never spoke about tactics, but would always try to give us a bit of a gee up. He'd say, "come on lads, we can do it". There was no ranting and raving, he would come in and say, "I've read the papers and they don't give us a chance. Now, go out and show them what we can do."

At first, I was homesick, the weather had a lot to do with it, being dark by four o'clock in the winter, but I stuck it out. I made my first team debut in a 2-1 win at Manchester United and stayed in the side until the end of the season. I returned to South Africa on holiday, but realised my life had moved on. My friends had got married or moved away. It was time for me to do the same.

In my first full season, 1950/51, we had some great matches against the likes of Tottenham Hotspur, Manchester United and Arsenal and I always looked forward to the local derbies with Preston and Bolton Wanderers. Before every game, we would limber up in the dressing room. Stan would have a massage before kick-off. He was older than the rest of us, so our trainer always gave him a good rub down on his calves and sides. At home, we got terrific support. There was always a big-match atmosphere and when we ran out from the tunnel around 10 minutes to three, a massive roar went up.

I played the majority of the season, which saw us finish third, Blackpool's highest ever finish in Division One. I also played in the FA Cup for the first time. We knew when the draw was coming up, so tuned in to the radio in the dressing room. During the run, I scored in a 2-2 draw with Charlton Athletic in the third round before we went through in a replay. Then I experienced the unique nature of the Cup when we struggled to overcome lower league opponents. Normally you would expect to ease past Stockport County and Mansfield Town, but in the FA Cup sides raised their games. Both were tough, but we came through.

The game I remember most was the semi-final replay against Birmingham City, especially the goal that I scored, because it proved to be the winner in the replay. England keeper Gil Merrick was in goal for Birmingham. I picked up the ball around the halfway line, made my way up the wing and beat the full-back towards goal. I was going to cross the ball because I could see Morty coming up behind me. I don't know why, but I changed my mind at the last moment and had a go at goal. The very fact that I'd assumed to send over a centre meant Gil came out anticipating it, was wrong-footed and the ball went in. Scoring the winning goal was special, but just to get through the cup-ties was the big thing.

In the dressing room, the realisation that I'd be playing in a Cup final was fantastic. Stan always used to say that the semi-final was the most important game because even if we didn't win at Wembley it was lovely just to get through and experience a great day. Getting to Wembley meant a lot to every player because apart from international football, that was your only opportunity. I played for England twice at Wembley and each occasion was special. For lots of other players, though, they never had the opportunity to play at the Twin Towers.

Joe Smith told me when the team for the final was chosen that I was a lucky lad at 20-odd years of age to play in a Cup final. He would say the same again in 1953. We travelled to London by train from Blackpool Central Station; the crowds were incredible. We stayed at Hendon Hall Hotel and made the short trip to Wembley, so we could walk around the pitch. It was awesome. On the day of the match, when the coach drove into the main entrance at Wembley towards the dressing rooms, all you could see was the crowd walking down Wembley Way; it was an amazing sight, all the colour. The atmosphere was electric.

When we got to the dressing room it was peaceful, so we began to relax with a few jokes, but as it got nearer to kick off the butterflies kicked in. Stan had his usual massage and, as much you could, we treated it as any other game. We did not have to wait long before we started to walk up the tunnel. You could hear the singing and when we came out of the tunnel, there was a tremendous roar. It was overwhelming.

The noise struck me forcibly and, of course, you are listening and looking around. There is excitement and trepidation, you feel whatever happens we must win, winning is the big thing. I was worked up, but as soon as we'd met the dignitaries and the referee had blown his whistle, I forget the 100,000 crowd completely.

On the day, Newcastle were the better team, it was an off day for Blackpool, no doubt about that. I remember the goals. Losing at Wembley is terrible; there is nothing worse. The winning team goes up to collect the Cup and you just hang around with your heads down. The best thing we could have done was get back to the dressing room. After getting our medals, we were really dejected. Blackpool supporters gave us a cheer, but you could tell it was a major disappointment for them. They'd lost in 1948 and it is not often you get a chance to play in another final, so many felt they'd had double the chance. We had a reception back in Blackpool, but it was an anticlimax.

Getting so close was heartbreaking, but Blackpool had a really good team, so I felt we'd get another chance. The following season expectations were high. I played throughout, but we only finished ninth in the league and went out of the Cup in the third round, which was disappointing.

Every season you start out and see what develops. We made a cracking start to the 1952/53 campaign, scoring goals for fun and winning matches. In the opening weeks, we thumped Aston Villa 5-1, Wolves 5-2, and Charlton Athletic 8-4. On our day, we were a match for anyone. Although we went through an indifferent spell and finished seventh in the league, our attention was diverting to the FA Cup and we were determined to have a real go to see if we could go one better.

The third round draw gave us an away trip to Sheffield Wednesday, who had defeated us at Bloomfield Road earlier in the season. It would be a test, but Wednesday were inconsistent. Morty was out with a bad knee injury, but we had a boost when Stan Matthews joined us at the Palace Hotel in Buxton the day before the match. Locally, the papers were not hopeful, but thousands of our fans made the journey to cheer us on. We always had a good following and they joined a crowd of over 60,000 at Hillsborough.

The traffic was so bad we had to get a police escort to the ground and when the match began, it was a tough encounter. Fog came down in the first half and got progressively worse, resulting in a white ball being introduced by the referee. Just before half-time, Stan gave us the lead after picking the ball up from a free-kick and lobbing the ball over a packed defence past an unsighted keeper. I remember the goal because it was not often that Stan scored. Wednesday came back in the second half and equalised. The match could have gone either way as both sides went for the winner, but two minutes from time, we snatched a great win when I headed down an Allan Brown cross for Ernie Taylor to volley into the net.

We listened to the radio anxiously for the fourth round draw on the Monday after training and received a better tie on paper against Huddersfield Town. Town had been relegated to the Second Division, but were riding high in the league when they arrived at Bloomfield Road. They would eventually gain promotion as runners-up. The night before the match, we went to the Tower Circus and the main thing I remember on the morning of the match was a gale blowing. We were told the wind had reached 70 miles per hour, so it would have a bearing on the match if it did not die down. Torrential rain fell before the match and with the gale still blowing Huddersfield had a hugely advantageous wind behind them. We dropped back to help our defence and I wasted a couple of openings, but we were satisfied to reach the half-time goalless.

In the second half, we gradually gained control but Huddersfield defended well. We eventually got the winner seven minutes from time with a freak goal. Tommy Garrett punted upfield from way inside our half, the wind got hold of the ball, the goalkeeper did not anticipate it, came out too soon and the ball carried over his head and dipped at the last moment into the net. It was a fluke and their keeper got the blame for it, which was unfair. It was a lucky break, but everyone says you need luck to win the FA Cup, and we had our share that day.

After the match, we were relieved and had no complaints when we were drawn to face Second Division Southampton at home. During the build up we prepared as usual in Buxton, but got stranded through heavy snow. Eventually, we managed to get a train to Manchester before a coach took us to Blackpool. Southampton's preparations were also hampered, but they made it in good time.

The match was an end-to-end encounter with both sides missing opportunities. Southampton had a goal disallowed, but they were lucky to escape an Ernie Taylor effort. I opened the scoring midway through the second half when I just beat the keeper and a defender to a through ball to hook the ball into the net from an acute angle. It looked like it would be sufficient, but six minutes from time Henry Horton grabbed the equaliser with a header from a disputed free-kick. We were disappointed, but there was no time to bemoan our luck.

Southampton supporters clearly believed a shock was on the cards because they snapped up tickets for the replay and they must have been delighted when Saints took an early lead through John Walker. By half-time it could easily have been 2-0, but for two desperate clearances by Tommy Garrett. We composed ourselves and took control of the game with two goals inside three minutes of the second half. I was involved in the equaliser when Henry Horton touched my cross past his own keeper for an own goal before Allan Brown rounded off a slick move with a cracking drive to give us a 2-1 lead. We never allowed Southampton back into the match after that. It was a solid performance as we were still without Morty.

It was a long journey home, but it gave us time to ponder the quarter-finals where we now faced league leaders Arsenal at Highbury. Cup fever was gripping Blackpool supporters. Throughout the cup run, fans queued for tickets the evening before a match. They used to bring old drums and make a hole to get a coal fire going through the night to make sure they got a ticket. This tie was a daunting challenge, but our fans were confident.

Arsenal had been on a terrific league run without losing, but we warmed up perfectly by winning a league match the week before the cup-tie at Highbury 3-2. Allan Brown got the winner. I remember Arsenal skipper Joe Mercer coming into our dressing room after the match, he was most upset, and said, "you lucky devils, wait until next week when we play in the Cup". The tie really caught the imagination. A crowd of 30,000 attended the league game, 70,000 packed Highbury for the cup match!

We saw the Crazy Gang the night before the game to help us unwind, but we knew this was our toughest test to date. Defences dominated and a replay looked likely until we took the lead 13 minutes from time; Allan Brown setting up Ernie Taylor with a brilliant ball before he crashed it home. We were ecstatic, but knew Arsenal were not finished. Six minutes from time, they lofted a ball into our penalty area; George Farm gathered it before two forwards barged into him, a legal challenge in our era. George spilled the ball for Jimmy Logie to score. Undaunted, we composed ourselves and hit back, Allan racing through to knock in a great cross by Jackie Mudie. Unfortunately, in the act of scoring Allan fractured his leg and, as in 1951, was ruled out for the rest of the season. That was truly terrible luck.

We drew Birmingham City or Tottenham Hotspur in the semi-finals. The other match was between Bolton Wanderers and Everton. If Birmingham won the game would take place at Goodison Park. If Spurs got through we'd play at Villa Park. As it transpired, Spurs triumphed. Two weeks before the tie I scored in a 2-0 win against them at home, but we knew it would have no bearing on the semi-final clash.

The good news for us was that Morty was back in the side. We arrived at Villa Park quietly confident and got off to the perfect start when I powered home a header from a Stan Matthews corner off the underside of the cross bar. Instead of dominating though, Spurs came back hard at us and were very unfortunate not to equalise before half-time because they had a good shout for a penalty and Len Duquemin struck the crossbar. Duquemin made no mistake early in the second half and Tottenham looked the more likely to take the lead as they surged forward relentlessly.

We were hanging on and had an escape again when Sid MacClellan hit a post. With 15 minutes to go Morty and Jackie Mudie switched positions in our attack. Leading the line, Morty looked more dangerous and almost grabbed a goal before Jackie scored the winner after a bad mistake by Alf Ramsey, whose attempted pass back to Ditchburn was not hard enough. Jackie nipped in and scored the winner. There was both relief and elation in our dressing room. There was also a determination to make it third time lucky at Wembley.

We had a few weeks until the final against Bolton and all you thought about was not getting injured. I was out with an ankle injury, but determined to make the final and eventually was passed fit. Sadly, for Hughie Kelly, an injury against Liverpool cost him a place in the final, but it gave an opportunity to young Cyril Robinson. Cyril had played only a handful of games and must have been shocked to all of a sudden be in the final.

A lot of the media attention focused on Stan, who was 38, and journalists wondered whether he would finally get a winners medal. Stan had a leg injury and was a doubt, but he was never going to miss out. Other players also gave interviews and it was a busy period with lots of interest from local and national newspapers, but it was nothing like it is today.

The routine for the final was similar to the Newcastle final and having played at Wembley before most of us knew what to expect. We stayed at the Edgewarebury Country Club as Bolton, who'd defeated Everton in the other semi-final, booked into the Hendon Hall Hotel. Bolton had finished fourteenth in Division One, but had class players including one of the best forwards around in Nat Lofthouse, who picked up the Footballer of the Year award that season. He was the England centre-forward and the main threat to us.

Going down Wembley Way, the sight of all the fans was fantastic once again and walking on the pitch and changing in the dressing room the expectancy grew. Walking out the noise was deafening and the atmosphere electric. I was fortunate to meet the King against Newcastle, this time I met the Duke of Edinburgh.

Suddenly it was game on, but we got off to a terrible start with Bolton scoring on two minutes when George Farm was deceived by a speculative shot from Lofthouse that bounced in front of him before going into the net off his arm. It was a shock, but the goal had come early so we had time to recover. We failed to settle, though, and Lofthouse almost made it 2-0. Fortunately, Nat hit a post. Slowly we found form. Jackie Mudie went close with a snap shot and Bolton had a problem because left half Eric Bell had torn a muscle, forcing him to switch positions with inside-left Harold Hassell. These were the days before substitutes, so we had an advantage as we had 11 fit men.

Taylor almost got Morty in the clear before we equalised on 35 minutes when Jackie flicked a ball through for Morty to fire home from 10 yards. His shot deflected off Hassell past keeper Stan Hanson. Unfortunately, our lead was short lived because Bolton went 2-1 ahead on 40 minutes when Willie Moir touched home a Bobby Langton lob. It was a poor goal to concede because George Farm should have cleared Langton's lob. We were disappointed to go in behind at half time after we had fought back, but we were determined to hit back in the second half. Within 10 minutes of the resumption though, our chances seemed over when Bell, making light of his injury, headed home a Doug Holden cross.

The thing I remember most about the final was this moment because I was really dejected and had the feeling that we would walk off the pitch having lost again. Bolton, though, were tiring and it soon became evident as Stan started to roam around the pitch looking for openings. A tactical change by Joe, 25 minutes from time, saw Jackie Mudie and myself switch positions, and it immediately paid dividends. Ewan Fenton and Ernie Taylor found Stan, who glided past Ralph Banks before sending in a terrific cross that Hanson failed to hold. In the scramble for the ball, Morty stuck out a foot to poke it into the net. That goal gave us a tremendous lift. One more nudge would put us on even terms.

We could sense that Bolton were simply trying to hold on. Stan was causing the Bolton defenders trouble every time he was in possession. They were so so tired and Stan stil had plenty of energy in those old legs of his. The pressure had to tell. Morty went close with a shot, I put another effort wide, Jackie Mudie was off target with another strike, and then a minute from time Jackie won a free-kick just outside the penalty area. Morty lined up his shot and blasted it straight through a gap in the wall past Stan Hanson and into the roof of the net for our third goal. Incredibly, we were level and I remember thinking, "now we have a chance, providing the final whistle doesn't go."

Historically, Morty became the first player since James Logan of Notts County in 1895 to score a hat-trick in a final, a feat that has still not been matched by any other player. Footage of that goal is always memorable, but also remarkable is the knowledge that Nat Lofthouse applauded at the very moment of his team's demise, an act of incredible sportsmanship.

Deep into injury time, Jackie Mudie was almost the hero, but struck a shot past the post and then in the very last minute, my moment came. George Farm cleared up field to Ernie Taylor, who in turn passed to Stan. Whenever Stan got the ball, all the forwards made for the goalmouth because nine times out of ten, Stan would beat his full-back and we knew the ball would be coming across. That is what I anticipated and sure enough, Stan got the ball on the wing, and crossed it, although he slipped as he did so, meaning he cut it back a little sharper than he had meant to. Morty let it go by at the near post as he wasn't in a good position and it came to me along the ground. It was just about on the penalty spot when I let fly with my right foot and I was so glad to see it hit the back of the net. For the first time in the match, we were ahead and we knew then that the Cup was ours. It was a marvellous moment and one I will never forget.

When the whistle sounded I thought, "We've won it!" There was elation and, of course, Joe Smith came running up onto the pitch congratulating everybody. The Bolton players took the defeat very well. Strange as it may seem, you do feel for the opposing team especially when you know what it is like to lose.

Receiving our medals from the Queen was memorable and there were great celebrations in the dressing room. We stayed overnight in London where we had a banquet at the Grand Hotel and then on Sunday an open-top bus met us off the train and we got a tremendous reception as we travelled through the streets from Preston through Lythym St Annes to Blackpool. At the Town Hall, Harry Johnston and Stan made a bit of a speech and then there was a reception.

For winning the FA Cup, we received a £20 bonus. During the summer, I got married and during a visit to South Africa for our honeymoon we were feted by the Mayor of Johannesburg. I was the first South African to win an FA Cup winners medal, which is something I'm extremely proud of. Over the years, everyone remembers it as the 'Matthews Final', but Morty deserves so much credit for his hat-trick. It was a match of high drama that had everything. I feel I was so lucky to play at Wembley twice within three years. Joe was right! It was absolutely fantastic and will be remembered forever more as a classic game, a magical Wembley moment. In Britain, 1953 was the year of the Queen's Coronation and Mount Everest was conquered, but for all Blackpool supporters it will always be associated with the year when we at last won the FA Cup.

JIMMY DUGDALE   1954
CENTRE-HALF 1950–1956

BORN   15 January 1932, Liverpool
SIGNED   From Harrowby FC, June 1952
WEST BROM CAREER   75 games
HONOURS   1 FA Cup, 1 Charity Shield (shared), 3 England B caps, Football League representative
LEFT   Transferred to Aston Villa, January 1956

A linchpin in defence during his brief tenure at the Hawthorns, Jimmy Dugdale played a key role in West Brom's most successful post-World War II Football League season. Finishing runners-up to arch rivals Wolverhampton Wanderers in the First Division, the Baggies claimed the FA Cup for the fourth time in their history in a thrilling final against Preston North End.

West Bromwich Albion 3 v Preston North End 2

FA Cup final
Saturday 1 May 1954

Wembley Stadium
Attendance 100,000
Gate Receipts £49,883

Frank Griffin's late winning goal tops a gripping West Brom comeback, including a seminal moment for the equalising penalty kick

Teams

	Managers	
Vic Buckingham		Scot Symon
Jim Sanders	1	George Thompson
Joe Kennedy	2	Willie Cunningham
Len Millard (capt.)	3	Joe Walton
Jimmy Dudley	4	Tommy Docherty
Jimmy Dugdale	5	Joe Martson
Ray Barlow	6	Willie Forbes
Frank Griffin	7	Tom Finney (capt.)
Reg Ryan	8	Bob Foster
Ronnie Allen	9	Charlie Wayman
Johnny Nicholls	10	Jimmy Baxter
George Lee	11	Angus Morrison

	Scorers	
Allen 21, pen 63, Griffin 88		Morrison 22, Wayman 51

Referee: A Luty

GROWING UP ON MERSEYSIDE, football was a major part of my youth, so I was thrilled to be able to make it as a professional footballer. West Brom was my first club and I was lucky enough to be part of the side that won the FA Cup in 1954. I went on to win further honours, which meant a lot to me, but that first major honour was particularly special.

I only ever wanted to be a footballer and played as a youngster in local teams, but I wasn't spotted by either Everton or Liverpool scouts. As a kid, I was an absolutely mad keen Evertonian and remember seeing Dixie Dean play. He was my hero and I went to every game at Goodison Park to watch Everton. You were Everton or Liverpool; the rivalry was intense.

By the time I was 16, I'd represented Liverpool Collegiate and Harrowby FC. A neighbour saw me play in the West Cheshire League and introduced me to West Brom. Their scouts watched me and must have been impressed because I met the manager Jack Smith and joined the club as an amateur before I went into the army for national service at 18 years of age.

I represented the army team and our manager bet with his opposite number on us winning. We had a useful side and won every game apart from one. Our manager was really annoyed that we lost one match and put me in jail as I was captain! I could not believe it. Following my army stint, I signed professional forms with West Brom. By now, Vic Buckingham had taken over as manager.

I made my debut during the 1952/53 season at home to Bolton Wanderers when regular centre-half Joe Kennedy picked up an injury. I was nervous, but coped, even though I was up against Nat Lofthouse. We lost 1-0 and I moved back into the reserves. I came back into the side with Joe sidelined again, for an FA Cup tie against Chelsea, and it helped me cement a first team place. As a kid, I loved the excitement of the competition. It had glamour and I listened to commentary of the cup finals on the radio. I was too young to remember when Everton won it in 1933, but hoped to play in a final when I signed professional forms.

It was my second game for West Brom and we went on to play Chelsea four times in the fourth round. I played in the opening clash at Stamford

Bridge and second replay at Villa Park, both matches ended 1-1, before we eventually went out in a third replay 4-0 at Highbury. The atmosphere in each game was fantastic and it made a great impression on me. Three of my first four professional games were FA Cup ties, which may be a record.

I kept my place for a league visit to Liverpool. We lost 3-0, but I stayed in the team for the remainder of the season. Things went well and we enjoyed good wins against Charlton Athletic and Middlesbrough. Two matches I recall were my first derby games when we faced Aston Villa during back-to-back clashes over Easter. We won 3-2 at the Hawthorns; Ronnie Allen scored twice and then drew the following day at Villa Park when again Ronnie scored in a 1-1 draw. I loved big derby games in front of packed houses. We gained revenge for our defeat at Bolton and a victory at home to Portsmouth brought a fourth place finish, West Brom's best for 20 years.

We had a good team that was developing. I lived close to the ground so travelled to training and matches by bus. Training used to be stamina based; we ran miles and miles. The atmosphere for players was wonderful. We socialised a lot together. We were close to a golf course and used to play every day. Whether we played home or away, on a Saturday night we headed straight to the dance hall.

On a match day, Vic Buckingham would give clear instructions on what he expected from every player. He'd put a board up and say, "you go here, you go there," tactics were important to him. Vic had played for the 'push and run' Tottenham Hotspur side which had won the league in 1951 and we played to that system, building from defence then spreading play accurate passes.

It was clear that striker Ronnie Allen and left-half Ray Barlow were the star players in the team and the supporter's big heroes, but they were only part of a terrific unit that we had. Norman Smith was a brave keeper, agile and with brilliant reflexes. Right-back Stan Rickaby was a strong tackler and had a great temperament, while at left back, skipper Len Millard was a great leader, who provided tremendous service for both the wing halves and forwards. In central defence, I always felt that I added balance, strength in the air and could bang them away.

At half-back, Jimmy Dudley played consistently, as did Joe Kennedy, which gave Reg Ryan and Ray Barlow the chance to cause damage. Joe switched to full back during the coming season and made a good job of it. Ray was for me the best footballer that I played with; he could make goals, score goals, put in superb crosses, in fact, he could do absolutely everything. Ray was a superb link player, helping defend then striding majestically across the pitch picking out the forwards with his passes.

In attack, Ronnie Allen led the line, while Johnny Nicholls was not only the Mickey-taker in the dressing room, but also a tremendous goal poacher who had a cracking shot with either foot. Ronnie was our key player and kingpin because he was the focal point in attack and also top goal scorer. Ronnie played deep and used his speed off the mark and strength to get past opponents. On the flanks, we caused teams a lot of trouble. Lighting fast and an astute footballer, Frank Griffin always had an eye for goal and scored some very important ones, while George Lee brought an extra dimension to the left flank.

The 1953/54 pre-season went well and I was in the team from the start of the new campaign. Our performances had made everyone optimistic about our chances of lifting a trophy. We'd seen the great Hungarian side demolish England at Wembley the previous season and in Ronnie Allen we had just the player to take on the now fashionable deep-lying Hidegkuti role as he had tremendous stamina and fine ball control. Johnny Nicholls played the Puskas part and Albion was seen as one of the most attractive sides to watch.

We made a fantastic start to the campaign following an opening day 2-0 win over Arsenal. Johnny Nicholls had been injured for periods during the previous season, but he got off to a flying start and was outscoring Ronnie, who had been top scorer for three consecutive seasons. We were unbeaten in our opening nine games, winning seven. Johnny scored in a number of victories and Ronnie was soon finding the target. Both came up with the goods in a 4-1 win at Burnley and 7-3 victory at Newcastle United.

That was a game in which I came up against the great Jackie Milburn for the first time. Newcastle could beat anyone on any given day and we had enjoyed a fine match a week earlier at the Hawthorns that finished 2-2. This would be tougher, though, as it was in front of their fanatical Geordie supporters. Jackie was a terrific player, but we had the upper hand that day. I managed to keep him out, but Vic Keeble and Bobby Mitchell (2) scored. For us, Johnny Nicholls scored three goals while Ronnie Allen grabbed two. Newcastle had no answer and the Geordie fans were left stunned.

Journalists said the win was one of the greatest victories in the club's history and one of the greatest attacking displays of football they had ever witnessed, so I was proud to have been part of that triumph. We tore into

Newcastle from the start; they did not stand a chance. At the end of the game, the St. James's Park crowd cheered us off, which was some accolade.

Our good form continued as we won 4-2 against Sheffield Wednesday after being 2-0 down and Ronnie scored also hat-tricks in wins over Huddersfield Town and Chelsea. I got injured at Blackpool in a 4-1 defeat and would not play again until the New Year. Joe Kennedy came back into the side and they continued scoring goals for fun. Ronnie struck four against Cardiff City in a 6-1 thumping and by the beginning of November; we were challenging local rivals Wolves for the title.

The atmosphere at the club was fantastic even though a 5-2 win over Liverpool on Christmas Day was our only victory in December. At the beginning of January, we were neck and neck with Wolves, so I was delighted to get back into the side for the third round of the FA Cup and would not lose my place for the remainder of the season. As a player, to win the FA Cup was one of my big ambitions, so I was hoping for a good draw in the third round.

But we drew Chelsea, which was incredible after our battles the year before. The odds on me playing them in my first four FA Cup ties must have been high. We knew that it would be a battle, though, but at least we did have the advantage of a home draw. Chelsea was a team on the up and they proved it by winning the league the following season. In a tight game at the Hawthorns we edged home thanks to an own goal by future West Ham and England manager Ron Greenwood. It was something of a relief to get through, particularly in just one game after the elongated tie of the previous season.

The fourth round was far more comfortable as we trounced Rotherham United at home 4-0, Johnny Nicholls (2), Ronnie Allen and Reg Ryan finding the target, but the fifth round was anything but easy even though our luck held with another home tie, this time against Newcastle United. Supporters went crazy for tickets and eventually over 61,000 packed into the Hawthorns and reports suggested over 20,000 remained locked outside.

This was, of course, the days before all-ticket matches and supporters crammed in through the turnstiles. The atmosphere was incredible and you could hear throughout the Geordie supporters singing *Blaydon Races*. We played in a changed strip and Ronnie gave us a 2-0 lead. Bobby Mitchell pulled one back, but Ronnie then completed his hat-trick. Jackie Milburn raised Newcastle hopes with a second, but it was too late as we held on for a famous win against the cup winners of 1951 and 1952. Both teams gave everything and our 3-2 win was a great team performance in front of one of the best atmospheres I played in at the Hawthorns. We were elated after the match.

In the quarter-finals, amazingly we received another home draw, this time against Tottenham Hotspur. They had been the side to beat a couple of years earlier when they won the League, but they were going through a transitional phase. We expected a battle, though in the end, we ran out comfortable 3-0 winners. Ray Barlow and Johnny Nicholls (2) did the damage.

The dressing room was a very happy place and we looked forward to the semi-final draw where we would play either Preston North End or Sheffield Wednesday, or outsiders Port Vale from the Third Division. Obviously, we were hoping for Vale, even though they had caused a major cup upset when they knocked out cup holders Blackpool in the fifth round. We got our wish. Freddie Steele's Port Vale was an efficient team which would win Division Three North that season, but we went into the match as overwhelming favourites. However, we could not take any chances. We gave them total respect and prepared as we would for any match.

The first team picked itself throughout the cup run and we had no last minute injury concerns. But at half time, we could barely believe that we were a goal behind. We had missed a number of chances and found ourselves 1-0 down following a goal by Vale's top striker. One of the biggest ever cup shocks was possibly on the cards, but we were not panicking. Vic Buckingham told us to keep playing our football and the goals would come. Jimmy Dudley grabbed the all-important equaliser when Vale's keeper missed a cross, and in the last few minutes, we were awarded a penalty following a foul on George Lee. Ronnie Allen, who used to play for Vale, slotted home the winner. There was a certain amount of controversy about the penalty because Vale claimed that the foul was outside the area. I was too far away to see, but I have subsequently seen film of the incident and it does look as if they had a point. Also Ronnie Allen was a former Vale player, so there was extra pressure on his shoulders as he ran up to take the penalty.

At the final whistle, we were relieved to be through because it had been a real battle. There was no time to ponder our big day at Wembley where we would face Preston North End, who'd defeated Sheffield Wednesday, because we had important League games coming up. We had stayed in the race for the title along with Wolves, but it all came to a crashing halt just before the Easter fixtures in April. We led the way and were on track for the double when we faced Sunderland at Roker Park, title rivals Wolves at home before travelling to Cardiff City. For all three games, we played without key first team players Ronnie Allen and Johnny Nicholls due to international call-ups for an England-Scotland clash. Today that would not happen as League matches are cancelled for such games, but we had to make do, so when we played Sunderland we knew it would be tough. It got impossible however, when our goalkeeper Norman Heath was badly injured in a clash with Ted Burden. Down to 10 men, Ray Barlow went in goal. Ray had a great game, but we lost 2-1.

Jim Sanders was a first class goalkeeper. A good shot stopper, Jim always made players shoot and would not sell himself. He replaced Norman, but four days later, we lost a crunch match in front of a capacity Hawthorns crowd to Wolves 1-0 and soon crashed at Cardiff 2-0. Our title challenge was over. To make matters worse, Norman was told that he would never play again. We only won one of our last seven league games and finished runners up to Wolves to complete a desperate end to our league campaign.

The focus now was totally on the FA Cup. We had the final to look forward to and were really determined to win otherwise the season would be a disaster. For me, I could not quite believe it as I was in my first full season at the club as a first team player. Was it always like this?!

Aside from the goalkeeping situation we had a few injury concerns. Joe Kennedy had come in for Stan Rickaby as right back. Frank Griffin was luckier, though, because he was passed fit to play after coming back into the side for the last few games after picking up an injury in the semi-final win. It was hard luck on both players who missed out on the final, but that is football. Injuries do occur, but you had to feel for both as they had played in every round and had contributed as much as anyone else had. That said, we had a job to do.

To date I'd faced all the great strikers of the day like Milburn, Mortenson, Lofthouse, Taylor; there were excellent. There was also Stan Matthews and whenever I came up against him on the pitch, he frightened me to death. Not that he was a physical player like some of the strikers, but his skill on the ball was exceptional and he had lightening pace of the mark. I'd go in to tackle him, but in a flash I'd go one way and he'd go the other.

Preston North End had finished as league runners-up the year before, but were disrupted with injuries and had ended this season in mid-table.

On their day, they could take on the best teams and had fine players such as half-back Tommy Docherty and forward Charlie Wayman. I was really looking forward to the final and knew we would have to watch Tom Finney, who was Preston's dangerman and had just picked up the Footballer of the Year award. Tom was an exceptional player; fast, skilful and a great striker of the ball. He was effective from both flanks, which made him a particularly difficult opponent to mark. Tom was carrying an injury and had missed a fair bit of the season, so we hoped he might not be on top form.

Our build up was terrific. The media wanted interviews; it was a really exciting time. We went down to London during the week and stayed near Wembley. On the day of the match, I was nervous, but determined to play well. We had a team talk before making the short trip to Wembley Stadium from our hotel. Seeing all the supporters making their way down Wembley Way was wonderful. This would be my first match at Wembley and I remember when we got down to the ground and looked around you could not help but think, "wow, this is fantastic, brilliant."

It was a fine day and Wembley was packed. When we walked up the tunnel and out onto the pitch, part of me was shaking like a leaf, but when the match started the brain stopped completely and I just concentrated on the game. I forget about the noise. Go here, go there, tackle here and tackle there.

We began well, but had to be alert to Tom Finney, who'd also started brightly, making light of his injury concerns. One of our main tactics was to cut the supply line to him and in Len Millard we had the player to make sure his efforts came to nothing. Supporting him was Ray Barlow, who helped snuff out the threat of the maestro, whilst joining the attack with probing balls.

On 21 minutes, we grabbed the lead after Willie Cunningham lost possession to George Lee. Taking his opportunity, George played a pinpoint ball across the face of the goal for Ronnie Allen to slide in and score the opening goal past Thompson. It was first blood to us and I learned later that it was our 100th goal of the season, which was some going. We were really excited, but made the mistake of letting our guard slip and inside a minute Preston drew level when Angus Morrison headed home a deep pass from Tommy Docherty.

The goal shook us and Charlie Wayman fired over minutes later. Bob Foster went close for Preston from a Finney pass and Johnny Nicholls almost edged us in front, but at half time it was anyone's match. Both sides had settled and the next goal would be important. We were determined to stay tight, but within five minutes of the restart, Preston edged ahead 2-1 with a controversial goal from Wayman, who I was marking. Docherty began the build up when he played a ball between Ray Barlow and Jimmy Dudley. I came out to cover, but Jimmy Baxter flicked the ball through to Charlie, looking yards offside. We appealed to the referee Mr Luty, but he signalled for play to continue. Clean through, Wayman scored with ease.

We felt hard done by, but refused to panic. Driven on by Ray, who was having a terrific match in defence, we pushed forward and got our reward just past the hour when Docherty fouled Ray on one of his surging runs forward for a clear-cut penalty. When Ronnie Allen lined up to take the spot-kick, he took his time, because there was a divot on the actual penalty spot. That added to the tension of the moment. It was agonising, although I think Ronnie was the coolest man in the house. It was the most tense moment of my life and I could barely watch as I waited on the halfway line. I was so nervous. There is a famous picture of the penalty taken from behind our goal. You can see me inside the Preston half, bending forward hoping Ronnie will score. Our goalkeeper Jim Sanders has his back to the goal as Ronnie is shooting, waiting for the West Brom supporters to roar. Thankfully Ronnie did not waste the opportunity and beat George Thompson with a great strike.

Level at 2-2, we felt confident. Both teams went for the winner, but defences smothered out any half chances. Nobody really wanted extra-time, but with the minutes ticking by it looked on until we got our opportunity two minutes from time. Joe Kennedy began the move with a pass to Reg Ryan, who found Frank Griffin with a terrific ball. Frank up until now had failed to make an impact on the game, but he grasped this opportunity, heading the ball beyond his marker to race clear and coolly fire home past Thompson for the winning goal. It was a marvellous moment; we were ecstatic and urged each other to hold on to what we had.

The final few minutes seemed to take forever, but there was no way that Preston were going to score. Finally, the whistle blew and we'd won the FA Cup. It was a fantastic feeling, one of pure joy and relief. Preston had taken us all the way and made it a memorable final, but we were deserved winners.

Getting my medal from the Queen Mother was thrilling and, of course, we went on the traditional Wembley lap of honour. Showing the cup to our fans was a truly magical moment. At one point I had captain Len Millard on my shoulders as we posed for photographs. Back in the dressing room, we celebrated before going back to the hotel for a banquet. We stayed the night and then went back home the following day where the fans came out in force to greet us as we went through the city in an open top bus.

Winning the FA Cup was the highlight of my short career and we received a bonus, which was welcome, but nothing like what the players earn today. The modern game is without dribblers, which is a shame. There are no stars like Stan Matthews or Tom Finney, now it is all pump, pump, pump and get the ball up quickly.

The following season, Charlton Athletic knocked us out at the fourth round stage and that would be my final FA Cup game for West Brom because by the start of the 1956/57 season I was playing for our Midland rivals Aston Villa. It turned out to be a great move for me as we won the FA Cup in my first season. There were some tough ties along the way, but the hardest by far was the semi-final against my old club West Brom.

It was strange facing Albion in such an important match, but I had a job to do. The first game was a stirring affair at Molineux that ended 2-2 and Villa were within two minutes of going out of the competition. Twice we came from behind to equalise, Peter McParland scoring Villa's goals. In the replay, we again stayed local by playing at St. Andrew's and there was a lot of controversy early on when I was involved in a collision with Ronnie Allen that saw him carried off. He wasn't the best header of a ball and when he leapt, Ronnie connected with my head and was knocked out.

West Brom went down to ten men because there were no substitutes in those days and we eventually edged the game. At the end, we were elated to have won, but I had to be escorted by police to the bus as a group of Albion fans were waiting to beat me up. I was frightened because they were yelling and screaming. I didn't injure Ronnie on purpose, it was accidental, but it was very upsetting at the time. I went to see him afterwards to apologise, but Ronnie would not see me after the game. I was not a dirty player and never went out to injure anyone, let alone Ronnie because he was one of my heroes.

In the final, we faced Manchester United's Busby Babes and they were some team, that would be cruelly ripped apart in 1958 by the Munich air crash. The likes of Duncan Edwards, Tommy Taylor and Eddie Coleman were fantastic players. I had to mark Tommy and he was a real handful. At Wembley, there was controversy too when Peter McParland fouled United's keeper, who had to be replaced by Danny Blanchflower. Two goals by McParland earned me a second cup winner's medal, but he'll tell you all about that incredible game later.

Winning the FA Cup twice was the highlight of my career and winning at Wembley is special, but I also tasted the bitterness of losing semi-finals twice at Aston Villa, against Nottingham Forest in 1959 and Wolves, at the Hawthorns of all grounds, the following season. There is no bigger disappointment of missing out on the big day and it made me appreciate the two occasions I did pick up an FA Cup winners medal. That first FA Cup final win for West Brom is still such a wonderful memory. We had some team and could beat anyone on our day.

VIC KEEBLE
CENTRE-FORWARD 1952–1958

1955

BORN   25 June 1930, Colchester
SIGNED   February 1952 from Colchester United
NEWCASTLE CAREER   120 games, 67 goals
HONOURS   1 FA Cup, Division Two Championship 1957/58
LEFT   Transferred to West Ham United, October 1957

During his peak years, Vic Keeble led the line during the mid-50s for Newcastle United and was the ideal foil for legendary striker 'Wor Jackie' Milburn. A strong runner, brave and brilliant in the air, during Newcastle's third FA Cup triumph of the first half of the fifties, Keeble was top scorer with five goals, including strikes in both the semi-final and semi-final replay. Keeble would have played more games for Newcastle, but for injury and he moved on to help West Ham claim a Second Division crown.

Newcastle United 3 v Manchester City 1

FA Cup final
Saturday 7 May 1955

Wembley Stadium
Attendance 100,000
Gate Receipts £49,881

'Wor' Jackie Milburn scores within a minute to set cup giants Newcastle on the way to a legendary third final victory in five years

Teams

Duggie Livingstone	**Managers**	Les McDowall
Ronnie Simpson	1	Bert Trautmann
Bobby Cowell	2	Jimmy Meadows
Ron Batty	3	Roy Little
Jimmy Scoular (capt.)	4	Ken Barnes
Bob Stokoe	5	Dave Ewing
Tommy Casey	6	Roy Paul (capt.)
Len White	7	Bill Spurdle
Jackie Milburn	8	Joe Hayes
Vic Keeble	9	Don Revie
George Hannah	10	Bobby Johnstone
Bobby Mitchell	11	Fionan Fagan
Milburn 1, Mitchell 53, Hannah 60	**Scorers**	Johnstone 44

Referee: R Leafe

WHEN I LOOK BACK at my football career, one game will always stand out above all others and that was the 1955 FA Cup final. It was my first final and indeed my only appearance at Wembley. For the club, though, it was a third visit and triumph in five seasons. You see, during the early 1950s Newcastle United dominated the competition. Our victory over Manchester City was a memorable day for everyone connected with the club and our fanatical supporters.

No doubt, the Toon Army looked forward to more glory in the world's most glamorous cup competition, but sadly, that has not been the case. Future sides have gone close, reaching three finals as the likes of Malcolm Macdonald and Alan Shearer succeeded 'Wor Jackie' Milburn as the Geordie fans' favourite, but over 50 years on, that glorious afternoon is the last time Newcastle triumphed in the FA Cup at Wembley, and for me the memories are still clear.

I was born in Colchester and educated at Colchester Royal Grammar School, which was a rugby school. I played rugby union until the age of 15 and represented the Eastern counties at fly half. The master in charge was a rugby man and aghast that I wanted to play football. He wanted me to win a blue at Cambridge University. I was determined, though, and one or two youth teams were interested.

To appease the school, I played rugby on a Saturday morning before then playing football in the afternoon for King George Youth Club, which was quite a good side. As a kid, I followed West Ham's fortunes, but rarely saw them play as I was myself playing rugby union, football, tennis, cricket and table tennis. I joined Colchester Casuals, who were a good amateur side and we won everything the season I played for them. Then I signed amateur forms for Arsenal after a local policeman who scouted for Arsenal, George Lesley, watched me a few times, but I didn't go to Highbury for training, although news got in the local papers, which was great for my esteem. Eventually, Ted Fenton at Colchester United signed me on as a part-time professional.

Colchester were elected to the Football League in 1950 and their centre-forward was Arthur Turner, who'd played for Charlton Athletic in the

1946 FA Cup final, so I heard all the stories about what it was like to play at Wembley. I eventually replaced Arthur in the first team.

During this time, I began National Service in the RAOC, so also played for the British Army. Some of my colleagues made it in football, among them John Charles. Big John was a centre-half in those days and such a strong player. In the air, John was unbelievable; he went up for corners, which opponents hated and also had a terrific strike on him.

At Colchester United, I began to score freely and Newcastle United's southern-based scout Bill McCracken, a former star defender at St. James's Park, followed my progress. In February 1952, I got a call from Colchester saying that Blackpool and Newcastle wanted to sign me. They both had England centre-forwards playing for them, Stan Mortenson at Blackpool and Jackie Milburn at Newcastle. Both needed cover.

Newcastle wanted to meet me in London. Three directors travelled down to negotiate with Jimmy and a couple of Colchester directors. When I arrived, I was told a £15,000 offer had been accepted. Was I interested in joining Newcastle? Of course I was. They were in the First Division and FA Cup holders. They also had great players such as Jackie Milburn, Bobby Mitchell and skipper Joe Harvey. I signed without my family, team-mates or friends knowing because it was too good an opportunity to miss.

I was stationed near Reading during my national service, so opportunities were often limited, but the officers were great and I never missed a weekend playing for the Newcastle reserves. Officers even booked my tickets; everything was done for me. I travelled from Reading to Newcastle and back the same day.

Chairman Stan Seymour looked after team matters; there was no official manager. Eventually, I made my debut at Chelsea when Jackie Milburn was injured. Another injury to Jackie gave me a four-match run in the side. I made my home debut in a win over Manchester City. St. James's Park was packed; the atmosphere was incredible with Newcastle fans looking forward to the forthcoming 1952 FA Cup final against Arsenal. I then found the target against Middlesbrough, Arsenal and Derby County in consecutive games.

I could not have faced Arsenal in the final as I'd played for Colchester in the first round against Port Vale. Even so, I really looked forward to the final because the FA Cup is such a prestigious competition. Before I arrived at Newcastle, I was playing in Colchester's reserves when they were a Southern League club and the first team had defeated Huddersfield

Town before losing 5-0 to finalists Blackpool with the likes of Matthews and Mortenson.

For the club and its supporters playing top-flight teams was everything. The matches attracted packed houses with supporters hanging off the trees! The gate was far greater than even a local derby against Chelmsford. The build up in the town was incredible. There were dinners and the players met the Mayor for their achievements. The whole town lived a different life for a few days, that was the magic of the Cup.

After gaining admission to the Football League, I played in the competition myself, indeed the year I joined Newcastle I scored in a 3-1 win over Port Vale. It was a great result, but we lost in the third round to Barnsley. Seeing the competition as a player was one thing, but in 1970, I saw the tournament as commercial manager at Colchester when they drew First Division champions Leeds United.

The directors were thrilled and planned how to generate the most money possible. It was hectic. We had extra tickets produced and held raffles on the day. Better still, Ray Crawford scored twice in a famous 3-2 win. Champagne flowed and the finance generated from that Leeds match and our quarter-final defeat at Everton was fantastic. We took busloads to Goodison Park and they had a day to remember despite a 5-0 defeat.

Back in 1952, as a squad member, I was in the crowd to see Newcastle win the trophy, which was a fantastic experience. It was my first visit to the stadium and it lived up to my expectations. All players wanted to play at Wembley because outside international games, there was only the FA Cup and Amateur Cup final. I hoped my day would come. Looking ahead, from humble beginnings at Colchester United I had progressed to playing against the great Wilf Mannion of Middlesbrough and walked through Highbury's great marble hall. It was hard to believe, but I quickly got used to playing against star names and alongside them in our team.

Newcastle finished in the top ten in the league, but were renowned as great cup battlers. During my first full season, again I deputised when Jackie was injured. We disappointingly finished sixteenth. I scored twice in a 3-2 win at home over Charlton Athletic, but was also in the side that lost 5-1 to Sheffield Wednesday at St. James' Park, which summed up our season. In the FA Cup, we were going for a third consecutive triumph, so the pressure was on and I noticed a different atmosphere for a cup match for players and supporters. We looked forward to the draw, despite our league form and our fans came out in force for a third round tie at home to Swansea.

Over 60,000 crammed into St. James's Park, but the match was abandoned after eight minutes due to fog. Newspapers said the match should not have started and urged supporters not to attend the replayed game, but 60,000 turned up again, which showed what the FA Cup meant to them. I was delighted to get a goal in a 3-0 win, but in the fourth round, we struggled despite having a home tie against Rotherham United. A gale got worse during the day and when our keeper Ronnie Simpson took goal kicks, the ball was blowing backwards. It put us under pressure. Before the game, due to frost, straw was pushed from the pitch to the running track. Kids sitting on the straw threw it in on the pitch when I scored in the second half. The match was held up to get the straw off, which benefited Rotherham. They got a second wind and with the gale behind them scored three goals. We were so disappointed afterwards. It was a poor way to lose our trophy.

Come the 1953/54 campaign we started well. I scored in a 2-1 derby win over Sunderland on the opening day in front of a packed house and struck again as we demolished Liverpool 4-0. The coming weeks, though, would be tough. I scored in 2-2 draws at West Brom and Preston, but my effort in the return against West Brom meant nothing as we went down 7-3 at home. Another loss at Tottenham would be my last action due to injury until the New Year.

Our form failed to improve and it was frustrating not being fit, but I was back to do my bit when the FA Cup came around. We drew non-league Wigan Athletic in the third round, so could not complain - especially as it was a home tie, but we struggled to a 2-2 draw.

I missed the game, but was back for the replay. Wigan was rebuilding a stand after a fire, but the changing rooms were not completed so there was a lot of press talk that the game may be moved, but it wasn't. Stan Seymour was accused of unsporting behaviour when he refused to let us change in Wigan's makeshift changing rooms and insisted we used the Corporation Baths. We got through 3-2, but it was a struggle and illustrated the unique nature of the Cup. Soon my season was over due to an ankle injury sustained at Preston. We reached the fifth round before losing at West Brom. They were such a pain that season. It was no consolation they won the trophy. In the league, we finished mid-table.

By December 1954, I was fit again and struck twice in a 2-1 win over Portsmouth and scored two more as we thrashed Arsenal 5-1, but it wasn't all going our way, especially on our travels as we experienced in a 6-2 thumping at Sheffield United and a 4-3 defeat at champions-elect Chelsea. As a strike force, we hit the target consistently, but had to tighten our defence. It was an era of attacking games and thrilling action for supporters. We also played on Christmas Day and Boxing Day, which was the fashion. No-one complained though, the stands were packed and supporters lapped up all the games.

Come the FA Cup third round we edged a tricky match at Plymouth Argyle when I was delighted to grab our goal during a 1-0 win. Most of the lads went back by the midnight train. I stopped at a local hotel as I was going home briefly and could not believe the behaviour of reporters. They were drunk and hitting each other on the head with newspapers. Happy days!

Next up was Brentford, another testing tie. It was a massive game for the Third Division side and they brought thousands to St. James's Park. We knew they would raise their game and they battled hard, but we came through 3-2 after a few scares with a Mitch [Bobby Mitchell] winner. Our luck held in the fifth round draw when we faced another Second Division outfit, this time Nottingham Forest. You could not help but think we had a chance of going far, but prepared for a battle, and Forest did not disappoint in three incredibly hard games. At the City Ground, Forest fancied their chances and took the lead, but Jackie equalised for a draw.

Our supporters celebrated as if the hard work was done, but we knew it wasn't and at half time at St. James's Park, Cup dreams were vanishing at 2-0 down. We'd let ourselves and supporters down. We went out in the second half and played superbly. Forest may have been a touch overconfident and paid the price as we battled back to draw. I scored our first before Mitch got the second. Neither side could break the deadlock in extra-time so it went to a second replay and unusually we tossed for home advantage. We won the spin, but I was carrying a knock so missed out. Alan Monkhouse was the hero for us with both goals as we went through in extra-time for a quarter-final against Huddersfield Town, our first top-flight opponents.

With all the replays, we seemed to do little training, but did not complain because we was making progress. We prepared differently for a Cup game and got ourselves in the right frame of mind by staying at the Norbreck Hydro Hotel in Blackpool right on the front. The hotel had a golf course, swimming pool and sauna, it was ideal.

At Huddersfield, we gained a creditable draw thanks to a Len White headed equaliser in front of a 55,000 crowd. We were battle-hardened and had a great team spirit. If we went a goal down we never panicked, we just got on with the game. The replay was a tight affair that again went to extra-time, but I managed to give us an important lead and a second by Mitch saw us through. Ten days later, we ran out for the semi-finals and faced giant-killers York City. We had no complaints even though we were over-whelming favourites, and knew that the other semi-finalists Manchester City and Sunderland would have traded places with us. It was a question of doing a professional job against the Third Division side.

York had knocked out 1953 winners Blackpool before earning a shock victory over Spurs on their way to the last four. It was a sensational achievement that captured the nation's imagination. Like all supporters, we had marvelled at their success and all romantics of the sport wanted to see the greatest shock in FA Cup history, but we was determined to break York hearts. I was really looking forward to the match, as it would be my first semi-final.

At Hillsborough, York sensationally took the lead, but we refused to panic and I was delighted to equalise and nearly put us through when I hit the crossbar in the last 10 minutes, but we settled for a replay at Roker Park. York battled well, but the first game was their best opportunity and we made no mistake, winning 2-0. I scored our opening goal and it was one of my most memorable. Mitch sealed victory with a second goal.

To York's credit, they had created history and had the consolation of becoming the first Third Division club to appear in a semi final replay. For Jackie, Mitch, Bobby and Charlie Crowe the feeling of reaching Wembley was something they'd experienced before but for the rest of us it would be our first final and we could not wait. The feeling afterwards was fantastic and we looked forward to playing Manchester City after they defeated Sunderland at the first attempt and end the possibility of the first ever North East final. We had a player's pool and made a few quid from pro-ducing a commemorative brochure to mark the occasion.

There was five weeks until the big day and we were determined to improve our league position. We enjoyed a great run, losing only two games from eleven and won our Easter fixtures against Everton 2-1, Sheffield Wednesday 5-0 and Everton 4-0. I scored the winner at Goodison Park, but got injured against Wednesday so missed the return clash with Everton. I was soon back as we finished eighth, so could now look forward to Wembley.

As a goalscorer, I picked up a few injuries because I went in where angels feared to tread at times, but that was my role. I rarely scored out of the box but struck my fair share. We had a formidable forward line and all scored goals. The first team on its day was a strong outfit and could give anyone a match. Like most teams, we played the W-M formation.

In goal was Ronnie Simpson. He was not particularly big but was very agile and could pull off great saves. Ronnie was also a funny lad, solid and of course went on play for Celtic, where he won the European Cup and played for Scotland.

Our full-backs were Bobby Cowell, who really liked to get forward, was fairly quick and gave 110 per cent in every game, and Ron Batty, who had been at the club a few years like me and came into the side during the season. Ron was a good steady player and never gave anything away. He was a good player to have in your side.

Jimmy Scoular was right-half and brilliant at finding Mitch with a passes. Jimmy was a hard man and terrific to have in your side. He was determined, took no prisoners and having him in our side gave you such confidence. I was one of his mates but he even kicked me in training but after a match was one of the nicest guys you could meet.

Bob Stokoe was centre-half and another lovely guy. We came through together and wound each other up during a match. He used to shout at me every game after around 25 minutes, get them f'ing going up there. I'd look back at him and say, Bob, you do your f'ing job at your end and I'll do my f'ing job at my end. After, he'd look at me and grin! Bob was a steady player and upset opponents with little digs.

Charlie Crowe played left-half and was a hard worker. In the second half of the season, Charlie picked up an injury and was doubtful for the final. Tommy Casey deputised and was an underrated player but gave everything in a game. We all appreciated his efforts.

I mainly led the line with Jackie feeding off me, but sometimes played on the inside. My partnership with Jackie was great. I'd nod them on and he could really move off the mark. Sides all look for balance and that is why we complemented each other. Jackie was a prolific striker, not great in the air, but had two terrific feet. Pace is everything and that made him very dangerous. He could really thump a ball. Even from 30 yards, the ball would go in like a rocket. Jackie would burst the ball today!

Bobby Mitchell was possibly the best in his country at the time. If you gave the ball to Mitch, he would hang on to it and they could not get the ball off him. Mitch caused a lot of danger to opponents and was a prolific scorer. Len White gave us balance on the wing that all teams look for as a unit. Fans loved his weaving runs and he had a powerful strike.

Then there was little George Hannah, who was such a clever player, he could beat people on a sixpence. George was not always a regular but when in the side, never messed around; he was a terrific one-touch player. During the campaign Jackie, Mitch, George, Len and myself scored 73 league goals, which was some going. We had a great side but for some reason was inconsistent in the league. It's just the way it goes.

We went to Brighton during the Wembley build up to keep our routine the same. The media came with us everywhere but our manager controlled it. A television company invited us to play a head tennis game at Manchester but City refused to attend. We travelled to London by train and played someone else instead, which helped pass the time. We only had light training. As it was the end of the season, we were as fit as we would ever be. Charlie Crowe was having treatment but failed to come through, which was devastating for him but an opportunity for Tommy Casey and we knew he would not let anyone down. Reg Davies also missed out because of tonsillitis. I really felt for Reg because he was twelfth man in 1952. George Hannah came in to the side.

I remember there was a big row over how many tickets the players should have and it got into the press. In the end, it got resolved but there was the usual scramble for Wembley tickets by supporters. It was a big day and supporters saved up to travel down. The ordinary worker was earning around half what we were on, we were a bit better off but our career was short. I was on £14 a week top whack. On top, if we won a league match we got a £2 bonus and £1 for a draw. For the cup final, we got a £25 bonus but nothing if we lost!

Manchester City had a gained publicity that season because they switched to playing with a deep-lying centre forward like the Hungarian side that thumped England at Wembley. They'd had some wonderful players. Puskas was out of this world and changed people's perception of football. At the centre of City's system was Don Revie, so their system was dubbed the 'Revie plan' and it worked for them. We lost at Maine Road 3-1 on Christmas Day before winning the return two days later.

Don was Footballer of the Year so we knew he'd be a danger but they also had the likes of Bobby Johnstone, Roy Paul, Joe Hayes, Ken Barnes and Bert Trautmann in goal so it had the makings of a cracking final. We knew how we would handle the 'Revie plan'. Wherever Don went, someone would pick him up. Duggie Livingstone had become manager halfway through the season but Stan Seymour was in charge of tactics and had us well briefed.

I roomed with Tommy Casey and we went for a stroll on the morning of the game. I was not too nervous but there were butterflies. I'd always done well against City so fancied our chances. Coming down Wembley Way, the sight was fantastic; so many supporters dressed up in our colours; it was a great sight. Supporters were mingling and there was not a sign of trouble. We were slowed down by the crowds and amazingly among all those thousands of supporters I saw my mum, dad, sister and brother-in-law. They tapped on the coach window to wish us luck.

We went to the dressing room, had a walk around the pitch to take in the atmosphere and then got changed. All the players had different routines though I did not have any particular superstitions. Jackie liked a cigarette and when we went from the dressing room to the tunnel, Norman Smith had a little flask of whiskey and two players had a cap to warm them up. We were told that when they played the hymn *Abide With Me* it would be time to walk out. The walk up the tunnel and out onto the pitch was unforgettable, the noise that hits you when we entered the stadium was incredible. You try and take it in but you just want to meet the dignitaries and get on with it. We were presented to the Duke of Edinburgh and he wished us luck. Then we were away to loosen up.

We were just about favourites but could not have dreamt of a better start. Jimmy Schoular combined with Jackie and Len White and immediately won a corner. We took up our positions and caught City cold because Roy Paul was marking me. Jackie was unmarked at the near post to head home Len's cross. Less than a minute gone and 1-0 ahead, it was amazing.

City almost equalised but Joe Hayes sliced wide an opportunity created by Paul and Revie. Mitch then hit the bar direct from a corner and then Trautmann made a brilliant stop from a Hayes shot that Paul deflected towards his own goal. We were on top and soon got an unfortunate assist when City full-back Jimmy Meadows departed on 20 minutes with ligament damage after he fell awkwardly when Mitch dummied his way past him. No substitutes were allowed so City were down to 10 men. You had to feel for them because no team likes to see this happen, especially in a cup final. It made their task really difficult. Bill Spurdle moved to defence and they played with four forwards.

Revie, Barnes and Johnstone worked hard, but we dominated although had a scare when Len picked up an ankle injury but was fine to continue. Chances came our way, but we failed to take them. Jimmy was left frustrated when Dave Ewing headed an effort off the line, Len saw a shot brilliantly saved by Trautmann after George Hannah and Mitch combined, then 10 minutes from half time I headed a cross from point-blank range towards goal but Trautmann clawed the ball clear. It was a great save but I should have scored.

City battled away and you have to give them credit. They created openings on the break, Hayes went close and, to our surprise, equalised on the stroke of half time through Johnstone. Revie and Barnes were involved in the build up before Hayes set up the Scot to head home from 10 yards. We were disappointed to let a goal in so late in the half but I fancied our chances as City would tire on the wide Wembley pitch.

In the dressing room, Stan Seymour said, "Stay in the middle, don't drift to the wing. Jimmy will supply Mitch, and Mitch will pick Revie up and tear them to ribbons." I pulled defenders away a bit and it worked a treat. Hayes gave us an early fright with a snap shot but space was opening up and our second goal came on 53 minutes when Mitch controlled White's centre, turned Spurdle, and caught Trautmann out by firing home from a tight angle instead of crossing the ball.

We were completely in control. Mitch forced Trautmann into a great save, but we were not to be denied and on the hour, Jimmy intercepted a City pass before crossing 40 yards over Spurdle's head for Mitch to control and square for George Hannah to fire home from 12 yards.

I knew that we had won the Cup; it was a tremendous feeling and before full-time, we could have had a fourth but Trautmann saved again from Mitch and I headed over when well placed. There was no way back for City. At the final whistle, there was total elation. We were dancing around the pitch. Collecting our medals was fantastic; I was so thrilled and George said to me he would be at the front of every picture, he was!

It was a record-breaking win for us. We was the first to win the Cup three times in five seasons, the only side to win at Wembley on every occasion we'd played there, the first side to play in 10 finals and our sixth win equalled Blackburn Rovers and Aston Villa. To cap everything, Jack's goal timed at 50 seconds was the quickest in a Wembley final.

In the dressing room, directors joined us and champagne flowed. On the Saturday night, we celebrated at the Savoy. We came back by train and had the Cup on display. Everyone at stations stopped to wave. Back in Newcastle, thousands turned out. We boarded a bus, came through the streets back to St. James, Park and walked around the pitch. It was an amazing sight and I will never forget Jackie throwing the commemorative brochure into the crowd.

The following season I top scored with 29 goals. Jackie scored 19 but played six more matches so I was delighted to finish ahead of Jackie for once. I opened my account in a 4-2 win over Sheffield United and our clash at Huddersfield Town was particularly memorable as I scored four in a 6-1 victory; it would be my only Newcastle hat-trick. During the festive period, I scored in every game. I struck two in a 5-0 win over Preston on Christmas Eve, two in a 6-1 Boxing Day win, our biggest win at Roker Park, and the opening goal in a 3-1 win at home to Sunderland 24 hours later. We was on a role and it continued into the New Year as I scored twice in a 4-0 win over Luton Town.

In our FA Cup defence we started with a 3-1 win at Sheffield Wednesday, I scored our second goal, then I played in one of the best matches of my career when we defeated Fulham 5-4. The great Johnnie Haynes reckoned it was the most exciting game he ever played in. We were 3-0 up and it could have been six. Fulham scored before half time and then went 4-3 ahead before I scored twice in the last 10 minutes to seal a famous win. We edged past Stoke City, but then suffered a disappointing 1-0 defeat at home to Sunderland in the quarter-finals. We were distraught. The season drifted and we finished in eleventh place.

We suffered a number of defeats; one I particularly remember was at Blackpool when Stan Matthews was playing. He was a superb player, always dangerous but he also had a great sense of humour. During the game, an attack had broken down so I began walking back to halfway when our bench had a go at me to get back and help the defence. I could run all day so ran back and tackled Stan, ran the ball into the corner to give the lads a bit of relief. Shielding it, Stan looked at me and said, "What are you doing, you should be in attack trying to score goals." He had the last laugh as Blackpool won 5-1.

The following season was my last at Newcastle United after I got injured. I played a few games in 1957/58 before joining West Ham in October 1958 to help their promotion push to the First Division. Ted Fenton was manager and knew all about me from my time at Colchester United. It was bizarre that I would begin and end my career with Ted.

I partnered John Dick and we clicked instantly, scoring 40 goals between us. I was really enjoying my football and grabbed a hat-trick in a 5-0 win against West Ham, two in 6-1 wins over Lincoln and Bristol Rovers, and further braces in a 6-2 victory over Swansea and 8-0 thumping of Rotherham United. The Hammers clinched the title in the final game at Middlesbrough, where we won 3-1. I knocked in the third goal.

I'd also enjoyed my return to the FA Cup, grabbing a hat-trick in a 5-1 win against Blackpool before we exited in an exciting derby clash at home to Fulham. We'd scored a club record 101 goals, which was phenomenal and I was so pleased to be able to play in the First Division again. I really looked forward to playing against my old mates at Newcastle United.

My partnership with John continued as we scored 47 goals and finished sixth in the First Division. I opened my account in a 2-1 win at Portsmouth before scoring twice in a 7-2 win at home to Aston Villa. I also scored four goals in a 6-3 win against Blackburn Rovers, twice in a 6-0 home triumph over Portsmouth and 5-3 win against Nottingham Forest. I'd been particularly pleased to score in a Christmas Day and Boxing Day double over Tottenham Hotspur but they gained revenge in the FA Cup. It would be my last match in the competition as a back injury ended my season and forced me to retire.

One of mainstays before I arrived was captain Malcolm Allison but he had been forced to retire also and went into coaching. His replacement was Bobby Moore, who made his bow against Manchester United. It was obvious Bobby had talent and as the game changed, it helped him, as he did not have great pace but his positional sense was superb. Also on the books was Geoff Hurst, who I used to give a lift in to training from Chelmsford.

Malcolm Allison was a real character. I lived with him for a year and he loved everything about football. He coached the kids, was a bit of a playboy, but developed well and went on to become a well known coach. Everything in the 50s was stamina-based, but Malcolm had great ideas and if you look at how the game has progressed, how right he was.

My days as a professional footballer were over, but I stayed in the game working at Colchester United, where I enjoyed their great day against Leeds in 1970, and Chelmsford Town. My fondest memories, though, are of my playing days and in particular that magical day at Wembley in 1955. Whenever I return to Newcastle, fans love to reminisce and I would dearly love to see them win it again. I can't believe the Magpies have not won a domestic trophy since that day. It was my one appearance at Wembley and it was a glorious day in every sense.

BERT TRAUTMANN 1956
GOALKEEPER 1949–1964

BORN   22 October 1923, Bremen, Germany
SIGNED   November 1949 from St. Helen's Town
MANCHESTER CITY CAREER   545 games
HONOURS   1 FA Cup, Division Two promotion 1950/51, Football League representative
LEFT   Retired, June 1964

Bernd (Bert) Trautmann gained world renown as a goalkeeper after suffering protests at the time of signing for Manchester City due to his nationality. A City legend, he appeared in two FA Cup finals, his finest hour coming in 1956 when he helped the Blues to victory against Birmingham City despite breaking his neck following a brave save. The first foreign Footballer of the Year that season, Trautmann was awarded the OBE for his services to the game. Following his retirement, he managed Stockport County and worked for the German Football Association. In 2005 he launched the Trautmann Foundation to promote British-German understanding through football.

Manchester City 3 v Birmingham City 1

FA Cup final
Saturday 5 May 1956

Wembley Stadium
Attendance 100,000
Gate Receipts £49,856

Bert Trautmann shrugs off an undiagnosed broken neck to star as City come back from the disappointment of 1955 to win only their second ever FA Cup

Teams

Les McDowall	**Managers**	Arthur Turner
Bert Trautmann	1	Gil Merrick
Bill Leivers	2	Jeff Hall
Roy Little	3	Ken Green
Ken Barnes	4	John Newman
Dave Ewing	5	Trevor Smith
Roy Paul (capt.)	6	Len Boyd (capt.)
Bobby Johnstone	7	Gordon Astall
Joe Hayes	8	Noel Kinsey
Don Revie	9	Eddy Brown
Jack Dyson	10	Peter Murphy
Roy Clarke	11	Alex Govan
Hayes 3, Dyson 65, Johnstone 70	**Scorers**	Kinsey 15

Referee: A Bond

GROWING UP IN BREMEN, I played centre-forward for local team Tura Bremen, and like many youngsters at the time joined the Hitler Youth. It was just something you did because we did not have a mind of our own. It was a chaotic way to grow up and frightening, but at least it took me off the streets and allowed me to compete in athletics, handball and football.

I was a motor mechanic when the war started. I became a paratrooper and served on the Russian front, earning my wings in 1941. After serving on the Eastern and Western Fronts, I was among troops abandoned in Northern France. We were captured and two Americans were designated to escort me to a PoW centre. I thought this was my last hour because I was told to put my arms above my head and walk across a field. I waited for a shot, but there wasn't one. I never ran as fast in my life. A British soldier eventually captured me.

At a PoW camp at Ashton-in-Makerfield in Lancashire, our Scottish major loved football. We played to keep fit and pass the time. The major got permission for our camp side to play local teams in Ashton and plenty of civilians came to watch. I was playing outfield, but picked up an injury. Our goalkeeper came from near my hometown and always wanted to play centre-forward, so I went in goal. It was pure luck, but I found goalkeeping came natural to me. My paratrooper training certainly helped me cushion the ball when I dived and I stayed in goal until I left the camp in 1948.

Then came an offer from the government to stay in Britain for 12 months, which I took up, as it was a good opportunity. At the same time, I joined St. Helen's Town and during 18 months in the Lancashire Combination, attendances went from 1,500 to 6,000. With the extra income, the club erected a new stand.

Rumours started that Burnley, Everton and Manchester City wanted to sign me. Eventually I signed for City, who needed a long-term replacement for legendary goalkeeper Frank Swift following his retirement. My arrival brought an outcry from fans. Nowadays, there are hundreds of foreign players, but in 1949, signing me was headline news, especially as I was an ex-German paratrooper. Season ticket holders threatened a boycott; the club was bombarded with protest letters and around 40,000 demonstrated in the streets. At the club, things were different. Eric Westwood was captain and along with other professionals, helped me settle, taking my mind of everything else that was going on. They were very good to me, though they did take the Mickey. They'd say, "Jerry, we won the war not you." It did take time to understand English humour, but there was no animosity.

I had expert guidance from the start in Frank Swift, who was a father figure at Maine Road. After five reserve games, I made my first team debut at Bolton Wanderers halfway through the 1949/50 season. Frank was there. He knew the supporters' expectations and that I was nervous. Frank was wonderful. He called everybody 'son' and came over to me before the game and said: "You're playing your first league game, son. When you go out, ignore the crowd completely. They're not there, just concentrate on your own game". I knew the crowd would jeer me and there were shouts of "Nazi" and "Heil Hitler", but I concentrated and simply let my football do the talking. It was great advice, even though we lost 3-0.

I kept my place for a home debut against Birmingham City. Over the years, I played over 500 games for City, but this was the most important emotionally. Fans were still protesting, but a Rabbi in Manchester said he felt that you cannot convict one person for the atrocities committed by Hitler. From that moment, my football career began. Home supporters accepted me, which meant everything. To cap a great day, we won 4-0.

City were a very inconsistent team. We were fighting relegation that season. Among many defeats, we lost 7-0 at Derby County, but there was no abuse thrown at me personally. Journalists were fair, they didn't look for sensationalism. Against Derby, I could not move in the mud, but still gave everything. Journalists recognised that.

I was a determined footballer and would always listen to sound advice. My father-in-law was club secretary at St. Helen's Town and told me from the start that you had not achieved anything in football until the London press recognised your talent. Manchester papers had a certain amount of power, but were nothing compared to London-based papers. My first game in London was against Fulham. We lost 1-0 at Craven Cottage, but it could have been eight. It was one-way traffic, but somehow I kept shots out. At the end, both teams applauded me off the field. I couldn't believe it. Every journalist praised my performance.

By the end of the season, City had suffered relegation and Les McDowall succeeded Jock Thomson as manager. We got off to a great start the next campaign and made no mistake, finishing runners-up to return to the top flight at the first time of asking. We played some terrific football, scored lots of goals and enjoyed excellent wins against Bury and Chesterfield 5-1, and Barnsley 6-0. There was also a thrilling 4-4 draw with Grimsby. I was ever-present and looked forward to testing myself against the best again.

The team was developing with the likes of Roy Paul, Jimmy Meadows, Dave Ewing, Don Revie and Roy Clarke coming into the side and City consolidated over the next few seasons. Before a match on a Friday, we had a short meeting. Our team talks were simple. Les didn't talk much about tactics, it was more man to man. If you were playing against Stan Matthews or Tom Finney, he would say, "Keep him on the outside, as he likes to cut inside." That was it.

Throughout my career, I never changed my approach to a game and I learned to play a match the night before in my mind. For home matches, I was always at Maine Road before 1pm. We were all on time. In the dressing room, I was peg number 32 and always wanted to go out correctly dressed. I put my right boot on first and shirt last and never wore a darned sock. When our socks had rings, some players had four, five, two or three showing. I always had to have the same number on each sock. I loosened up 20 minutes before kick off. Some players ran out in a particular place in the line-up. Most goalkeepers came out behind the captain, but it did not bother me. That wasn't one of my superstitions.

I followed Frank Swift's advice and it never let me down. When I went out, I put my head down, threw my cap in the net; that was it. Some people thought I was high-handed as I didn't acknowledge the crowd, but I was just concentrating. Defensively, I commanded the area and playing outfield in my earlier days helped me react to certain situations. I positioned defenders on both posts at free kicks and corner kicks because I was never a goal line keeper. I tried to claim or clear a ball and only stood on the line for a penalty. It is nice when the likes of Bobby Charlton described me as the greatest goalkeeper of all time, but, of course, I admired other goalkeepers like Ted Ditchburn, Gil Merrick, Ronnie Simpson and Jack Kelsey.

In my era, it was tough because a centre-forward could barge a goalkeeper if both your feet were on the ground. In the air, they couldn't. Football is a game of bodily contact, so you had to prepare yourself. Instead of going for a ball straight, I went in sideways so met an opponent at an angle with my shoulder at the ready. There were times when I got hurt. I remember once Trevor Ford of Aston Villa was having a right go at me. I told him, "next time you barge me, I will put you in hospital." Trevor left me alone for three years until a game at Maine Road when he was playing for Sunderland. I caught a cross and left him behind me. In those days, we bounced the ball before kicking it away. Anyway, I bounced the ball, and Trevor came from behind me and nicked the ball. It ran loose and he scored a goal. I thought, "you cheeky bugger." We still won 3-1.

Football then was very different to the modern game. We went out to win every game and entertain, whereas today sides go out not to lose. Defend, defend, defend; how can you win a game if your priority is on not losing? Teams also had six or seven personalities, whereas many teams now have only ordinary players. Training was stamina-based and there was no specialist goalkeeper training. During pre-season, we ran miles and miles. We did interval training up the stands 30 or 40 times in a session and 20-odd miles on the road. We also had five or six players who could run 100 yards in under 11 seconds. We were tough, had endurance and stamina, which you needed because the pitches were full of mud, often waterlogged and there was no grass; only the areas by the corner flags were green. Today, pitches are like a snooker table, anyone can play on them. It was a great era to play, though, and often we went back to the training ground to work on things. We enjoyed ourselves and put plenty of effort in.

The 1953/54 campaign saw the 'Revie plan' evolve at City after Hungary beat England 6-3 at Wembley that November. Hungary played brilliantly and their system suited us. When a ball was crossed into our penalty area, I always went out to claim it. Now, our half-backs could watch the flight of a ball, turn and go on the attack waiting for me to release the ball to a deep centre-forward like Hidegkuti. Most sides employed a centre-forward leading the line like Trevor Ford, Nat Lofthouse or Stan Mortenson but we had Don Revie, who played like Hidegkuti.

We tried the system with Johnny Williamson in the reserves. Freddie Tilson was in charge of the team and approved. Freddie discussed it with Les McDowall and Don brought it to the first team for the opening game in 1954/55 at Preston. It didn't work straight away as we lost 5-0. The coach was very quiet coming back through the Blackpool holiday traffic and, of course, the papers hammered us. Credit to Les, he stood firm and we thumped Sheffield United 5-2 in the next game. Results picked up, especially with Ken Barnes now offering balance after breaking into the side.

We enjoyed fine wins at Arsenal 3-2 and at home to Manchester United 3-2, although there was the odd setback such as a 5-1 defeat at Charlton Athletic. I did not have time to dwell on that result, though, because I was set to visit Wembley as Germany, who became world champions in 1954, were playing England and I was attending as interpreter. I'd been to the 1949 FA Cup final and also when Blackpool won in 1953. Both occasions I got goose pimples when supporters sang *Abide with Me* and really enjoyed the experience. I now understood FA Cup fever.

The night before the England v Germany game, I went with the squad to Wembley, and, of course, was impressed when I walked out onto the pitch for the first time, even though there were no supporters in the stands. I stood under the goal and thought, "wouldn't it be marvellous to play here just the once." National coach Sepp Herberger had a policy of not selecting German players who played in other countries so my only opportunity would be an FA Cup final.

Within weeks, we embarked on another FA Cup run. I'd only reached the fourth round to date, so hoped for better things. I would not be disappointed as we defeated Derby, Manchester United, Luton, Birmingham City and Sunderland to reach Wembley. The derby win was memorable because almost 75,000 supporters packed Maine Road to see Don Revie and Joe Hayes score crucial goals, and to cap a great season of derby clashes, we won 5-0 in the league at Old Trafford to complete a clean sweep; the only time in my City career.

Reaching Wembley was something special, and in our final league games, we persevered and finished seventh. We prepared at Eastbourne and, at the end of a training session, I asked the players to hammer shots at the same time. I caught one at a stretch, went to the ground, and ricked my ruddy neck. I thought my Wembley dream was over. I could not move my head for three days, but we found a physiotherapist who gave me intensive treatment and got me fit.

As the day approached, nerves increased. The journey to the stadium was a spectacle. Seeing all our supporters it was obvious what the match means to fans. In the dressing room, I kept the preparation as close to a league game as possible, but it was not easy. Les gave his final instructions then we had to wait in the tunnel, which was nerve wracking. I had goose pimples when I heard *Abide with Me* as at those previous finals. Suddenly we walked out and heard the crowd roar. The size of the stadium hit me. You're so small with so many people around you, it was a magnificent sight. The feeling inside, it was tremendous. We met the Duke of Edinburgh and he asked how I was in German, but I just wanted to start the game.

At last, we kicked off, but Jackie Milburn headed a goal from a corner in the first minute, which caught us by surprise. We lost Jimmy Meadows through injury, which was a real blow, but we battled hard and Bobby Johnstone scored before half time to level things. Wembley is a big pitch and we tired. Newcastle were the better team and won comfortably 3-1. Of course, there were tears because you never know if you'll get the chance to go back again. But our captain Roy Paul stood up on the journey home and stated that he knew we'd be back the next year. The same had happened when City lost to Everton in 1933 and came back a year later to defeat Portsmouth. Hopefully history would repeat itself.

It took us some time to get going in 1955/56. Don Revie was struggling to recreate the form of the previous season when he was Footballer of the Year. We suffered heavy defeats, including a 7-1 drubbing at Wolves and 5-2 defeat to Charlton Athletic. Jack Dyson came into the side and Bobby Johnstone replaced Don in the deep-lying role. Results picked up around Christmas and just as well because we were determined to make an impact in the FA Cup.

We always listened to the draw on a Monday lunchtime after training. Someone would bring a radio in and we'd cram around to hear whether we'd been lucky. The third round draw gave us a home tie against 1953 winners Blackpool. It would be tough. Mist settled over Maine Road before kick off. The match should not have started. In the end, we were relieved when the game was abandoned with the score at 1-1after an hour. Joe Hayes had equalised an Ernie Taylor first minute strike, but a replay would have been a real battle.

The re-match took place in atrocious conditions on the Wednesday afternoon. Bobby Johnstone opened the scoring for us in the first half, but Bill Perry equalised immediately. Finishing the match was in question because the referee was struggling to see the line markings, but we carried on and Jack Dyson scored the winner. We were delighted.

Next, we faced a tricky match at Southend. Facing lower league teams was always hard as we'd experienced when Luton defeated us 5-1 in 1953. The weather was also not a great omen because it rained for three days on the Essex coast. The drains failed to get rid of excess water, so groundsmen dug trenches across the pitch, which filled up with cockleshells. The pitch was a quagmire, but we had to get on with it even though our feet sank a few inches in the mud. Joe Hayes gave us a first half lead. From then on, we had to close down their attack. It was hard work. A muddy pitch can be a goalkeeper's nightmare, but then there are days on a perfect pitch when you drop every ball. I had to concentrate and enjoyed one of those days when the ball stuck to my hands like glue. I received praise in the papers, but it was a great performance by the whole side to come away with a 1-0 win.

In the fifth round, we faced Liverpool, who were battling for promotion to the First Division under new manager Bill Shankly. It was not going to be easy. The first match took place at Maine Road in front of almost 70,000 fans. Snow had fallen heavily, but it had been pushed to the side of the pitch by kick off. We came out early to get used to what could only be described as treacherous conditions. With ice underfoot, controlling the ball and timing tackles was difficult. It turned into a battle, which ended goalless, but we should have won because we had our chances.

At a snowbound Anfield in the replay, Liverpool fancied their chances and I almost gifted them a first minute lead, but Dave Ewing denied Billy Liddell. Liverpool did take the lead in the second half before Jack Dyson equalised. We grabbed the initiative two minutes from time when Joe Hayes scored. It was a great relief, but deep into injury time, Liddell skipped past our defence to fire home with the last kick of the match. I could not believe it. I was devastated. But when I looked up, I noticed that some of our players had left the field, so I joined them. Mervyn Griffiths had blown his final whistle as Liddell began his run. Liverpool players complained bitterly, but we were through. The controversy raged on for days, but pictures in local papers showed the referee signal the end before Liddell scored. Every side needs luck to win the Cup and we had enjoyed plenty in the opening rounds. Just maybe, this was going to be our year.

We drew Everton in the quarter-finals. Cup fever was gripping the club as 76,000 fans packed Maine Road. I was doubtful on the morning of the game, but our trainer Lawrie Barnett declared me fit after a test. Early on, I had to be on my toes to keep out Tommy Eglington, but was unable to prevent Jimmy Harris scoring. It was a worrying time because Everton were in control, so were relieved to reach half time. Slowly we got back into the match and equalised 20 minutes from time when Joe Hayes squeezed between two Everton defenders to head home a Roy Paul free kick. We sensed the relief among City supporters and Bobby Johnstone soon headed the winner from a Roy Clarke cross.

Into the semi-finals and the draw gave us another tough clash, this time against Tottenham Hotspur. Although fans talked about a return to Wembley, we thought of nothing further than the next game. Playing the 'push and run' style of football, Tottenham were going to be testing and they did caused us problems. Danny Blanchflower went close early on, but we edged ahead before half time. Bobby Johnstone set Roy Clarke free down the left flank, sprinted ahead and out-jumped two defenders to head home Roy's cross for a fantastic goal.

We controlled the second half with Ken Barnes and Roy Paul dominating midfield, but late on there was a melée of players on the edge of our penalty box. I dived in and brought down George Robb. It could have been a penalty, but the referee let play continue. It was one of those things. During a game, you do things instinctively as you have less than a second to decide what to do. Yes, I fouled him, but it was instinctive not malicious. We held on to win, but Tottenham felt aggrieved. There was tremendous relief in our dressing room as we celebrated our promised return to Wembley. More important, there was a steely determination to bring the Cup home.

The papers were full of the Robb incident and a week later, we returned to London for a league match at White Hart Lane. Before the game, we went to a local picture house and to my amazement; the incident was on *Movietone News*. The reporter said, "Watch German goalkeeper Bert Trautmann foul George Robb by holding his legs". I couldn't believe it; of all the news stories available and they included this incident. Tottenham supporters were still bitter and I received the worst abuse at a game I can recall during those 90 minutes, but it just made me more determined to play well, although we went down to a 2-1 defeat. We finished the league campaign in fourth place following a 4-2 win over Portsmouth, our highest position since my debut.

Matt Busby's Manchester United won the league, so we were determined to make it a Manchester double as media attention turned to the FA Cup final. We faced Birmingham City, who had gained promotion the previous season from Division Two and finished sixth in the First Division, two points behind us. It would be tough because few sides had outscored Birmingham, who'd had forwards Eddy Brown, Noel Kinsey, Peter Murphy and Gordon Astall finding the target regularly. We'd lost 4-3 at St. Andrew's early in the season and drew 1-1 at Maine Road shortly after both of us reached Wembley. We respected them because they had won all their cup ties away from home, including against Arsenal and Sunderland. They were favourites to many pundits, which suited us as it put pressure on them, but we did not think it would be a harder final than Newcastle. After, all only Gil Merrick and Jeff Hall of their team had Wembley experience, whereas most of our side had played at the Twin Towers.

For supporters, getting Cup final tickets was always difficult. City were allocated 30,000, but as we'd had two home gates in the Cup over 70,000, thousands would be disappointed. All players were approached for tickets, but there was little we could do, as we needed ours for our own families.

As in 1955, we stayed at the Queen's Hotel in Eastbourne during the build up. Bill Leivers (ankle) and Bobby Johnstone (thigh strain) were the main injury concerns, but both responded to treatment. Don Revie had been in and out of the side, but travelled. Bobby was pencilled to play the deep-lying role with Bill Spurdle on the right wing, but an attack of boils for Bill brought a eleventh-hour return for Don, with Bobby returning to the wing. Johnny Hart, who'd missed out against Newcastle with a broken leg, also failed to make the line up and you had to feel sorry for both Bill and Johnny, but injuries are part and parcel of the professional game. We had an experienced outfit with plenty of pace and I was confident we would triumph.

I had complete confidence in all my teammates. Bill Lievers was a tough footballer who never shirked a tackle. Bill talked about what he would do to opponents, but that was it. He was a great team player and could read a game well. Roy Little was very tenacious and a great man-marker. He stuck to his opponents like glue and was the joker in the side.

Our captain Roy Paul was an exceptional footballer. He might not have been the fastest player around, but he could read the game brilliantly. Roy was a beautiful header and deliverer of a ball, but we did have our misunderstandings on occasion. Against Birmingham in a cup tie the previous season, I went out for a cross, shouted loud and had the ball in my hands. Roy came in kicked the ball out from my hands and it hit the crossbar. I screamed, "You Welsh B*****". He replied, "You German B******; get back into goal!" Roy was the best centre half and skipper City have ever had. He was an amazing man and a big influence on the team. He would say, "Come on lads! You have the ability to win." He was so inspirational.

Dave Ewing had one of the biggest hearts in the game. When things weren't going well and we were under pressure Dave was a tower of strength. Many times we won by a single goal and Dave secured the win. He was a pure stopper, but not the greatest back-passer; in fact, some of the best saves I made in my career were from Dave! Half-back Ken Barnes was the best in his position not to play for England. Ken would see me coming out for a cross, turn and go for the open spaces. Ken was a great team player, a beautiful stroker of the ball and the linkman. Ken for me was the key to the Revie plan. When he played, so did City.

I looked for Don Revie when I had the ball most of the time because when he came deep he always found space. Don would have his back to an opponent and because he knew how I threw, would immediately spin round knowing the ball would end up in front of him. Then he could go forward and ping a ball 40 or 50 yards. He was a very good footballer and an expert at the banana pass or shot. Joe Hayes was a great goal scorer. Joe never looked like a footballer, but was sharp and sensed the right place to be to stick the ball away. Jack Dyson was a natural footballer and had terrific ball control, but before a match was always nervous.

Bobby Johnstone read the game brilliantly, was a great distributor of the ball and technically was the perfect footballer. Bobby was brilliant, one of the best I have ever seen. Roy 'Nobby' Clarke was direct, determined, tricky and a fast footballer. Roy was a classical winger, always aiming to get to the dead ball line before pulling the ball back across the face of goal. He also scored his share of goals, but mainly had that ability to turn a game our way.

Going down Wembley Way again was special. Having done it the year before you tend to take more in, but you are concentrating on the game ahead. We knew the feeling of losing and did not want to experience that again. Our jerseys were out waiting for us in the dressing room, we were ready to go. Les McDowall went over our roles and reminded us of the early goal we let in against Newcastle. We must not get caught cold again. He also told us not to carry the ball too much because the pitch can sap your energy. Play to our strengths and we'd win.

Waiting in the tunnel, *Abide With Me* completed the community singing and it was time to walk out onto Wembley. Roy Paul gave a final rallying call. He was in doubt that we would win. I was fifth in line behind Don Revie. Again, we met the Duke of Edinburgh and had a brief chat. Then it was game on and just as we hoped, we made a terrific start, scoring on three minutes. After collecting a pass from Bill Leivers, Don began the move with a sweeping 40-yard pass to Nobby Clarke. Racing forward to take the return pass, Don dragged the ball back with the sole of his boot to Joe Hayes, who gave Gill Merrick no chance with a great left-foot strike.

The goal gave us confidence, but you don't think, "oh we'll beat them easily". If you do, you're dead - and sure enough Len Boyd and Eddy Brown were proving a handful. Brown made Birmingham's equaliser on 15 minutes when he evaded Roy Paul and Dave Ewing to set up Noel Kinsey to score. I thought I should have saved it, but my reactions were a split second too late. Both sides tested each other defensively, so Gil Merrick and myself had to be on our guard. Although level at half time, we still felt very confident we'd come through.

Bobby Johnstone and Nobby Clarke had caused Birmingham full backs Jeff Hall and Ken Green problems, while centre-back Trevor Smith had struggled. It had been an open game and must have been entertaining for supporters. Ken Barnes had been marking Peter Murphy tightly as instructed by Les, but Don wanted him to link up more and made his feelings known. It was time to play and take the game to Birmingham.

We took a grip on the match and closed Birmingham down at every opportunity. Bill Leivers controlled the impact of Murphy and Alex Govan, enabling Ken to get forward and attack. Meanwhile little was getting past Dave and Roy. Don Revie was playing superbly, linking up play. It seemed only a matter of time before we took the lead and eventually the pressure told as we struck two goals in five minutes midway through the half.

Don, Bobby and Ken combined to give Jack Dyson the chance for our second goal on 65 minutes, which he took. Then, on 70 minutes, it was 3-1. That came about from a long clearance after I collected the ball from Brown's feet. Launching the ball forward for a counter-attack, which was integral to the Revie Plan, Don found Jack, who nodded on to Bobby Johnstone to thump past Merrick. That was it, two moves and we scored. We led 3-1 and I felt confident.

The game was not over, though, as Birmingham would have to press forward. Fifteen minutes from time, came the incident that changed my life. I sustained a neck injury that would still be talked about 50 years on, when I dived at the feet of Birmingham inside-left Peter Murphy as he raced into our penalty area and looked like scoring. It was an instinctive save and I did feel a hell of a bump as his knee struck my neck.

If I were a line goalkeeper, I would not have sustained the injury. The impact was tremendous, but no-one could have detected it was a broken neck. If they had, I'd have been off like a shot. I was told later that whilst I was on the ground, City fans were chanting 'We want Bert' and then when I staggered to my feet the chant changed to 'For He's a Jolly Good

Fellow'. After I recovered, I went on to save at Brown's feet, but then broke down when I collided with Dave Ewing. My neck hurt like hell.

Our defenders did everything to shield the ball from me because there were no substitutes allowed. They knew I wasn't well, but nobody knew I could not see properly. At first, it was foggy then, two minutes from time, it was clear. I was very groggy and was fighting hard to concentrate. But the boys did so well to keep Birmingham away from my goal.

At the end of the game, it was not joyful for me; I was in so much pain. I went for my medal and the Duke of Edinburgh asked if I was OK. I told him it was like going to the dentist with bad toothache. I did not join the players when they showed off the FA Cup and enjoyed the lap of honour. I walked slowly back to the dressing room.

No doctor examined me before we headed off to the Café Royal. On the Sunday, before going back to Manchester by train, I went to see an osteopath. He told me I had five vertebrae out of place. He tried to manipulate them back into position and told me four were back in. He had another try at the fifth, pushing my head back. It was very painful, but he couldn't do it. He wanted me to return so he could have another go, but there was no way I was going back. I wasn't going to miss the victory parade around Manchester.

The crowds were amazing and the event was covered live on Granada Television before a civic reception, but I was still not feeling great. Frank Swift came over and slapped me on the shoulder to congratulate me. It's amazing I didn't pass out. During the week, I went to Manchester Royal Infirmary where an X-ray revealed the full problem. A vertebrae had been pushed out of alignment, crushing several nerves. I was fortunate the osteopath had not caused permanent damage. They operated immediately. My future was uncertain as I recuperated over the summer, but I was utterly determined to play again even after one of our sons died in a car accident, which was such a shock.

It had been a traumatic time, but I was back in the side by Christmas although we had slipped down the league. Our FA Cup defence ended in the third round when Newcastle United overturned a 3-0 deficit in an incredible replay at Maine Road to win 5-4 in extra-time. The Cup final team had begun to break up and by the end of the season, Don Revie had joined Sunderland, Roy Paul had departed to Worcester City as player-manager and Jack Dyson's appearances would be restricted. My remaining years at City would bring no more FA Cup glory. In fact, we got no further than the fourth round, and our exits included 5-1 defeats to West Brom and Southampton. I was also in goal on the famous occasion when Denis Law scored six goals against Luton Town in a fourth round clash in 1961 before the match was abandoned 20 minutes from time with us 6-2 ahead. We obviously fancied ourselves in the rescheduled game, but somehow lost 3-1.

In the league, we experienced highs and lows. In 1957/58, we finished fifth, scoring and conceding 100 goals. We enjoyed terrific wins including a double over Everton 6-2 and 5-2, yet went down to heavy defeats against West Brom 9-2 and Leicester City 8-4. The following season we just avoided relegation, yet defeated Tottenham, Chelsea and Newcastle 5-1.

By 1962/63, the maximum wage had been abolished and as players we had to negotiate our own terms. I'd started on £10 a week back in 1949, which went up slowly, but now I was my own agent, and could only manage to negotiate £35 a week, although new players were earning more than twice my salary. My City career was ending. The season began with an 8-1 defeat at Wolves followed by a 6-1 loss at home to West Ham. Harry Dowd replaced me. City suffered relegation and I would play just three more matches the following season. George Poyser replaced Les McDowall as manager, and I soon left.

When I look back at my football career, I was very fortunate. People talk about great players and every team had stars. There were the likes of Tom Finney, Wilf Mannion, Stanley Matthews, Tommy Lawton, Nat Lofthouse, Trevor Ford and John Charles. All were exceptional talents and I am able to say, "aren't I a lucky fellow" because I played with or against them.

Receiving the Footballer of the Year award the year we won the Cup and my OBE were wonderful highlights, but my testimonial match also stands out. It was raining heavily. I thought, "no-one will come tonight," but Maine Road was packed, it was magnificent. I stood there, tears running down my face; there was joy, appreciation and a feeling that is difficult to describe. Of course, I had ability, but without people's help and acceptance in the early days, I would have packed my bags and gone home. Of all the games though, winning the FA Cup in 1956 will always be special. It was such a highlight for every professional footballer. It was a day I will never forget.

Over fifty years have passed since I won the FA Cup with Manchester City and became the first foreign player to win the Footballer of the Year award. So much has happened since, yet whenever I visit Manchester to attend a function, fans still talk about that match when we defeated Birmingham City and I broke my neck. Painful though it was at the time, the memories are still clear.

PETER McPARLAND 1957
LEFT-WING 1952–1962

BORN 25 April 1934, Newry
SIGNED September 1952 from Dundalk
VILLA CAREER 341 games, 120 goals
HONOURS 1 FA Cup, 1 Division Two Championship, 34 Northern Ireland caps, Football League representative
LEFT Transferred to Wolverhampton Wanderers, January 1962

A Villa legend, Irishman Peter McParland brought pace and power to the left wing during a 10 year spell at Villa Park. His bullet left foot provided crosses and shots, both with deadly accuracy. He was a renowned goalscorer and topped the Villa scoring charts twice, netting over a century of goals for the club. But his two most famous goals came at Wembley in 1957 in a game perhaps just as famous for his challenge on Manchester United goalkeeper Ray Wood, which left United down to ten men for much of the game, but was considered fair by referee Coultas.

Aston Villa 2 v Manchester United 1

FA Cup final
Saturday 4 May 1957

Wembley Stadium
Attendance 100,000
Gate Receipts £48,816

Peter McParland courts controversy and scores twice as Villa deny the Busby Babes a first double of the twenty-first century.

Teams

	Managers	
Eric Houghton		Matt Busby
Nigel Sims	1	Ray Wood
Stan Lynn	2	Bill Foulkes
Peter Aldis	3	Roger Byrne (capt.)
Stan Crowther	4	Eddie Colman
Jimmy Dugdale	5	Jackie Blanchflower
Pat Saward	6	Duncan Edwards
Les Smith	7	John Berry
Jackie Sewell	8	Liam Whelan
Bill Myerscough	9	Tommy Taylor
Johnny Dixon (capt.)	10	Bobby Charlton
Peter McParland	11	David Pegg
McParland 65, 71	**Scorers**	Taylor 83

Referee: F Coultas

YOU ALWAYS FEEL THAT you're going to win the Cup. As you get ready for that Third Round tie on the first weekend of the New Year as a top flight player, you're thinking "This will be our year."

But I really had the feeling that Villa could be a decent cup team that year and I did actually say that to people. I thought we were developing into a team that was very hard to beat. In fact we were never beaten until the very last second. There was that feeling amongst us, that we were all decent players and we were looking to be successful. I think we were top half of the table most of the season and we finished tenth. We didn't win enough matches to be any higher, but we also didn't lose many. In those days, of course, it was a much more level playing field when it came to winning things. Even though Wolves and Man United were the best two league sides in the 1950s, it was rare for the same teams to make it through to Wembley. Often clubs from lower down the league got through and once you are there, who knows what can happen.

And our run to the 1957 final was a hell of battle. We started off at fellow top flight side Luton Town and when the 90 minutes was up we were out of the Cup. There wasn't a big deal made of injury time then. That's something which has come into the game more due to the likes of Alex Ferguson insisting that it's played when his team need it! In those days the referee would just add whatever. So we're deep into what little injury time there was and this corner came over and we were all jumping for it desperately trying to get something on it. The ball dropped down about two yards out and stuck in the mud and I landed down on my knees right on the ball with a lot of players all around me, boots flailing, mud flying, bodies toppling. I dragged it over the line amid this melée with our right-back, Stan Lynn, behind me and he later told me "If you hadn't have taken it over the line I'd have kicked you into the net with the ball." He wasn't joking either. That was the equaliser and the relief was incredible. Luton kicked off and the ref blew the final whistle. Then we beat them 2-0 on the Monday at Villa Park. We were off and running.

When our run in the FA Cup started I'd been in the team as a regular from 1954. In August 1953, Villa had brought in Eric Houghton as manager to replace George Martin, who had signed me the previous summer as an 18 year-old from the Dundalk club in Ireland, where I'd proved myself an attacking player of some promise. Eric brought a trainer with him called Billy Moore from his previous club Notts County. Billy was a no nonsense kind of bloke and he rejuvenated the whole club with his ideas and personality. Billy was absolutely marvellous. He had great variety in training and knew a great, great deal about injuries. He could diagnose you on the spot, whatever the problem was. At Notts County he'd looked after Tommy Lawton, the great Tommy Lawton and Tommy always rated Billy as the best trainer he'd ever worked with. The best person to get you fit and get you moving.

Billy was a Newcastle lad whose experience was playing for Stoke City. Under him we became a dogged sort of team that didn't give up easily and we'd be fighting and battling to the end. Billy would give you tremendous confidence. In fact he used to say to me, "when the team are on their knees, I want to look out and see you going like a bomb because you're so fit." His ways got into you mentally. He'd make you believe that you were strong and could do things and not to be afraid to try things. He'd also give you confidence by putting you into a good physical condition. Billy made us work physically hard in training, but we also had a great amount of ball work as well. That was unusual then when many clubs kept the ball away from players during the week, believing that they would be more hungry for it at the weekends!

I was a winger. The game then was about wingers. I had been a goalscoring inside-forward at Dundalk, but George Martin had decided to turn me into a left winger when I arrived. I think it was because of my pace. It was a case of developing more strength and skills after that; running at full-backs a bit more. I was playing on the left, but I was always a naturally right-footed player. As a 10 year-old I had developed my left foot by kicking the ball against a wall and by my early teens, when I was playing seriously, my left foot was equal to my right and so, having good ability with both feet as a left winger, I developed into coming inside and letting fly with my right and that helped me get goals. But I could also get to the byline to cross the ball and create goals for other people. I could do both things, where many wingers could only do one or the other. That was a strong point for me. George Martin always told me, "You get to the byline four times and pull the ball back in a game and one of those chances will get converted into a goal." That's all my thoughts were then. Four times down the line and one will end up in the net.

I grew up with the legendary Danny Blanchflower in the team as left half-back, what you would call left midfield today. Danny always wanted the ball. He used to say to me, "If you're ever in trouble, look up and I'll be inside you. Just give it to me. I'll help you out."

And you know with fellows like that around to help you it wasn't too hard coming into the Villa first team. And it did help that a few of them were Irish. There was a fellow called Con Martin, an Irish international centre-half, who also, rather strangely, played in goal too. Con was great to me. I'd been living in these digs and I didn't really like the fact that the landlady was bringing in more and more people and it was becoming crowded. Con said to me that I could go and live with him and his wife. He had a couple of kids and I ended up acting as babysitter for them. He helped me to settle and feel at home. He'd been a Gaelic football player in Ireland and had played centre-field for his county. That involved a lot of high jumping and catching. And he'd been a basketball player when he'd been in the Irish Airforce (they only had one plane at the time). So he had that ability to get off the ground. It meant he was a great centre-half and played against all the top centre-forwards of the time. He developed a big, big reputation as a centre-back with two good feet and strong in the tackle. Because he could jump and handle as well, he actually ended up playing in goal for Ireland as cover on a foreign trip to Portugal and Spain.

Then there was another Irish half-back, Pat Saward, who we signed from Millwall that also went on to play for Ireland. He came from Cork. But my big mate in the Villa team was Welsh international wing half Vic Crowe. He arrived at the same time as me. We had a good solid bunch of players, without any superstars. And we became very difficult to beat with Billy driving us on.

In 1955/56 Villa only survived in Division One by the skin of our teeth after finishing level on points with Huddersfield Town. That was nerve-jangling I tell you. With three games to go we looked doomed, having only won just three games out of 14. Mind you it was a funny old season that year as Spurs, who'd won the title a couple of years before, and Chelsea, who were reigning Champions, were also in the mire and I remember that Arsenal were struggling for quite a while as well. We only got out of it by winning all three of those remaining games, rounding it off with a 3-0 win against West Brom. And it's a good job we did as Huddersfield also won their last three matches, but thankfully our goal average was better than theirs, so we just survived.

That really gave us the kick up the pants we needed to improve. Our league form in the 1956/57 season wasn't bad. I remember hammering Everton, Sheffield Wednesday and Wolves by a few goals. And Wolves were a great side under Stan Cullis. We ended up finishing in mid-table, as I say, but there was only one team in the title chase – and that was Manchester United, the Busby Babes. They won the Championship by a street, eight points ahead of Spurs, I think. And that was after winning it by even more the season before. They were a fabulous side and because of what happened to them the following year when their plane crashed, they were never allowed to truly fulfil their incredible potential.

But the fourth round FA Cup draw paired us with Second Division Middlesbrough, rather than one of those big clubs. That didn't mean it was any easier, though. We had to keep battling as we had all season, making sure we were hard to beat. And thankfully the goals kept going in at the other end. It was a cracking game at Ayresome Park. Jimmy Dugdale was playing centre-half for us and he had Brian Clough, who had a phenomenal goalscoring record, in his back pocket all game. But Cloughie still somehow managed to score two goals. They lead us once, but we beat them 3-2 and we had a good feeling after that game, because they were a top Division Two side and it gave us plenty of confidence.

Next we drew Bristol City, who were a Third Division team, at home. On the Friday, our scout, Jimmy Eason, who watched opposing teams for us, came in to give us a talk, because we didn't know anything about them at all. And he went through the team telling us about them and he came to their centre-forward, John Atyeo, who'd played international football for England and scored a few goals for his country as well [5 in 6 games], and Jimmy said "forget about this bloke when he's on his right foot. Stick him on his left. He's completely left footed."

So come the game, about 20 minutes in and City were playing well, backed by about 20,000 fans who'd travelled up from Bristol. Atyeo comes inside onto his right foot, with Jimmy shuffling him that way as he's been told and Big John lets fly with his right peg from all of 20 yards and the ball fairly flew into the top corner of the net to put them ahead! And then they were at us. They gave us a bit of a going over to half-time and their supporters were up and pushing them on. Eventually, though, we got the equaliser and then Jackie Sewell got the winner from one of my crosses. That was a tough old battle. But we scraped through. Mind you we didn't let Jimmy forget about John Atyeo's right foot!

Now we were into the quarter-final. I remember the BBC broke into the six o'clock news to make the draw for that round - that was how big the Cup was in those days. And I was sitting listening having my tea in the house. We had all talked about it during training and we'd said we don't care who we get as long as it's not Burnley at Turf Moor. Burnley was one of the toughest places to go to play football. Their side was full of little tricks and particularly adept at free-kicks. If anybody slept in they would catch you and break your offside trap. You had to be on the alert all the time. They would go on to win the title shortly afterwards and get to the Cup final themselves, so they were a good side. No teams liked going there and Villa hadn't won there for 25 years or so. They really had it over us at their place. And as the draw goes on we haven't come out. Until there's two teams left. Us and Burnley. We were OK against them at home, but that away record was a bit of a thing. And, of course, we drew Burnley at their place. I nearly swallowed my sausage whole when Burnley came out first!

But we managed to draw up there. They went into the lead just before half-time when their blond centre-forward Ray Pointer scored. And we had a bit of backs to the wall to hold on to the 1-0 deficit for quite a time. We had a right winger called Leslie Smith, who'd joined us from the Wolves in early 1956. Wolves had always been known in the 50s for their great wing play and Les had been the deputy to the great Johnny Hancocks. He was a great crosser of the ball. He used to drive balls across hard, just above head height and I'd come in on the back post and head them in. I had to work on the timing to get in front of my defender. And at Burnley, we broke away with about ten minutes to go and Les hit a cross spot on and I got between two defenders, I think one was Tommy Cummings, and met it full ball with my forehead and it rocketed into the back of the net. It was the most rewarding sort of goal you can watch going in because you've actually worked at it. And that move would prove crucial in the final too.

We battled it out to the end to take them back to Villa Park. And it was always on the cards that we would win. They were the same as we had been. They didn't want to come to Villa Park. And sure enough we beat them 2-0 on a Wednesday afternoon. I'll always remember that day. It was a dull March afternoon, forty odd thousand at Villa Park and the crowd looked really black in the background and lo and behold if Burnley don't come out wearing black shirts. The referee had to change his shirt to white. He had to take one of our change shirts and wear that. I made jokes that you couldn't see their players at all against the background. It was like a few years ago when Manchester United had those infamous grey shirts. Well just before they got hammered 6-3 at Southampton wearing them and changed them half-time, they wore them at the Villa. I was sitting watching with a young couple of Man United fans next to me, and I said as they came out, "What a horrible outfit." And the girl said to me "Yes, terrible." How anyone thinks those kind of kits are going to help a team, I don't know.

So by now we were in the semi-final, and boy had we had to battle to get there. As it happened there were three Birmingham teams in the hat for the draw - ourselves, Birmingham and West Brom, the first time ever three from the city had reached the semi-finals at the same time. I can remember having a photographic session at Villa Park with all three teams together. It had been arranged by the Midland papers, but all the national boys turned up as well. And I remember when these other photographers came in we all turned our backs on them, because we had agreed to this especially for the Midlands newspapers. It was a special thing for the area, so we turned our backs to the photographers from the national papers and it annoyed them so much that the next day they ran with the shots of our backs in the national newspapers. We did it because these other photographers were all freelance and would make plenty of money out of circulating our photographs and in those days we had no control over that kind of thing. There were no image rights or anything like that. And because it hadn't been set up for the national boys we turned our backs. I suppose player power was just really beginning at that stage and it was a small indication that we were unhappy with everyone making money out of us left, right and centre.

We came out of the hat with West Brom. It would have been something had it been Birmingham, but they got Manchester United! West Brom were a good team, an excellent team, and a lot of their side had won the FA Cup in 1954. They had great cup pedigree and had been together a number of years. There was a great rivalry between us, particularly after we had stopped them winning the Championship in 1954 when we took three points off them right at the end of the season. We had drawn 1-1 on Easter Monday at the Hawthorns, but then hammered them 6-1 the following evening at Villa Park. That allowed Wolves to win the Championship and, as West Brom went on to win the FA Cup, it meant that we'd denied them the double.

That was particularly relevant to us as Villa were the last club ever to achieve the famous double and that had been back in 1897. So, we were defending Aston Villa's double. The feat had passed into folklore by now because no-one had emulated it in 60 years and we loved the fact that we had scotched West Brom's chances of doing it in '54. That meant a lot to us then and it would mean a lot to us in the final, when we got there, because Manchester United were also trying to win the double and it gave us yet another reason to try and stop them.

In the league games against West Brom much earlier in the season we'd failed to score against them, drawing at home 0-0 and losing away 2-0. They'd ended up finishing only one place and a point below us in mid-table, so we were fairly well matched teams. We were always playing catch up in the first game at Wolverhampton. They took the lead through our left-half, Pat Saward, making a horrible mistake. He mis-trapped the ball and their centre-forward Brian Whitehouse went through and scored. Then, just before half-time, I hit one with my head again just inside the penalty area and beat Jim Saunders the goalkeeper. It was a really good header, you know, from a good distance out with power.

Then we came out in the second half and the same lad, Pat Saward, made another mistake and it also ended up in the back of the net and we were 2-1 down. He was a worrying type of feller and his whole game went to pieces. You could see him thinking "Oh, no! I've shot the boys. We're not going to get to Wembley now." So we pressed West Brom back again and we had them on the back foot and a ball was crossed into the goal-mouth and I was running in about the six yard line. And I knew this was a goal, but I was thinking to myself "I've got to keep it down" And with trying to keep it down I hit on top of the ball and it bounced up and bobbled towards the line, with the keeper on the floor. It took such a time to go in and the left-back was diving towards it full-length to try and get his hand to the ball. But thankfully there was enough on it to get it into the corner.

There was only six minutes left to go. We had them on the run after that and nearly won it. I got a ball with Barlow and Kennedy chasing me through the middle. I knew I had the pace to keep clear of them, but I didn't have the power to get away. I'd run myself into the ground and didn't have the energy. The semi-final of the cup is such a tense thing and we'd put so much effort into getting back level, that I couldn't burst away from them like I normally would have, so I got tackled and the chance went. But I could have had a hat-trick there and we would have been in the final straight away, but as it was we had to go through a replay.

But this was the sort of team we were. We knew we had that sort of comeback in us. Getting the result at Burnley had given us so much confidence and we knew we could take anybody on. So in the replay at St. Andrew's we took the lead after about 20 minutes. I clipped the ball into Billy Myerscough, our centre-forward, and he got down on his knees and headed it in to make it 1-0. Being in the lead is probably one of the harder things in a semi-final, because we were thinking "We're on our way to Wembley now" and we let ourselves be pushed onto the back foot and the Albion were really chucking it at us. We fought and battled to hold on. I found myself in our own penalty area defending, which I shouldn't have been doing, so I went and stood back up field as the outlet for the defence.

I always remember there were fans sitting on the top of the stand on the roof and I looked around while they were laying siege to our goal and there was this feller shouting from the rooftop "Don't go back in defence!" I was thinking "You'll topple down if you don't watch it," but all he cared about was Villa getting to Wembley. We survived an onslaught and towards the end of the game the pressure lessened as West Brom tired. It was more relief than celebration when the whistle went. Definitely relief that we'd made it, because we'd clung on to this lead for so long.

One of the funny things about it was that you didn't really realise what you'd done until ten or twelve days later. I was walking in town with Pat Saward and he suddenly said to me, "I can't believe it. We're in the final!" Yes, we had a celebration after the semi-final win, but it really comes into you a few days later. And he just kept saying, "We are in the final!"

There's a lot of time before the Cup final, once you've won the semi. Five weeks or so. It's a real long time and you are just hoping, "Please God it will all go OK and I won't do anything silly and get an injury." Some times it affects a team's league form badly, but we had a half decent run. We beat Birmingham, Sheffield Wednesday and Wolves and we had to play at Burnley about three weeks before the final and they weren't too happy about us beating them and they just came at us kicking lumps. Their manager was telling them to get stuck in and we didn't like that and lost 2-1.

We were facing Manchester United in the final as they'd beaten Birmingham 2-0 and they'd pretty much already wrapped up the league title. This, of course, was the original Busby Babes team. Actually it was funny, we'd played them at Manchester when we'd both won our quarter-finals with everyone saying that this could be the Cup final rehearsal. We'd played really well and drew 1-1 - and United didn't drop too many points at Old Trafford. We took a lot of confidence from that result.

We were so aware that we had to defend Aston Villa's proud boast of being the last team to win the double. That was at the front of our minds. We had to keep that record against the best team in the country. We knew a lot about them, of course. But you don't talk about how good teams like that are because it would scare the life out of you. They had the likes of Duncan Edwards, Dennis Viollet [Viollet missed the final through injury allowing a 19 year-old Bobby Charlton to play] and Liam Whelan, who were all great creative players. They had dangerous wingers, Johnny Berry, a good runner, going down the line and crossing and David Pegg, who was a young boy, going all the time. And they had this great centre-forward, Tommy Taylor, the England centre-forward. So there were threats every-where in their side.

We went down to London on the Friday morning on the train and stayed at Brent Bridge Hotel, near Wembley. Because there was a clash of shirts it was decided we both had to change and Eric Houghton, immediately on the ball, said, "No team in stripes have lost the Cup Final" making sure that the United boys knew this. Just recently Newcastle had won three times, so it was sort of true! So we had a blue outfit as our usual change kit and their kit was white, but Eric went and had some Claret and Blue pin-striped shirts made for us. You'll try anything to give yourself the smallest edge.

The FA Cup Final is steeped in superstition; Jack Tinn's famous spats which won the Cup for Portsmouth in 1939, for example, or Jimmy Melia's suit during Brighton's run in 1983. We were quite a superstitious bunch and Eric Houghton wore this Crombie coat, which he'd worn at Luton on that cold January day when it all started. And he kept wearing it all the way through the run until he wore it at Wembley – this great huge coat on a boiling summer's day! Steaming hot he was!

Another one for Eric started against Bristol City in that Fourth Round tie when he sent his wife outside when we were a goal down and thereafter during the run if we were losing he would say to her, "Go on. Get out of the way," and she would have to leave the ground! It worked, though, didn't it! Eric was a very superstitious fellow. I was a bit too. I carried bits of green in my pocket just for luck. I had a piece of green tape and little shamrock thing I kept on me during the run. Of course, I carried them on plenty of other occasions and they didn't work for me, but you forget about those don't you!

We got to Wembley at around 1.30pm. There was no such thing then as going out and having a look at the pitch, so we mooched around the dressing room, you know, hands in pockets waiting so as we could start changing. There were tons of telegrams waiting for us from well-wishing Villa fans. That was wonderful and helped pass the time too. As we finally got ready, everybody goes through their own little routines to prepare. And it's a funny thing. You're getting ready and there's a knock on the door and they shout "Get ready to come out" and there's a feeling then that comes into you. The thing that makes the Cup final the most special of all days. It's just this feeling that this is the one. This is it.

Some of the boys were diving for the toilets. Wembley had huge dressing rooms with about twelve toilets and they were all full about ten minutes before the kick-off! I really found the nerves when we heard *Abide with Me* being sung. In fact Jimmy Dugdale was being sick during it – and he'd won the Cup in '54 with West Brom!

We stood at the end of the tunnel and United came out of their dressing room and immediately the mind games began. "Look at their faces" was going down our line. Up and down between us, so they could hear. I think it was Stan Lynn who started it. He was a big hard player – a tough full-back. The United players did look as if they were a bit uptight and we took that out onto the pitch with us. They probably weren't, you know, but it geed us up no end. We were feeling good.

The most sensational feeling is to come up the dark tunnel and go out into the stadium when it hits you. It's just a big roar, you know, Whooom! as you arrive onto the pitch. As soon as I put my foot on the grass I felt, "this is it now, I'm here and I'm ready to go". They say that some players wilt at that very moment. You can either cope with it or not. It made me grow just that little bit in stature.

I had played at Wembley for Ireland and we had also been to the ground the day before the final to sort out what stud we would wear in the one pair of boots we owned. But little things make such a difference at Wembley. I remember Wally Barnes, the old Arsenal and Wales captain, was there when we arrived. He was covering the game for BBC television and he came over to us and made a good little point. Wembley was noted then for people getting injured. There was a succession of finals in which players got hurt or injured themselves and one side had to play with ten men. It eventually led to the introduction of substitutes. But Wally came over to us and said "When you get out here, don't go tear-arsing around all over the place in the warm up. Save it for the match when you really need it. You could pull a muscle if you do too much too soon." That was his little bit of advice. Well, I knew he was right as when I'd played there for Ireland I'd found the second half tough. We'd been beaten by England at Wembley in '55. As it happened we would record one of the Northern Irish international team's few victories at the old stadium later in 1957, so it was a pretty good year for me!

But the way the final panned out we were always in the lead, so we had no worries about the strength being sapped from us, because, of course, it's always the team that doesn't win that complains about that phenomenon. Did you ever notice that? Not the winners. It's as much mental as it is physical.

Fairly early on in the game we were playing well and had a grip on them and looked the far more likely team to score. Then the incident happened. That incident. The one for which the final will always be remembered.

We made a movement on our right hand side and Jackie Sewell came up the right edge of the penalty area and he crossed the ball and I am coming in on it and I thought "this is a goal", but instead of placing my header into a corner of the goal, I headed the bloody ball straight into Ray Woods' hands as he came out. I kept running as my momentum took me forwards. I was going a fair pace I can tell you - and Ray come out with the ball he'd just caught. I decided I was going to shoulder charge him. I knew Ray. He was the type of goalkeeper who would take you on. We did it then in the game. It was part of it. Everyone knows about Nat Lofthouse and Tommy Lawton banging into keepers. Well they weren't the only ones. But as we were going to make contact, Ray pulled away at the last minute and unfortunately we clashed our heads together. The side of my head hit Ray on the temple and he came off worst from it.

When I went down, 100,000 people were going round and round and I thought, "I'm finished." Things were just going round and round. But the trainer come on and sorted me out. Ray was in a much worse state. He had a damaged jaw and went off for a time before eventually coming back on to play on the wing.

Jackie Blanchflower went in goal and we played ten men for quite a while, but we didn't actually score. When he returned just before half-time to play out on the wing, Ray caused a few problems for our full-back. I thought "He should be back in goal", he was taking on our full-back and dribbling, so he must have been OK. But their bench must have thought that he wasn't fit enough. After the game several observers thought that

United should have put him in goal and left Blanchflower as an outfield player. I agree.

Halfway through the second half we finally made the breakthrough. Johnny Dixon crossed it from the right just like Les Smith had at Burnley. Low and flat, just above head height. And I ran in and just hammered it with my head into the net. It's a case of getting your timing right and getting the full power behind it and I was lucky enough to be able to do that when I was heading and do it on the run too. We'd practiced it a lot. I was always working at heading and getting the timing right, not getting in too early which is what a lot of modern players do. They're jumping from standing starts and craning back to try to reach the ball. I was trying to come onto it and head it on the run, getting across the front of a defender to beat him to the ball. It is quite rare for a winger to score goals with their head, but it's just something you sort of develop. I had a strong neck. I'd been a goalscorer all my career, even from the boy's club. Not prolific in the way a Greaves is, but getting enough goals here and there. I was noted during my time at the Villa for scoring the winning goal. And there's nothing more important in football matches than the winning goal. I was noted for that. It became a mental thing with both our team and the opposition, that if I put us ahead often it would prove to be the winning goal. So I had that in my armoury, which was a bit of luck to be able to do that. Especially in the FA Cup final.

I got so much power behind that header that it wouldn't have mattered who was in that goal. It fair flew in I'm telling you. I'd got in front of Foulkes and Duncan Edwards to make that header and there was no chance for any keeper. Banks, Shilton, Jennings – no-one was going to save that header because it was right in the top corner.

I fell forward when I headed it and got up and I was standing for a few seconds and I'm saying to myself, "I've scored a goal in the Cup Final!" When I went home in the summer a chap in Ireland said to me "You didn't know you'd scored, laddie!" I said "I did, but I was just standing there saying it myself." And then I've put my arms up and everyone came jumping around me.

Everyone wants to do that. Score in the Cup final. I just had.

We didn't want to just hold on to that lead. We just kept playing and we got our reward for staying positive shortly afterwards with a second goal. Another ball came from the right wing to the far post. This time I was there to head it back into the goalmouth. Johnny Dixon jumped to head goalwards and smacked it onto the crossbar. It went up in the air and came back down towards the penalty spot. I still congratulate myself for the speed that I got across from where I was to the middle of the goal to crack a volley into the back of the net. I beat Billy Myerscough to the ball. In fact he was underneath me as I landed, having jumped to strike the ball. I gave it a full right foot volley. No keeper would have ever saved that either. It was absolutely bang on. It had to be because if you get that wrong it ends up at the back of the stand. But it went like a rocket. I've got photographs of the goal and in them Billy is falling to the deck, so I think if I hadn't got there he may have got underneath it and skied it, so I'm glad that my reactions allowed me to come across and hit it. It was in the net. Again!

2-0. Two goals by me. Then it is a case of you want to get three. You are so high.

But then they scored.

Tommy Taylor netted from a corner kick with a looping header that Nigel Sims just couldn't reach. And then we were thinking, "Oh, God. We had a two goal lead and now we might lose it. We'd better hold onto this now." So we set our sights on defending. They threw everything at us. There were about seven minutes left and they chucked the kitchen sink. But they didn't create a chance. By now Ray Wood had finally returned to play in goal allowing Blanchflower out to give them ten fit outfield payers. They murdered us for those last few minutes. Our legs were starting to go. It hadn't affected us at 2-0, but as soon as it went to 2-1 people started getting cramp. I was fighting it. And I got dragged back into defending again. Billy Moore was shouting at me from the bench to get upfield to wait for a loose ball. It was wrong for me to drop back because when we got the ball the defenders needed someone to aim for. I was one of the most fresh and if they hammered the ball upfield I could race after it. But you get dragged into it when it's the Cup that's at stake.

We had three players that played brilliantly in defence. Stan Lynn, Peter Aldis and Jimmy Dugdale commanded the whole middle of the field. They had a good centre-forward in Taylor, but Jimmy battled him all the way through and the only chance Taylor got was the one he scored with. A bit like with Cloughie in the earlier round. Jimmy was good. I saw him do the same with all the best centre-forwards – Lofthouse, Steele, Lawton. And Jackie Sewell and Johnny Dixon worked and created and kept the ball when they could. They were on top form. Remember they were facing Colman, Edwards, Whelan and a young Bobby Charlton. That was some United team I tell you. They'd won the league by so many points that I think everyone expected them to do the double, but we won that battle and then clung on for dear life. On the day you have to say that our fellers produced better than them

Then the whistle went. "We've done it!" And we all ran to each other and hugged each other. Brilliant. We were very much a team and we all met up and congratulated each other and then commiserated with them. I spoke to Ray Wood to say "hard luck" to him.

Then you go up to collect the cup and shake hands with the Queen. I remember she had a very light touch. But this was the part for me that you don't take it in. Trevor Brooking has said that he wants to go back and do it all again so he can take it in, because when you're so involved all that just passes you by. It did for me anyway. I would love to be able to go back for a second time to soak it in. These days Arsenal and Man U players will be able to take it in time and time again

We did the lap of honour with the cup. The end where the Villa supporters were... my word. That was something special. To stand in front of them. They'd followed the club through thick and thin and they were going crackers. They were screaming out to you as you were going past. Remember they hadn't won anything since the first season after the First Word War. It was a big, big thing for them. Most of them had only heard of success, so they were going delirious with the excitement.

And it was the same when we went back to Birmingham on the train. We stopped at a few stations on the way and the crowds were there to welcome us home with the Cup. Remember only 15,000 Villa fans had tickets because of the ridiculous situation with Cup final tickets, so most had watched the game on TV. Coming out of the station to get onto the bus, thousands were waiting for us. All the people who couldn't go to Wembley. We drove through the whole town to the Civic Hall for a reception and then on to Villa Park where the place was packed. There must have been four or five hundred thousand people on the streets of Birmingham that particular day.

The Press reports in the nationals concentrated on United losing the double rather than us winning the Cup, but we didn't care about them. In the Midlands it was all about Villa. The sport edition of the local paper on Cup final night was printed on claret and blue paper. There was naturally a lot of comment about the incident with Ray Wood and I had to stand up in front of the papers and give my side of the story and I suppose that was always going to be a big controversy. The Manchester papers were on about it, because it was a daft sort of challenge and all that. Of course they ignored the two good goals that I had scored and the fact that United had eleven on the pitch then. I still think Ray Wood should have been back in goal. So that's Busby's decision which maybe cost them. Mind you, Ray should have said, "Hey, I'll go back in goal now. We're losing 1-0, let's get Jackie out onto the pitch." But it didn't happen until they went 2-0 down and that's not our fault.

I still watch the FA Cup because it is so special. Even in the qualifying rounds. You take a team from somewhere like Helston in Cornwall. They draw a big club for them like Bournemouth, or if little Chasetown in 2005 reach the first round of the Cup. You get real cup conditions and that's their day out. That's the Cup. Fellers get stuck into you. Reputations are forgotten. That was the magic of the Cup through Yeovil way back and Sutton. The FA Cup is littered with all that magic and now it's happening again. Exeter, Tamworth, Nuneaton. They give a good account of themselves. But since the big money has come into the Premier League they've tried to push the Cup aside a wee bit and I don't think they've succeeded, because the Cup has always been magical. When you get these fairytale draws with Manchester United having to play at Burton Albion in 2006. It's fantastic. It captures the imagination and you side for the underdog. That's what the Cup is all about. And don't forget it's magic to a lot of the foreigners because wherever they've grown up they've seen the Cup final as the most glamorous event of the year in British, possibly world, football. It's a marvellous pageant and occasion and they want to play in it. You ask Dennis Bergkamp or Freddie Ljungberg. They wanted to win the FA Cup final. You could see that when they battled their way to victory in the 2005 Final with Arsenal. They should have lost that game, but somehow they clung on and won.

The FA Cup is too big and too famous to be pushed aside. And I think its going to blossom out again now with the new Wembley, which looks magnificent. The Premiership and the European Cup are massive events, yes, but playing at that new Wembley will be so special to these megastars. To be honest I felt before the last final at Wembley, which Villa lost to Chelsea, that the Twin Towers of the old stadium shouldn't go, but I now think the big arch is magnificent, isn't it? It's the new landmark for the 21st century and long may it continue. No other stadium in the world holds a candle to Wembley.

TOMMY BANKS

LEFT-BACK 1948–1961

1958

BORN   10 November 1929, Farnworth, Lancashire
SIGNED   October 1947 from apprentice
BOLTON CAREER 255 games, 2 goals
HONOURS 1 FA Cup, 6 full England caps, Football League representative
LEFT   Transferred to Altricham , July 1961

Emulating his elder brother Ralph, who marked Stan Matthews in the 1953 final, Tommy Banks was renowned as one of football's 'hard men' during the 1950s. An outstanding youth player who represented the Boys Club of Great Britain, Tommy developed into a tough-tackling, formidable character, who took no prisoners and used his muscle and pace to get the better of wingers. A stalwart of the Bolton Wanderers side that claimed the FA Cup against Manchester United in 1958, Banks represented England at the World Cup finals in Sweden.

Bolton Wanderers 2 v Manchester United 0

FA Cup final
Saturday 3 May 1958

Wembley Stadium
Attendance 100,000
Gate Receipts £49,706

*Amidst a welter of sentiment following United's incredible resurrection
after the Munich disaster, Bolton steal the show to win their first
FA Cup in 32 years*

Teams

Bill Ridding	**Managers**	Matt Busby
Eddie Hopkinson	1	Harry Gregg
Roy Hartle	2	Bill Foulkes (capt.)
Tommy Banks	3	Ian Greaves
Derek Hennin	4	Freddie Goodwin
John Higgins	5	Ron Cope
Bryan Edwards	6	Stan Crowther
Brian Birch	7	Alex Dawson
Dennis Stevens	8	Ernie Taylor
Nat Lofthouse (capt.)	9	Bobby Charlton
Ray Parry	10	Dennis Viollet
Doug Holden	11	Colin Webster
Lofthouse 3, 55	**Scorers**	

Referee: J Sherlock

DURING THE 1950s, Bolton Wanderers were renowned for having a defence that gave opponents a tough game. Together with Roy Hartle, Derek Hennin and John Higgins, I enjoyed great battles against the likes of Stan Mortenson, Jackie Milburn, Tom Finney and Tommy Lawton. I always liked the opportunity of marking Stan Matthews of Blackpool because I was a bit of a rabbit so had a good game against Stan, who found my pace difficlt to deal with.

It was such a great time to be a footballer. Whenever I chat with Bolton supporters about my playing days they always mention our FA Cup final win against Manchester United in 1958. Our side cost a total of just £110, so it really was some achievement and the memories are still clear after all these years.

I was born less than three miles from Burden Park and was the youngest in my family. My eldest brother represented Manchester United's 'A' team, but an injury cost him a chance of first team football. Ralph, though, did make the grade. He was nine years older than me and signed for Bolton before the war broke out. I lived at home during the war; it was sparse, but I enjoyed my football and played for a local team called Partridges.

I was a fair player and Wolves, Manchester United and Leeds United took an interest in me after I picked up a winner's medal in the Boys Club of Great Britain tournament between the army, air force and naval cadets. I was 17 at the time. One day I came home from the pit at Moseley Common, where I was working, and my mother said that a fellow had been over in a motorcar. He was the Manchester United chief scout and wanted me to have a word with Mr Matt Busby. I had the opportunity to play with the Busby Babes, but my mother said it was too far to Manchester, so I signed for Wanderers, my local team. I was the first lad to sign amateur forms for the club after the war.

Arthur Rowley had played for Bolton and was now secretary-manager, a behind-the-desk man. He always called me Thomas. One day he said, "Thomas, I want you to come out of that pit and sign professional." It was top money then, £10 a week, far more than £3 in the pits, so I got very excited. My father had died in 1945, so now it was just my mother and me at home, as everyone in the family was married. I asked if I could play part-time. Mr Rowley said, "Thomas, I can't give you top money like Matthews, Finney, Lofthouse and Lawton. They are on £10 a week, £2 for a win and £1 for a draw." I told Mr Rowley my circumstances at home and he thought about it. He said: "Thomas, I want you to get the army out of the way. If you go in when you are 18, we'll have you back when you are 20." He obviously liked me and was planning ahead. I would be in his team by my early 20s. I asked again if I could be part-time and Mr Rowley offered me £6 a week plus the same bonus as the other players. So I clocked it up. I'm a young lad earning £3 in the pits, now I could be on £9 a week when Matthews and players like that are on £10 plus bonuses. I thought, "there's no justice for those star players," but I was not complaining and signed.

I gave my notice in at Moseley Common on my 18th birthday then did my national service in artillery. I gave £6 a week to my mother; she could live on that, and I lived on my army wages. I made my first team debut at Wolves in May 1948, but opportunities were few. I played in the Central League side with some of the youngsters and also more experienced players. It was a good standard and I developed. Wanderers were going through a transitional period as Mr Rowley and his successor Bill Ridding moved on the likes of striker Ray Westwood and captains Don Howe and Matt Gillies. Mr Ridding was also a secretary-manager, popular with the players and stayed in the post throughout my Bolton career.

By the time I came out of the army in '53, I'd only played a handful of league games, but they included 1-0 wins over local rivals Manchester United and Manchester City. Nat Lofthouse scored the winner in both games to send all Boltonians home happy. My football career had started and I was earning £12 a week plus bonuses.

Bolton were in the middle of an FA Cup run that would take them all the way to Wembley. I played four league games during all the excitement and almost broke into the cup team because the manager was not satisfied with our full backs, who were my brother Ralph and George Higgins. Following the win over City, I pulled a muscle at Cardiff, which was the week before the semi-final against Everton. I was disappointed. The manager brought George back into the side and Bolton won a thrilling match 4-3. Nat scored twice.

The week before the final against Blackpool, we played Newcastle at St. James's Park. It was the last league match and I replaced Ralph. A local reporter Hayden Berry, we called him 'The Tramp', was covering the match and said he knew what was going on at Bolton behind the scenes. He said to me, "good game today, Tommy, and you're in next week". I said, "it's too late, Hayden, they've all been fitted out with suits."

I was right. Ralph got the nod. I'd only played a handful of games, so it was right. The final was Ralph's last match for Bolton before he ended his playing days at Aldershot and Weymouth. Ralph was unlucky as he lost the peak years of his career to the war. Another change had seen Johnny Ball return after injury for Roy Hartle. It was tough on Roy because he had played in the every round of Cup including the semi-final. Roy and I were in the army together, but he'd come out 12 months earlier than I did. My mother said to me, "don't worry Thomas, it'll come your turn," and by Jove it did!

All the family went to Wembley and we watched from the stands. It was my first game at the famous stadium and oh, it was wonderful place. It was not a classic game for me because there were too many mistakes, but it was a thrilling final. Without the bad goals, Bolton could have won 1-0. I've often joked that we'd have won if I played because I always did well against Matthews. I wouldn't dream of denying Stan his winner's medal, but I would have done if I'd played! People used to say Stan never played well against Bolton because he didn't like facing Banksy. That's rubbish, Stan Matthews didn't fear anyone. In fact I have a photograph of Stan going past me. Roy Hartle used to joke, "I see you missed him again, Bansky!" The banter at Bolton was good. There were quite a few jokers in our squad; they were all good lads.

Our trainer George Taylor had played wing-half for Bolton pre-war and knew all about football. We played the W-M formation as pretty much every team did then. We had a centre-back, two full backs, two wing halves and five up front. Our inside forwards played back a bit, the wingers brought width and Lofty led the line. All our forwards used to run up and down that bloody field, in fact we all did, so we had to be fit. They had us non-stop running in training and we finished up by playing five-a-side on a cinder pitch at the back of Burnden Park. That was our practice ground. The pitch was no more than 60 yards long with only one goal post. We daren't go on the ground, we daren't touch the pitch, we'd have been slaughtered by the groundsman! We used to run around that track 40 or 50 times a day.

Every Tuesday morning we had a full-scale practice match, but it was really a tactical match. We never had quite enough players for two teams, so we'd get two or three local lads to take off work and join the 'A' team.

They were all amateurs and it gave them an opportunity to shine. George Taylor was old-fashioned. He would stop the match and say, "do this or do that." I liked attacking opponents, but George disapproved. He always went on at me not to go over the halfway line because if I was caught, our wing half had to cover, which left us open, but we all covered for each other in defence. If opponents were attacking down our left hand side, I'd move two or three yards towards our centre-half. Anything loose and I was in to tidy up, no danger.

I was married by now and I used to keep hens and then got some pigs. T'other lads used to go golfing, but I was not interested in that. There were not many cars around and I used to walk to the ground. On match day, if one car used to stop and offer me a lift, 20 would stop, and it was only a couple of miles. I used to say, "I'm getting warmed up." When I arrived at ground, I was ready. A few, including Roy Hartle would already be stripped off. I'd say, "what time we kicking off? I've done my warming up!" We'd do stretching exercises before the game and that would be it. It was ancient, not like today.

I replaced Ralph at the start of the new 1953/54 season and it was great to get a run in the side at last.

Bolton were quite a dour side. George Taylor was of the defensive mould and our inside forwards never stopped running. We got off to a great start in the league that season and, apart from one spell before the festive games, played consistently all season to finish equal on points with Manchester United and Blackpool in fifth place. We had some great wins. The highlight was a 5-1 victory at Old Trafford in front of a capacity crowd, which pleased all Boltonians. The top side was Wolves and they won the league, but the Busby Babes also were exceptional. United was something special with the likes of Roger Byrne, Duncan Edwards and Tommy Taylor in the team.

I played in the FA Cup for the first time and we were determined to get back to Wembley and make up for losing to Blackpool, but it was not to be. I loved the tournament, and so did our supporters. Every match was a sell out and the atmosphere was electric. I experienced playing against non-league opposition and Headington United gave us a right run for our money before we claimed a 4-2 win. We should have won the Cup that year and really fancied our chances, but only drew at Sheffield Wednesday in the quarter-finals when Willie Moir missed a penalty late on after scoring one earlier. In the replay, there was only me and our goalkeeper in our half. We murdered them, but Wednesday scored two breakaway goals. It was a missed opportunity, but I hoped to win the Cup won day.

That season everyone was talking about Hungary after they defeated England 6-3 at Wembley in November 1953. I had watched that game on television. We didn't know anything about Hungary beforehand, but they were the best side you had seen in your life up to then. They were all over England and their system of play would influence how the game developed tactically, especially the role of the deep-lying centre forward.

After a bright start in 1954/55, we fell away badly. It was frustrating for me because I picked up an injury in a 2-0 defeat at Sheffield United just before Christmas and did not return until the final few games. I wanted to help, but couldn't and to cap a poor season I missed out on the highpoint when we defeated the reigning champions Wolves 6-1 at Burnden Park. They went on to finish runners-up behind Chelsea.

We opened up the new campaign by defeating the champions 2-0 at Stamford Bridge. It was a great result for us, the perfect start. We continued our good form with wins over both Wolves and Manchester United before completing doubles over Chelsea and Spurs. Four defeats over the festive period checked our progress and we went out of the FA Cup in the fourth round, but we stayed in the top 10 as the Busby Babes clinched the title.

Willie Moir and Nat Lofthouse were our main strikers, but Willie, who had served Bolton well, moved on at the start of the 1955/56 season after Dennis Stevens broke into the team. Nat topped the First Division scoring charts and was a real handful for defenders. I was pleased he was on my side! Dubbed the Lion of Vienna following his match-winning display for England against Austria in the early 50s, Lofty would be un-buyable today. He was some footballer. As good as his scoring record suggests. Nat was top scorer at Bolton 11 times and, of course, became assistant trainer, chief scout, manager and, latterly, club president. You can't compare Nat to other centre-forwards of his era because of his size. Lofty was under six foot, he was only an inch taller than I was, but he was strong as an ox and great in the air.

Our side was taking shape; in fact, by the start of 1956/57 campaign only Doug Holden and Nat remained from the Cup final runners up side as Roy Hartle, Bryan Edwards, Dennis Stevens and Ray Parry cemented first team spots. Bryan had missed out in '53 due to National Service. He was a terrific wing half, but could also play full back and deputised for me when I was injured. All these lads are Bolton legends, as would be new keeper Eddie Hopkinson.

Each season we had to get fit in three weeks. George Taylor used to referee our six-a-side games in training. He never blew for a foul and we kicked lumps out of one another, but we enjoyed it. My side rarely won because we never had the first team keeper. I used to say we were the ball players, the others were all roughens and that is how Hoppy got in the team. Hoppy had come out of forces and made up the numbers in my side. George decided to give him his debut at Blackpool on the opening day of the 1956/57 season. We won 4-1; Hoppy played well and kept his place.

Nat scored a hat-trick that day and was on fire early on, but even his haul over the season could not push us above mid-table. We were simply not as consistent as United, who won the title again. We did have the upper hand on them though in our games, though, which pleased all Boltonians and for the only time in my Bolton career, I was in a side that claimed a double over them. We won both games 2-0 and the latter one at Old Trafford was the first match under floodlights at the stadium watched by over 60,000. Unfortunately, I was in and out of the team through injury and missed our FA Cup exit at the third round stage to Blackpool.

I was fit again for the 1957/58 season and we made a promising start after a 6-1 defeat at Wolves. I played in two brief spells and particularly enjoyed a 3-2 win over Tottenham Hotspur and 5-4 triumph against Wednesday at Burnden Park. Before Christmas, I returned to the side and missed just one more match. Our inconsistency was there for all to see as we lost 5-1 at home to Everton on Boxing Day before picking up a 3-2 win at Blackpool, *BBC Radio FiveLive* commentator Jimmy Armfield scoring our winner with an own goal.

The FA Cup had again come around and as with each season, we fancied our chances because on our day we could give anyone a game. Most of the players listened to the draw on a Monday lunchtime after training, but I didn't. Someone told me the draw at the farm where I was checking my pigs. I always preferred it that way.

Would we be lucky with a home draw? No, we came out having to travel to high-flying Preston North End. It was a shocker on paper because we never had much luck at Deepdale. Since signing for Bolton, we'd picked up just one victory and I was not in the side! The omens were not good, Preston had claimed a 3-0 league victory a couple of months earlier, so we knew it would be tough, but we went in determined to change our luck. I got a ticket for a pal of mine and he managed to slip into the direc-tors' box. He told me after the game that at half time a Bolton director said

Preston were murdering Bolton 2-0. My pal was stunned because Bolton was winning 2-0, we'd changed our strips! It shows what some directors know about football!

In the dressing room, we were delighted, but we were a shade fortunate because for some reason Preston decided to play Tom Finney on the left wing and Roy Hartle marked him out of the game. Tom was a great winger. I always struggled against him when he moved to my flank, but he'd been devastating in the deep-lying centre-forward role that season, so we had anticipated he'd be playing there. Tom, in my humble opinion, had the edge on Stan Matthews as an all round player. Tom was good in the air, had a natural left foot and you didn't know if he was going outside or inside. Stan was sheer speed, good on the ball and the best crosser of a ball I've ever seen. Never mind Beckham, Matthews was crossing in the '50s. Oh, Stan could cross a ball. By half time the game was over due to a tactical error on Preston's part. Ray Parry scored two and Dennis Stevens the other. That victory would be the only time I played in a winning side at Preston.

Lofty had been in fine form and was on target when we suffered a 7-2 defeat at Old Trafford. The Busby Babes were leading the First Division and trailing a blaze in the European Cup. Little did I know this would be the last time I'd face this terrific side. The defeat spurred us on as we faced a tricky fourth round clash at York City. I'd played against lower league opponents before and it was tough. Plus this York side had reached the FA Cup semi-final in 1955, only losing in a replay to Newcastle, so they were a good team. True to form, we had a battle on our hands and ended up the luckiest team in the world. The match would have been postponed today because the pitch was frozen before thawing overnight when it snowed. It was like a skating ring, honest to God, the ground sank near the penalty box and inside the 18-yard area.

The conditions actually saved us because inside two minutes, York broke clear and John Higgins couldn't get anywhere near his opponent, but the ball got stuck under the attacker's feet, it was that deep in water. By the time he got the ball from under his feet, we'd cleared it. A cup-winning team needs luck and this game was our lucky day, no doubt about it. Of course, our boots didn't help. Those buggers we used to play in made it hard work. Anyway, we played it up in the air the whole match, kept them out and won the replay 3-0.

Only five First Division teams had made it into the last 16, so we were pleased to receive a home draw against Second Division Stoke City, but ten days before the match the football world was in mourning following the Munich Air disaster. Manchester United were returning from a European Cup match in Belgrade, but the plane crashed on take-off in Munich and it cost the lives of Roger Byrne, Geoff Bent, Eddie Colman, Mark Jones, David Pegg, Duncan Edwards, Bill Whelan and Tommy Taylor. They were all great lads and it hit me hard like every professional footballer and supporter of the game. Of the survivors, Matt Busby was fighting for his life, while amazingly, considering the wreckage, Bill Foulkes, Harry Gregg and Bobby Charlton returned to action.

Bolton always had a good game against United and just two weeks earlier Byrne, Colman, Jones, Edwards and Taylor had been in the United side that had hammered us 7-2. They were a fabulous side. If that team had carried on, never mind Real Madrid, the Busby Babes would have dominated the English and European game. It was a bloody shame and an absolute tragedy. I found out about the disaster in the Black Horse pub the following day when someone came in and said, "look at this newspaper, Banks." I could not weigh up what I was seeing at first, but through television and radio we learnt the full extent of the terrible news. Quite rightly, the club received the sympathy of the nation. They certainly had ours.

Boltonians came out in force for our fifth round clash with Second Division Stoke because cup fever had gripped the town, but everyone had a thought for the Busby Babes. On a terrible pitch, we adapted better. I gave away a penalty; the referee said I dived for the ball. I didn't agree, but we came through 3-1. Lofty, Dennis Stevens and Ray Parry scored. Ray's goal was a beauty. It came from a free kick. Now Ray could hit a ball, but this effort was 35 yards out. I went over to him as he stood over the ball and said, "have a dig, Ray." He did, and it went in like a rocket!

It was four years since we'd been in the quarter-finals and I was hoping to God that we got a home draw. We did, but it could not have been much tougher as we faced Wolves. They had a strong team that would be thereabouts in the league throughout the '50s. Billy Wright was skipper and inside forward Jimmy Mullen was as good as anyone was. I faced little Norman Deeley, their right winger, and used to tower over him, but he was a good, speedy player.

We had the perfect preparation for the match when we claimed a 2-1 win at Arsenal. It was our first win at Highbury since we'd won the FA Cup in 1929. Maybe it was a good omen. Following a 2-2 draw with West Brom we were ready for our clash with the Baggies' great rivals. In an epic encounter, Wolves murdered us. Eddie Hopkinson was that tired from making saves he couldn't take goal kicks; Roy Hartle and I took them, but we battled away for a great 2-1 victory. It wasn't end to end, it was more end to our end, but somehow we were in the semi-finals. Dennis Stevens and Ray Parry came up trumps again with the goals. This was the third round they'd seen us home; they were real warhorses. Everyone was buzzing.

There was always a different atmosphere for cup-ties. The colours and rattles never came out as much for league matches, but they did in the Cup. There was an expectancy, a magic and for a player it was different, too, because each game is a one-off and every team had a chance. For smaller clubs it was especially important because one good gate could carry them for a season. The FA Cup was a great competition, it had so much history and for most players was the only chance to play at Wembley. Outside internationals, this was the only game at the Twin Towers.

The draw for the semi-finals pitched us against local rivals Blackburn Rovers, while Fulham drew Manchester United. In Matt Busby's absence, coach Jimmy Murphy had incredibly put together a United side capable of reaching the last four, with emotionally charged wins over Sheffield Wednesday and West Brom.

Leading into the Blackburn clash, our form was patchy. We defeated Birmingham City 1-0 and were confident in spite of Lofty being sidelined after picking up an injury in a 1-0 defeat at Sheffield Wednesday. In Lofty's absence, reserve winger Ralph Gubbins deputised. Blackburn were pushing for promotion from Division Two. I was facing winger Brian Douglas, who went on to play for England. We knew that we had a battle on our hands and Blackburn emphasised that when they took the lead, but Ralph proved to be the hero with two goals to book our place in the final. In the dressing room we were all ecstatic.

United overcame Fulham after a replay to reach a second consecutive FA Cup final, having lost controversially to Aston Villa in '57. Before the build up to the final, we had our final league fixtures to play. We won one, at home to Aston Villa 4-0, and drew two of our final six matches. It was a poor end, but we knew that we were safe. Naturally all our thoughts were on Wembley.

There was the usual commotion in trying to get tickets for all the family, and supporters continually asked if we could help them out, but there was little we could do. Before we knew it, we were on our way to London by train. We knew the public would back United, there was nothing we could do about that, what they had achieved in adversity was incredible, but we had to concentrate on our own game. We stayed at Hendon Hall Hotel and trained in the grounds, but it is not the same as being at home. I preferred going down to London the day before a game because you can get a bit bored, but there was plenty of press around and our club officials organised interviews. That kept us very busy.

We had our team talk on the Friday. United had performed a miracle in reaching Wembley, but their league form had dipped and they eventually finished ninth. Of the side that we faced in January only Bill Foulkes, Bobby Charlton and Dennis Viollet faced us at Wembley. Ernie Taylor and Stan Crowther had received permission by the Football Association to join the club in the special circumstances and play in the FA Cup, even though both were ineligible having played for other clubs in previous rounds. Numerous youngsters made up the United team, but the additions were not in the same league as the players who'd died.

In our team talk, George Taylor told Bryan Edwards to mark Ernie Taylor tightly and if he did we'd win because Ernie was their playmaker. Even though our league form since the semi-final had been poor, we had a stronger team and if we played to our potential we would win. This was the match that we'd been waiting for; we were raring to go. Throughout the competition, we'd played a settled team and had no major injury worries. Eddie Hopkinson, Roy Hartle, myself, John Higgins, Dennis Stevens, Brian Birch, Ray Parry and Doug Holden had not missed a tie, while Nat Lofthouse, Derek Hennin and Bryan Edwards played in all but two matches. Our two goal hero from the semi-final, Ralph Gubbins, missed out because Lofty was fit again, but we all knew that was going to happen. It was not a surprise.

I had confidence in all my teammates. Hoppy was brilliant when one-on-one with an opponent. He was also acrobatic to say the least. Roy Hartle could thump a ball and used to stop wingers in a nutshell. I was a bit of a rebel. Derek Hennin was a warhorse, John Higgins a stalwart; you had to run 10 yards to get around John. Bryan Edwards was a great defender; Brian Birch was solid, while Denis Stevens and Ray Parry were the unsung heroes. Then there was the incomparable Lofty and Dougie Holden was a great player too.

We went to the pictures the night before the game and, as usual, I roomed with Bryan. I was never a great sleeper and it was the same before the final. After relaxing in the morning and taking a stroll, the journey to Wembley went quickly. We always had a card school, which included Bryan, John, Ray and Dennis. Lofty didn't play and I was a crossword fiend; I'd try and do *The Telegraph*. This journey though, mostly we watched the fans making their way to the ground. It was a wonderful sight and going down Wembley Way was special.

The police escorted our coach in and closed the gates behind us. We could not hear a thing. I wasn't too nervous looking around the stadium and checking out the surface. Then it was time to get changed. George Taylor came over individually and had a few words. Bryan Edwards always went out behind Lofty. We all had our set position; I came out last. The walk out at Wembley was special and the noise came to a crescendo as we took the field. It was a special moment and one I'll never forget. Lining up we met the dignitaries and that is when I saw Matt Busby. It was incredible that he had made it. He must have been so determined to sit on the bench and watch his side, but you could see he was still weak.

At last, it was kick off and we got the perfect start when Lofty opened the scoring after just three minutes. I actually began the move that resulted in a corner conceded by Stan Crowther under no pressure. Crowther's clearance from Doug Holden's kick fell to Bryan Edwards some 30 yards out. An accurate through ball by Bryan caught United flat and Lofty easily side-footed into the net past Harry Gregg, who clearly had started the game nervously. It was a simple goal, but well executed. We were ecstatic and the goal settled us down.

Soon both Lofty and Brian Birch almost added a second goal, but Gregg saved well. Derek Hennin and Bryan Edwards were dominating midfield and United rarely threatened apart from the occasional burst from Bobby Charlton. I made sure their forward Alex Dawson, who'd scored a hat-trick in the semi-final win over Fulham, had no opportunities down my wing and Roy Hartle did likewise with Colin Webster. Anyone trying to break through the middle came up against John Higgins, who was in fine form.

Eventually, United carved out a few openings. Dennis Viollet shot wide following good play by Ernie Taylor, and then Hoppy saved a Taylor header acrobatically before making an amazing save from a Charlton screamer. We may have been on top, but we could not relax. At half-time, we were content in our dressing room, but felt a second goal was needed to secure the Cup.

We began brightly again, but seven minutes into the second half, we had a right let off when Charlton struck an upright with a great effort before the ball dropped safely into Hoppy's hands. This was United's last chance as we responded in the best manner by scoring again.

Bryan Edwards, Dougie Holden and Derek Hennin began the move before a Ray Parry dummy allowed Dennis Stevens to fire in a shot, which Harry Gregg could only knock into the air. As Harry tried to catch the ball, Lofty, quick as a flash charged him and the ball over the line, legal in our day. United players protested, but the referee awarded a goal. It may not have been a classic strike, but it was crucial. Today, of course, it would have been disallowed, but the game was all but over. Gregg took time to recover.

The goal finished any fight that United had and they failed to trouble us in the rest of the game. Late on there was a bit of a scuffle involving Dennis Stevens and Colin Webster, but the referee quickly resolved it. In the dying seconds, Bryan Edwards sent Lofty clear, but Gregg saved his goalbound effort, so Nat missed out on his hat-trick.

We were elated at the final whistle and in the end, ruined the fairy-tale cup win that everyone wanted outside of Bolton, but we had a job to do and performed it well. We dominated the match throughout and deserved our victory. The match was labelled dull, but in truth, there was only one team in it. Prince Philip gave out the medals, which was a special moment, as was the lap of honour.

We were unpopular winners, but that was only natural. We'd been in a similar position in 1953, because in the build up the papers all wanted it to be the year of conquering Everest, the Queens Coronation, Gordon Richards winning the Derby and Stan Matthews winning the FA Cup. They got what they wanted then, but we were determined to make the headlines this time. We had a player's pool, made a few bob, and received £100 from the club, exactly what we were entitled to and no more. We wanted a watch to commemorate the win, but the chairman refused, which was disappointing because the club did very well financially.

After the game, trainer Bert Sprotson said, "you may never have anything like this in your life again," so we went back out onto the pitch and ran around again. The United fans had gone, but we did another lap of honour. It was fantastic.

Back in the dressing room, champagne was in the trophy with manager Bill Ridding handing it round. Then, Matt Busby came in to congratulate us all, which was a wonderful gesture. Great memories.

After the club reception, we went out, but could not get into the club we'd planned to visit as it was jam full with supporters. Lofty, bless him said, "come on, we'll go back to the hotel and celebrate." When we arrived, George Taylor was going to bed. I said, "champagne for everyone" and then we ordered another. We had a great time; I remember drinking champagne out of my wife's slipper! I can't remember much else, mind!! Next morning there was a meeting arranged about our celebrations. Me being a Big Time Charlie, I asked how much the bill was. I had £5 in my top pocket, so got it out, but it turned out it was £70! In the end the club paid.

We travelled back to Bolton by train, but I got off at Rugby, as I had to meet up with the England squad to prepare for the World Cup finals in Sweden. I missed the coach trip through the streets with the FA Cup, but heard it was fantastic. I did ask England manager Walter Winterbottom if I could go, but he refused. On the post-season tour, I didn't play against Yugoslavia, but made my debut against Russia. I was so proud.

In Sweden, I kept my place for all the games. We drew pool matches against USSR, Brazil and Austria, but lost a play off to USSR 1-0, so returned home. It was disappointing. Essentially I was on the trip because of Roger Byrne's death. Our biggest problem was that we didn't have a recognised centre-forward. Bobby Charlton was with us, but there was no intention of playing him. In my humble opinion, England would have won the World Cup if Tommy Taylor had been there. We should have beaten Brazil; in the first 20 minutes their heads had gone. Then we should have easily beaten Austria, but drew 2-2; we walked all over them. But we couldn't finish these teams off.

At the start of 1958/59, Lofty got us going in a 4-0 win over Leeds United, who were struggling after John Charles had joined Juventus in 1957. Big John was a colossus of a footballer. He started out as a centre-half, but switched to centre-forward with devastating effect. Early in the season, we claimed the FA Charity Shield when we defeated defending champions Wolves 4-1.

We stayed consistent and enjoyed four-goal victories over Manchester City, Luton Town, Tottenham Hotspur, and Leeds again. We also hit six past Manchester United and Chelsea, but endured some heavy defeats, notably a 6-1 loss at Arsenal and 4-0 defeat at Blackpool. We finished on a high, though, with four wins in our final six games to finish fourth, our best during my Bolton career. The only disappointment was that we failed to equal the club's best ever league finish of third place due to Arsenal having a better goal average.

In our FA Cup defence, we really fancied our chances, especially after defeating Wolves at Molineux 2-1, which was a fantastic result. It took three games to get past Preston before we travelled to Nottingham Forest in the quarter-finals. Forest had claimed a 3-0 win the week before, which was their first triumph over us since promotion the previous season. We were jaded after three tight games against Preston, but it was still a huge disappointment to lose 2-1 and no consolation that they went on to lift the Cup.

Lofty got injured in our post-season tour to South Africa and missed the whole of the 1959/60 campaign, when we finished sixth. I also picked up an injury along with Hoppy and Bryan Edwards, which sidelined us all for a long period. We were back, though, for the new campaign, but neither Lofty nor I featured often. Nat only played a handful of games before an injury at Birmingham ended his illustrious career, while I played 11 games to take me past the 250 appearances mark and made one last appearance in the FA Cup when we suffered a 4-0 defeat at Blackburn Rovers in a fourth round replay. It was not the ending I'd planned at Bolton and I finished my playing days at Altrincham in the Cheshire League, but I would not change anything about my career.

Supporters always ask me whether players in my era could have played in the modern era. In my humble opinion, good players can play at any time. In my day, the best thing about playing was the camaraderie. It was the way we were brought up; there were not a lot of transfers. Many of us played out our careers at one club. I was also fortunate to play against all the greats of the era, appear in a World Cup finals and won the FA Cup. Along with winning my first cap for England in Russia, that occasion at Wembley was the highlight of my career and an unforgettable day.

CHIC THOMSON 1959
GOALKEEPER 1957–1960

BORN   2 March 1930, Perth
SIGNED   August 1957 from Chelsea
FOREST CAREER   136 games
HONOURS   1 FA Cup, 1 League Championship 1954/55
LEFT   Retired, July 1960

Chic Thomson won a championship medal with Chelsea before joining Nottingham Forest after they clinched promotion to Division One in 1957/58. Following a season of consolidation, Thomson played his part as Forest claimed the FA Cup for the second and last time in the club's history. Remarkably, the same Forest XI played in every round. A reliable goalkeeper with terrific reflexes, Thomson was respected by his peers in an era packed with outstanding strikers such as Jackie Milburn, Stan Mortenson, Tommy Taylor and John Charles.

Nottingham Forest 2 v Luton Town 1

FA Cup final
Saturday 2 May 1959

Wembley Stadium
Attendance 100,000
Gate Receipts £49,708

The Wembley injury hoodoo strikes again, but not before Forest's two early goals secure the FA Cup for the first time in the club's history

Teams

Billy Walker	**Managers**	Managerless; led out by Chairman Thomas Hodgson
Chic Thomson	1	Ron Baynham
Bill Whare	2	Brendan McNally
Joe McDonald	3	Ken Hawkes
Jeff Whitefoot	4	John Groves
Bob McKinley	5	Syd Owen (capt.)
Jack Burkitt (capt.)	6	Dave Pacey
Roy Dwight	7	Billy Bingham
John Quigley	8	Allan Brown
Tommy Wilson	9	Bob Morton
Billy Gray	10	George Cummins
Stuart Imlach	11	Tony Gregory
Dwight 10, Wilson 14	**Scorers**	Pacey 62

Referee: J Clough

OVER FIFTY YEARS AGO, I was a member of the Chelsea squad that won the First Division title for the first time in the clubs history. Four years later at Nottingham Forest, I won the FA Cup, which was a tremendous thrill and a day I will never forget. Being in the right place at the right time was the story of my football life. At the beginning of my career, a Clyde scout saw me playing for Scottish border team Blair Gowrie Rangers in a Junior Cup clash. He actually wanted to see another player, but got on the wrong bus in Edinburgh. He thought, "I've come this far I may as well watch this game." It turned out to be a stroke of luck for me.

I was 17 at the time and an apprentice engineer earning 26s 9d a week. An average weekly wage was £5. My wages went up to £8, expenses from Perth to Glasgow and a bonus took me to £12. I felt like a millionaire but my father quickly taught me a lesson. I spent my wages on shoes, flannels and sport jackets. The second week I did the same, then the third week, I got a three-piece suite at an auction. The fourth week, I went for my wage packet, but there was only expenses in it. I enquired why. My father had written to Clyde requesting my wages go direct into a bank account. He was sensible, but at least he gave me a few weeks enjoyment.

I made my debut against Rangers in the Charity Cup at Hampden Park. I was set to play for the reserves the previous day when a police car drew up. The sergeant asked for Thomson the goalkeeper. He explained Clyde had rung to tell them that I was playing against Rangers, but could not contact me. I was nervous up to kick off. Rangers had many stars including Scotland captain George Brown. We drew 2-2, but lost the replay. Young got both Rangers goals from penalty kicks, scoring with his right and left foot. He was some player. My four years at Clyde included National Service, where I won an Army Cup winner's medal. Back at Clyde, I won a League 'B' Division title in 1951/52, edging Falkirk by a point.

In October 1952, Chelsea signed me for £5,000. Ted Drake, a legendary Arsenal striker, was manager and I was one of his first signings. Ted had spotted me when he was manager of Reading and I was playing for the army. Chelsea had nothing resembling a championship team; in fact, we only just escaped relegation in my first two seasons. I was deputy to goalkeeper Bill Robertson, but played my part when called into the first team.

Ted was a man's man and attitudes changed immediately at the club. He got rid of the Chelsea Pensioner from the club badge, which he felt was a negative influence, and that helped ditch the 'music hall' image which had seen the club constantly ribbed for never having won anything and he was always at the training ground. The youth scheme gained momentum and his knowledge of the lower leagues gave players such as myself opportunities at a higher level. Ted was a motivator and a hard taskmaster. Team spirit and total commitment was everything to him and we went out determined to win.

Roy Bentley led us. He was inspirational as captain, a prolific marksman as well and a pioneer of the deep-lying centre forward role in the English game following Hungary's demolition of England in November 1953. The Chelsea lads all went to that game because Roy was playing. It was my first visit to Wembley and it was an impressive stadium. What I remember most was the skill of Puskas; he seemed to have the ball attached to his boot and he was simply unstoppable. Hungary's 6-3 win changed English football beyond all recognition. Within weeks, we all had our own ball and practiced skill, and stopped pounding round the pitch. We learned to 'talk' to the ball and it made a big difference.

Our squad was built on a shoestring and during the 1954/55 campaign we started slowly as defending champions Wolves and Sunderland set the pace. During inconsistent form, Seamus O'Connell made an incredible debut, scoring a hat-trick against Manchester United at Stamford Bridge, but somehow we lost 6-5. I came into the team during January, which coincided with us forcing our way into the title race. Roy scored a hat-trick in a thrilling 4-3 win against Newcastle United, but our season would not turn until a re-arranged fixture against FA Cup holders West Brom when only 7,000 fans attended the game on a snowbound pitch.

Ten minutes from time, we trailed 2-1 when Peter Sillett smashed in a free-kick before slotting home a penalty. Roy added a fourth in the last minute. The result sparked an unbeaten 10-match run in which we claimed seven wins. That gave us impetus. During Easter, we defeated Sunderland 2-1 and title rivals Wolves 1-0, Peter scoring a penalty in front of 75,000 fans, before drawing at Portsmouth. We clinched the title in the penultimate game at home to Sheffield Wednesday 3-0, finishing four points ahead of Wolves, Portsmouth and Sunderland. There was a tremendous feeling of achievement coming top over a whole season. Roy finished as leading scorer with 21 goals. You would have thought we'd get a bonus, but we didn't - we received a new suit!

A highlight every season was the FA Cup, but we didn't get past the fifth round during my time at Chelsea. I experienced the magic of the Cup during some incredible ties. My first ever FA Cup tie was a 4-4 draw at Derby County. We went through 1-0 in the replay. It then took four matches to get past West Brom before we won 4-0 at Highbury. But then Birmingham City knocked us out by the same scoreline. That was the year of the 'Matthews final', when Blackpool defeat Bolton Wanderers 4-3 in a fantastic game.

The following season West Brom lifted the Cup, knocking us out in the third round. When we won the league, Notts County defeated us. It was a shock result as County were a Second Division side. The result rocked us and allowed us to concentrate on the league, but we were not thinking about that in the dressing room afterwards. Twelve months on, it took five games to despatch Burnley. I played in the last two clashes; we eventually won 2-0 at White Hart Lane before Everton knocked us out.

I would play just two more matches for Chelsea as the title side broke up. At the time, I was earning £20 a week plus bonuses, but realised that I'd be moving on as the club had paid £20,000 for Reg Matthews from Coventry City, a record fee for a goalkeeper. During pre-season training in 1957/58, Ted told me Nottingham Forest wanted to sign me. They had just been promoted to Division One after an absence of 23 years and required experienced players. I travelled to Nottingham, agreed to join, and moved into a club house in Beeston.

Billy Walker had been Forest manager since 1939 and was very different to Ted Drake. Billy hated long balls; he didn't want anything over 30 yards, a bit like the old Tottenham 'push and run' tactics of the early 50s. Our trainer was Tommy Graham; he would put you down and lift you up. I was amazed when I started because training was so different. I was used to running lots of laps, then quick sprints. The first week I put my spikes on, but was promptly told spikes were not required. It was all ball-work and that is why we were a good footballing side.

I made a winning debut against Preston as we enjoyed a fantastic start to the 1957/58 season, claiming seven victories in the opening ten games to top the league. In a great run, we defeated Portsmouth 7-1 at the City Ground before away wins at Birmingham City 4-1 and Tottenham Hotspur 4-3. We definitely surprised teams before going through an indifferent spell until a 4-1 triumph at Newcastle United on Christmas Day.

Disappointingly, after New Year, we only won three games to finish in mid-table. In the FA Cup, we were disappointed when West Brom knocked us out by hammering us 5-1 in the fourth round following an exciting 3-3 draw at home.

At Forest, life was very different to Chelsea, but I was not complaining. At Chelsea, we travelled everywhere first class. For my first away game at Forest, I was stood around with Joe Macdonald at the station and Billy Gray said, "let's go have a cup of coffee." They said we should wait for our tickets; third class tickets eventually arrived. We had to go down the train looking for our seats. The organisation was like a Third Division club, but there was a great team spirit.

The side was taking shape. Bill Whare had reclaimed the right back spot, John Quigley replaced Jim Barrett in attack, while right half Jeff White-foot succeeded Bill Morley to form a terrific partnership alongside centre-half Bob McKinley and wing half and captain Jack Burkitt. Bob would set the record for making most appearances for Forest, followed by Jack.

Tommy Wilson led the scoring charts supported by winger Stuart Imlach. Tommy lived around the corner from me, so we travelled in by bus. On match day, we went in with the supporters, so there was a bit of Mickey taking. During the close season, winger Roy Dwight arrived. The dressing room at Forest was great. There was always good-natured banter. Jeff was one to have a word, as did John and Stewart Imlach.

We experienced an indifferent start to the 1958/59 campaign. After losing the opening game at Wolves 5-1, we defeated Portsmouth 5-0 then West Ham and Manchester City 4-0, but remained inconsistent. The festive games brought a double over Newcastle United, which took us into the New Year in good heart with the FA Cup around the corner.

I'd won a league championship medal, so naturally wanted to add the FA Cup to my collection. For me it would be the icing on the cake, but our third round tie was awkward as we faced Isthmian League side Tooting & Mitcham at their ground. Tooting had knocked out Bournemouth and Northampton in earlier rounds, so had nothing to lose, whereas we had everything to lose as everyone expected us to win. We had to do a professional job.

Waiting in the hotel, word came back that the game may be off as the pitch was unplayable. We were told to have a full lunch. I had steak and then we got word that the game was on. We could not believe the pitch when we got down to the ground. It was rock hard. Ground staff threw sand about, but it frightened the life out of some of our players.

Tooting chased everything. Centre-forward Paddy Hasty did their groundwork, knocking everybody about and we were 2-0 down at half time. Billy Walker was not a ranter. He said, "keep hitting the ball at the goal; we could still get away with a result." The tactics worked. There was a patch of ice inside the penalty area I'd been defending, and in the second half Murphy, who scored one of Tooting's goals, made a routine back pass, but it jumped five feet over his keeper's head for our first goal. Then we got a penalty when the ball bobbed up and hit a player's hand. There was no intent; it was just a bad bounce and Stuart Gray scored.

We'd got away with it and knew we had been lucky. In the dressing room, there was a real sense that we could win the FA Cup, even though it was an early stage of the competition. Every team needs luck and we had certainly had it that day. The replay was easy, it was on our nice flat surface and we won 3-0, Dwight, Wilson and Imlach scoring. Our supporters got quickly into cup fever because over 40,000 turned up.

In the fourth round, we faced Grimsby Town. Jeff Whitefoot loved that because he had been a Busby Babe at Manchester United, winning a league championship medal, but he'd lost his place to Eddie Colman and eventually moved to Grimsby before his arrival at Forest. The clash went according to the formbook as we won 4-1 and Jeff grabbed one of the goals, which he was chuffed about.

There were a few hard opponents that as goalkeepers we had to face. The one that knocked me about was Dave Hickson of Everton. I liked playing against him despite the fact that he'd thump you, because you knew he was coming and it was nothing nasty. Then there was Morty (Stan Mortenson), he was a real handful. Trevor Ford had a reputation, he was a bit of a moaner, but never troubled me, maybe our centre-half sorted him out!

The rules meant I ended up doing a few backward somersaults, but it was part of the game. When I first became a professional, I had sound coaching. My father, Chic, was a keeper for 20 years, playing for Falkirk and Brighton & Hove Albion. Provided an opponent jumped with you, there was no problem, but if he jumped after you, it was a foul. You were also chased all around the box when you had the ball, though you could bounce the ball three times before getting rid of it, which I always did.

The fifth round took us to Birmingham City, who had lost at Wembley in the 1956 final. We knew it would be a tough encounter. Before that match, we lost in the league at West Ham 5-3. It was one of the best games that I ever played in. There was end-to-end football and terrific goals. We then defeated Bolton Wanderers 3-0 to take us into the Birmingham clash in confident mood.

As expected, we had to battle. Birmingham scored before Tommy Wilson nodded in a free kick. A draw was a fine result and we soon discovered that if we progressed we would face cup holders Bolton at home in the quarter-finals. At the City Ground, Birmingham again scored first prior to Roy Dwight lobbing Gill Merrick before the ball slowly bounced into the net to earn another replay.

Before the second replay at Filbert Street, the referee came into both dressing rooms and said, "lads, it's a man's game, but I'll look after you," and twice he penalised the intention not the actual foul on me. Whether it affected Birmingham, I'm not sure, but it helps when you know that you are not going to get clobbered every time. At the third time of asking, we cruised into the last eight. It was one-way traffic in a 5-0 win. Roy Dwight got a hat-trick. In the dressing room, we were elated. We now faced Bolton and realised it would be a harder task than in the league.

We had played to packed houses in every round and the atmosphere was building. The clamour for tickets against Bolton was incredible. There was a real buzz in the city and a capacity crowd packed the City Ground. The players believed that this would be our year no matter what obstacles were in front of us. When Danny Wilson scored, I felt that was it, this was our day. I was right as we won 2-1, Danny scoring again.

Aston Villa, Luton Town, Norwich City and ourselves remained. One or two of the lads were concerned about drawing Villa as there was a general feeling they were the side to beat in the FA Cup. They were winners in '57 and renowned as a good cup team. For me, though, the team I wanted to avoid was giantkillers Norwich City. The Third Division side had enjoyed a great run. They were a physical side; all appeared to be over six foot tall and ran themselves into the ground. I didn't fancy playing them until the final. We drew Villa, but there was one game to fulfil before the semi-final at Hillsborough. Billy Walker rested a few of us, myself included, and we went down 7-1.

I remember two things in particular about the semi-final, John Quigley's winning goal and Villa winger Peter McParland. I never liked playing against Peter because he was a sneaky attacker; goalkeepers were not fond of him. If it was face to face or shoulder to shoulder, no problem, but he used to catch you a half second from behind after you had kicked the ball and would not often be pulled up by the referee.

John's goal was not one you could count as memorable, but he was in the right place and found the corner of the net. It was a tremendous feeling at the final whistle; I would have hated to have lost at the semi-final stage.

During the build up to Wembley, where we would play Luton Town, we lost at Luton 5-1 in the league. That didn't exactly bode well, but again Billy Walker rested Joe McDonald, Ted Burkitt, Roy Dwight and myself. It was a turning point in our tactics for the final. I sat with Joe and watched Luton winger Billy Bingham closely. He made three goals from crosses. I told him that he could not let Bingham fly down the wing at Wembley and get crosses over as he was doing. A couple of times during the game we managed to push him inside and it didn't come to anything, so that was part of Joe's task for the final.

Billy Walker always did things deliberately and was very secretive to avoid local reporters tracking us to our cup final base at the Hendon Hall Hotel. A fan took our luggage to the bus while we made our way to a back street near the City Ground. It took around three or four miles until a couple of cars with reporters inside tagged along behind us. We stopped at Northampton for lunch, and we suggested Billy asked them to join us but he refused. When we arrived at the hotel, of course, it was all flash bulbs as they were waiting for us!

We had suits made by a local tailor for the final and set up a player's pool. The tailor wanted to organise it for 10%, but we did everything ourselves. We made a few hundred pounds each and had a lot of fun. Billy kept us laid back and we had great fun practicing at a local park. We had committee members then, not directors, and they joined us in a seven-a-side game with the coaching staff. That was all the training we did.

A couple of days before the final we went to Wembley to get used to the surroundings. We looked at the dressing room and went on the pitch. Billy Gray had a tennis ball, so we had an impromptu game of cricket on the 18-yard line then walked up the royal box and pretended to get our winner's medals and spot where our wives would be sitting.

We had two injury scares, Billy and myself. Billy was nursing an ankle problem and had an injection on the morning of the final. I had a toothache throughout the week. I roomed with Bill Whare, who tried to treat it. He bought a half bottle of sherry and told me it would sooth the pain. I wanted to spit the sherry out, but he said, "don't do that, its good sherry, swallow it." So I did and had one of the best night's sleep with a toothache I've ever had! I had the tooth taken out on the Thursday. It wouldn't stop bleeding, but nobody was going to play in goal but me.

On the day, we were relaxed and had our final team talk. Billy Walker was again playing his tricks as we were late leaving our hotel, which meant we went down Wembley Way with the crowds flocking the area. We were

30 minutes late, which did not allow us time to get nervous. That was deliberate. We went straight in the dressing room. One of the committee members who owned a lace factory gave us pair of ladies knickers as a present, which helped break the tension.

After looking around the ground and waving to a few people, we got changed. All the lads had some superstition, whether it was what boot to put on first, the order we took the field or something obscure. I always went out third and before a game had a massage. Billy Walker was full of information, whom to mark and so on. He gave everyone final instructions. Captain Jack Burkitt, as always, said a fair bit to encourage us.

Then we got the signal to wait in the tunnel, which was the worst part for me. I just wanted to get out there because you could hear the hulla-baloo outside. Being third in line, you could see the pitch, but we had to wait until we got the signal as everything is timed to coincide with when the dignitaries arrive. Walking out, of course, is one of the highlights of the day and as you see the crowd, the noise is unforgettable. After chatting briefly to the dignitaries, finally we could have a brief kick about before kick off.

We started superbly and I thought that after 30 minutes we could score four or five goals. It was beautiful to watch the lads stroke the ball around. We looked comfortable and Roy Dwight went close early on with a header before meeting Stuart Imlach's pulled-back centre with a sweet strike on ten minutes to open the scoring. Tommy Wilson doubled our advantage four minutes later with a terrific header from Billy Gray's diagonal centre. I thought, that's it we've won the FA Cup.

We were completely on top when Roy broke his leg on the half hour while tackling Brendan McNally. Roy was a bit late into the challenge and was then stretchered off to hospital. We were down to ten men and it was now a new match, but we weren't in any danger up to half time. We looked solid. Roy was the sixth player injured in seven years at Wembley in an FA Cup final and there was a lot of talk afterwards to allow substitutes. At the time though, we had to soldier on. We discussed what we were going to do; it also gave Luton time to rethink. 2-0 up with an hour to go, but a player down, do we kick for touch or keep the ball? The general opinion was that we were a footballing side, so we should keep the ball and let them do all the running. It may be that with ten minutes to go we start kicking the ball out as we would be tired.

Luton had to attack and Allan Brown forced me into a couple of smart saves. Eventually, they got a goal back from a Billy Bingham corner on the hour. Passing short to Hawkes, the centre evaded our defenders and went loose to Dave Pacey standing to the right of the goal. His shot hit the post and went in. There was nothing I could have done, I didn't see it and even if I did I doubt if I could have stopped it. Luton took heart.

The last few minutes I had to avoid making any mistakes. There were quite a few balls in the area that I had to deal with, but they didn't trouble me, then six minutes from time we were all breathing a huge sigh of relief when a Brown header from a cross by Bingham hit my knee and went inches past the left hand post. Joe had been marking Bingham well, as we had discussed during the build up; it was one of Billy's few crosses and showed how dangerous he could be, but Joe did a great job.

My wife Pat, father and father-in-law were in the stands. My father told me afterwards that it was the first game that he was screaming at the referee to blow for full time. Stewart Imlach's wife tore up her programme, while Pat shredded her hat with the tension. Without a doubt, it was worse for our family's than ourselves, as we could do something. I knew there could not be long to go when I heard Jack ask the referee to blow his so and so whistle and he said that only a few minutes remained.

At last, the final whistle and we'd won the Cup. There was elation and relief in equal quantities, but the funny thing about the moment was something my wife and Stewart's had said beforehand. They told us that we could not meet the Queen without our teeth! There were four or five of us missing bits and bobs. I was going to leave mine in my sunhat in the goal, but someone said, if the ball strikes it we'd be in trouble. Tommy Graham had a handkerchief, which we used. Sorting the teeth out before walking up those steps was comical.

Jack Burkitt had been immense and a real inspiration, Bill Whare and Joe Macdonald had kept a check on Luton's wingers, while Bob McKinlay had blocked out the middle. Everyone contributed to make sure Luton failed to take advantage of the wide-open Wembley spaces. The pitch sapped a player's energy, so they did remarkably well. Stewart Imlach in particular ran his socks off; I have never seen anybody cover the pitch as he did that day. He played wing half, left back, inside left, outside left, right wing. Stuart was everywhere and put it down to a diet of sherry and eggs! We deserved our win.

Eventually it was time to collect the FA Cup. For me, it meant so much because I'd finally won both major domestic honours. After receiving the trophy there was a little celebration lifting Jack up for a group photograph for the media, then Bob McKinley and I walked back to the dressing room during the full lap of honour. It was a bit mad in the dressing room. We had individual slipper baths and there was a lot of water thrown about before we eventually got ready and went to celebrate at the Savoy Hotel.

The players sat together, kept a chair for Roy, and tossed up to see who would visit him in hospital. Jack, Billy and Tommy Wilson took his medal over. Roy told them that when he got to the hospital they were going to take him straight into X-ray, but he wanted to watch the end of the game. They wheeled him into a horseshoe of patients, he still had his strip on and by the end of the game, he had tears running down his face.

We went to Brighton with our wives on the Sunday and saw the game replayed on television at a friend of Billy Walker's before the civic reception in Nottingham on the Monday, which Roy was able to join.

During the summer, we went on a post-season tour to Portugal, France and Spain. Then I had a family holiday in Devon. We received the official bonus only. The club committee let us down because they'd said they would organise commemorative pictures and the like, but we got nothing.

The following season we got off to a reasonable start, but faded away badly and only just avoided relegation. Our biggest win was a 4-1 victory against relegation rivals Leeds United, but we lost far too may games, including a 5-1 defeat at home to Manchester United and 6-1 reverse at Everton. A 3-0 win against Newcastle United in the penultimate game of the season secured our safety as Leeds lost at Blackburn Rovers. They defeated us in the last game, but their fate was sealed and they went down with Luton. Sheffield United knocked us out of the FA Cup in the fourth round. Thatwould be my last FA Cup tie as a player.

During the close season, Andy Beattie replaced Billy as manager. Billy had suffered from ill health and died in 1963, which was a sad loss. Andy did not believe in swearing, drinking or having a laugh and the Cup final team quickly split up. In fact, after that team played in every round during our cup run we never played another first team game together again. In 1960/61, I picked up a knee injury and retired. My final game was a 5-3 defeat at Wolves, which was fitting as they had featured in so many league and cup battles during my career.

I was very fortunate because I won a League and FA Cup winner's medals. The league medal was more of an achievement as the slog through the winter months is something else, but the Cup is so full of excitement. I still miss the dressing room banter like many ex-players. The everyday craic is what the game was all about for us. They were very special times.

NORMAN DEELEY 1960
RIGHT-WING 1948-1962

BORN 30 November 1933, Wednesbury

SIGNED July 1948 from school

WOLVES CAREER 237 games, 75 goals

HONOURS 1 FA Cup, 3 First Division Championships 1953/54, 1957/58 & 1958/59, 2 full England caps, England Schoolboy international

LEFT Transferred to Orient, February 1962

Built like a whippet, with pace to burn and a heart to match, Norman Deeley took on the seemingly impossible task of replacing the legendary Johnny Hancocks on Wolves' right wing. But he was always one of the unheralded heroes of Wolves fabulous team of the late 1950s – that was until he took the 1960 FA Cup Final by the scruff of its neck and wrote his name into Wolves and FA Cup folklore by being involved in just about every significant incident.

Wolverhampton Wanderers 3 v Blackburn Rovers 0

FA Cup final
Saturday 7 May 1960

Wembley Stadium
Attendance 100,000
Gate Receipts £49,816

Unsung hero Norman Deeley stars as the team of the late 1950s,
Wolves, romp to their first FA Cup in 11 seasons

Teams

Stan Cullis	**Managers**	Dally Duncan
Malcolm Finlayson	1	Harry Leyland
George Showell	2	John Bray
Gerry Harris	3	Dave Whelan
Eddie Clamp	4	Ronnie Clayton (capt.)
Bill Slater (capt.)	5	Matt Woods
Ron Flowers	6	Mick McGrath
Norman Deeley	7	Louis Bimpson
Barry Stobart	8	Peter Dobing
Jimmy Murray	9	Derek Dougan
Peter Broadbent	10	Bryan Douglas
Des Horne	11	Ally MacLeod
McGrath (og) 41	**Scorers**	
Deeley 68, 88		

Referee: K Howley

I WAS ONLY 4 feet 10 inches when I left school, although I grew to a whopping 5 feet 4 eventually. But I was never worried about my height. I had bags of skill and plenty of pace and I knew I was a good enough footballer to be able to make it in the game. After all I'd played for England schoolboys at wing-half in a team containing Albert Quixall [Sheffield Wednesday], Ray Spencer [Aston Villa] and Bryan Brennan [Stockport], who would go on to have good careers in the game.

I'd played for South Staffordshire and Birmingham and District representative teams and the Wolves' Chief Scout, George Noakes, came to see me when I left school at 15. He asked me to join the groundstaff at Molineux, but when he went to speak to my parents Dad initially said "no", because he wanted me to go to West Brom! But I wanted to go to the Wolves. I'd made my mind up and Dad agreed in the end. It was something special to sign the forms and become a Wolves player.

That was in 1948 and in the same intake were George Showell and Alan Hinton. Wolves won the FA Cup final the following season, Stan Cullis' first season as manager, so I knew I was in the right place. I was in the reserves by the age of 16. We won the Central League three years on the trot. The team was mostly made up of first teamers vying for a spot like Ray Chatham and Billy Baxter.

At this stage I was still a wing-half, but my lack of inches was beginning to be a problem playing there. The philosophy of the club was for us to be able to fill in at our position if an injury occurred in the team above us. Well that would mean me replacing Bill Crook or Billy Wright. I just didn't play in that style. Cullis brought me along slowly. I made my debut at Molineux in 1951. I marked Arsenal's Doug Lishman and we won 2-1, but, of course, Billy was back in the side the next week. I only made a few appearances and then I was called up to do my National Service when I reached 18.

I entered the South Staffs regiment and was allowed to play for Wolves if I got leave. Mostly I played for the reserves, but then we got posted to Balakinley in Ireland, by the Mountains of Mourne and later to Linden in Germany. I played in the Battalion team and really enjoyed it. I scored bags of goals thanks to my pace and shooting ability and really changed myself into a more attacking player. My game then was all about pace and passing, so perhaps it wasn't such a surprise that when I came back from serving in the Army I was converted into a forward. Stan and Joe Gardiner saw that they could use my pace on the wing and trained me to replace Johnny Hancocks, who was just coming to the end of his career. I was actually a tiny bit taller than Johnny, so I knew then there would be no barriers to me getting into the first team.

I was now 20 and I knew that I had to get my career moving again. I'd signed up to the Army Engineering Reserve to get an early discharge from National Service and that came back to bite me when I got called back because of the Suez crisis, which flared up in February 1956. I was taken out to Egypt and we had to work 12 hours on and 12 off stevedoring. Thankfully we weren't out there too long.

In the summer of 1956 Wolves went on a tour to South Africa when, incidentally, Stan signed outside-left Des Horne. That tour was brilliant for me. It really made my career. It went really well for me and I think it made Stan Cullis sit up and take notice.

I played 41 games in the 1957/58 season and scored 23 goals from outside-right. I was off. The team took off too. We won two consecutive titles and scored 100 goals three seasons in a row. We were a really good side and it was nice to play that kind of football with those players. If one man was having an off day all the others rallied round to help him out. The dressing room was electric. I was always quite chirpy and loved cracking jokes. I'd do things like put freezing cold water in the bath after training!

One of the greatest things that Stan Cullis did to build that Wolves team was to sign Peter Broadbent. He spent £13,000 on him from Brentford in 1950. I'd actually played left-half against him at schoolboy level in the England trial in 1948 at Portsmouth when the South played the Midlands. He was only six months older than me, but he got a regular place in the Wolves side a few seasons before me. Now I formed a great partnership with him on the right hand side. We set up a pattern that only we knew. Often I would come inside and he would cross me and I would leave the ball for him to take on up the wing and then he would play me in with a reverse pass. His running off the ball like that was fantastic. Mind you, he wasn't bad on the ball either!

You only get out what you put in. It's a simple motto of mine, but over the years I've found it to be true. I trained so hard and put every possible effort into both my training and every second of every game and it paid off for me. We'd won two successive League titles and in 1960 we were in line for the double. We hadn't started well in the League – I remember losing 5-1 at Spurs and 4-1 at Burnley – but when Bill Slater returned to the side we kick-started a run which took us right into the title race. Our main rivals were Burnley and Spurs as it happens, so those defeats caused us big problems.

Our FA Cup campaign started well, though. We drew at Newcastle and won the replay easily 5-2. I scored in that game. In the next round we saw off Charlton, who were a Second Division side, 2-1. Then we had two away matches at Luton and Leicester. We won 4-1 and then 2-1 and got to the semi-final having played well, but without truly being tested.

Stan Cullis was a hard task master. He was like Manchester United boss Alex Ferguson in some ways. He would have a go at you to give you a kick up the rear. He was strict and hard, but to be successful you have to be. He had some strange ways of motivating you. Before the Cup semi-final against Second Division Aston Villa he called me into his office. I'd had a groin strain and I thought he wanted to find out if I was fully fit again, which I was. I sat down and he told me that he believed I had put some money on Villa winning the match. He was accusing me of gambling against us and planning to throw the match! He said he knew I'd been offered £500. I was shocked and I said "Well, you'd better leave me out then, if you think that."

After that I went for a drink in the pub as I thought I wouldn't be playing the next day. I played dominos and had a couple of bottles of beer, but when I went back to look at the team sheet that George Noakes always pinned up in the corridor on a Friday, I found that instead of dropping me, Stan had moved me from outside right to outside left and dropped Des Horne. I think that was to motivate Des for the coming games as he was then scared he'd miss the final. As it happened Des had a great game at Wembley. Stan put me up against Villa's right-back, Stan Lynn, who was a rock hard defender and he knew I wouldn't be intimidated by him.

So, come the semi-final the next day at the Hawthorns, I was so determined to prove Stan wrong that I scored within 10 minutes and we held on to win 1-0. The next day I went into Molineux to get some treatment on my groin, which had flared up again a little bit during the game, and Stan was there. As I walked past him I said "I threw the game then, didn't I?" I don't think he really believed I was going to throw the game at all. That was simply a way of motivating me to up my game in a big match. And you have to say it worked didn't it?!

The only goal of that semi-final came because I was on the left wing actually. Jimmy Murray was put in down the inside-right channel and he shot across the goal. Nigel Sims, the Villa goalkeeper, who had until recently played for Wolves, parried the ball out. I always came in off the wing when I knew someone was going to shoot, so I could pick up the scraps and this time it fell perfectly for me and I smacked it in. No-one had tracked me into the area.

The semi-final turned out to be our toughest game of the Cup run. Villa played well and gave us a few scares. My groin pulled again just after the goal and I ended up as a bit of a passenger. I just tried to make a nuisance of myself on the left wing, but mostly the rest of the game was about us defending well. Malcolm played really well in goal. There were a couple of near things, but we hung on.

There was quite a bit of controversy around the final. For the Wolves' part, Stan Cullis took the decision to drop Bobby Mason, who had played in every round of the Cup, in favour of young Barry Stobart. I can't tell you why particularly. In fact I don't think we'll ever know the reason why. It was just something Stan chose to do. Barry had only made something like five first team appearances prior to Wembley. We'd played at Chelsea in our final league match on the Saturday before the final and Barry was in the team. We won 5-1 which meant we finished our league programme on top of the table, one point ahead of Spurs and Burnley, who had one game still to play. Unfortunately for Bobby I think Stan thought Barry had played so well in that game he couldn't drop him.

By then we had lost the League title as Burnley had won their final match at Manchester City. It would have been three championships in a row, of course, and the double too, because we then won the Cup, so we'd have beaten Spurs to the achievement of being the first twentieth century team to manage that feat. But that's football.

Of course I was worried I'd miss the final with my injury, but actually that manipulation broke a blood clot up in my groin. The Wolves club doctor was called Dr Richmond. He used to stretch my leg around my neck – see it does help having a short body sometimes! He worked wonders on me and when he'd finished and I'd rested up I couldn't feel it at all.

We were massive favourites for the final as Blackburn had only finished 17th in the First Division. Everyone expected us to win, but Wolves had been in this position before in 1939 when Stan Cullis had been in the team and so he did not allow us to consider anything other than that this would be a very tough match and we would have to go all out to win it.

On the Friday night before the game, we were all in bed by 11pm after having some tea and biccies! I had a couple of bottles of Double Diamond and they helped me sleep really well. When we got up for breakfast some of the players were complaining about not being able to sleep, but I'd had a wonderful rest! I remember the waitresses wishing us all the best for the game and then it was onto the bus for Wembley. I had a few butterflies as we drew up to the ground. I don't believe anyone can say that they don't get butterflies on a day like that. All along Wembley way there were Wolves fans with scarves jumping up and down. They kept trying to jump and touch the coach's windows. We had to go so slowly down Wembley Way I thought we'd never actually get there! We looked at each other then and said "We can't lose this for them."

It's traditional to go and walk out onto the pitch before the FA Cup final. We never really used to do that anywhere else. We were all wearing our club blazers, which we'd been measured up for at Lew Bloom's in Wolverhampton. But we walked around at Wembley and began to get ready about three quarters of an hour before kick-off so we weren't sitting around in the dressing rooms for too long. None of us were particularly superstitious and we had Bill Slater as our captain. He'd only just got back into the side and been part of our tremendous run which nearly saw us take the title. He'd been a great player, but was now coming to the end of his career. He made a great captain, though, after Billy Wright had retired. He wasn't one to go round geeing players up. His leadership was more on the field.

Then you get the knock on the door and it really is something very different to walk down the tunnel at Wembley and into the light of the stadium. It's a long walk to the halfway line, so you have plenty of time to think, which sometimes gets to people. I remember, after shaking hands with the Duke of Gloucester, we broke away to warm up and when I put my ball down onto the pitch it actually ran away from me. The pitch was like glass. It just rolled away. I'd chosen to play in a medium stud, which was a good choice because the pitch was too hard to take a long one.

You don't tend to settle down in the first five minutes or so. My stomach butterflies stopped after that and I felt much more with it, settled and concentrated. Blackburn did create one decent early chance when Peter Dobing went through on Malcolm Finlayson, but Malcolm saved at his feet and that turned out to be their only real chance. We started to play a bit then too. My job was always to get into the box from the right-hand side when the ball was on the left wing. It had worked the opposite way round for my goal which won the semi-final. Anyway, Barry Stobart made a good run down the left and got to the byline and whipped a cross in. I'd charged into the middle and Mick McGrath, the Rovers left half, went with me. He actually reached the ball just before I did by stretching and sliding. With their keeper coming out to collect the cross I watched as the ball beat the keeper and rebounded off McGrath and into the net.

It didn't really matter as I would have scored anyway. Once the ball had beaten the goalkeeper, if Mick had missed it I was only a couple of yards behind him waiting to tap it in. But own goals are a nightmare to put behind you at the best of times and this one was in the biggest game of all. As it turned out that cost me a hat-trick in the FA Cup final. If only you'd missed it, Mick! I'm sure you wish you had too.

As I was racing in behind him ready to score I couldn't stop myself from following the ball into the net and clinging onto the rigging in celebration. I didn't normally celebrate too much, not like they do these days, but a goal at Wembley is special.

Blackburn weren't without a bit of controversy themselves, although we didn't know about it until after the game. It turned out that their star forward Derek Dougan, who of course later became well known to Wolves fans, had put in a transfer request the night before the game. That must have unsettled them quite a lot.

The controversy didn't stop during the game either. Obviously having lost the League like that we wanted to win all the more. Now we were a goal up, our first thought was to defend the lead and so we made sure we won every tackle we could. It was around then that the incident the game is now most famous for happened. The ball was knocked out towards me as I ran inside off my wing. It was a bit short and so tempted Blackburn full-back Dave Whelan into the tackle. I might only be small, but I could tackle as well as any Wolves player, because I'd started out as a half-back. Dave and I went for this ball and we arrived at speed pretty much together. Crunch. I heard this crack as we collided and I thought "That's my leg."

When I looked down in my dazed state there was duck-egg shaped bump already forming on my shin. Then I looked across at Dave's leg and there was no flesh on it for about four or five inches. He barely moved and it was obvious straight away he had done something bad. It was a really awful incident and in a way it still overshadows the success we had in the Cup final to this day.

Dave was carried off and it turned out that his leg was so badly broken it ended his career. My leg was sore, but I could jog on it. It certainly didn't help Blackburn as, playing against ten men, we just kept the ball and tried to work openings. That huge pitch took its toll on them as they chased us around. There'd been this succession of injuries in Wembley finals which had started a debate about substitutes. It was known as "the Wembley Hoodoo". We hadn't given it a thought.

But it didn't necessarily help us either. Sometimes ten men play just as well as eleven as they try so hard to make up for the loss of a body. We didn't find it easy, but all the same we didn't find it too much of a problem. Still with only a goal lead, we couldn't be complacent.

As we walked off the pitch after the half-time whistle, BBC TV asked me if it was actually my goal. Live on air, at half-time! I told the nation that Mick had scored it. I could have claimed the goal then and I would have had my hat-trick, but I knew Mick had got the touch not me and I thought it was obvious. I also didn't know what destiny had in store for me in the second half.

When we got into the dressing room all Stan said to us was "Keep going". I saw him change his shirt as the one he was wearing was wringing with sweat. It was a hot day, but I think he was so nervous, with us being favourites and then having the man advantage. He didn't want us to make any silly mistakes. We didn't have that luxury. I remember my shirt was wet through too, although at least I'd been running around! But we couldn't change. To be honest I had been hotter the previous summer when I'd played for England on tour in South America.

We played extremely competently in the second half. Blackburn didn't really threaten us. But we still needed another goal before we could say "That's it." And it came my way. Des Horne crossed from the left towards me. I was running into the area and hammered it first time. I knew it was in as soon as I stuck it and when it hit the back of the net it felt tremendous. There was even some controversy about this goal as Blackburn claimed Horne was offside. But what happened was that McGrath was

BILL PERRY – 1953
BLACKPOOL 4 v BOLTON WANDERERS 3

Wembley gave me the chance to score the winning goal in an FA Cup final, something I'd always dreamed about, and I gladly accepted.

The celebrations afterwards were incredible and rightly centred on Stan Matthews' (on shoulders, right) fabulous performance.

JIMMY DUGDALE — 1954
WEST BROMWICH ALBION 3 v PRESTON NORTH END 2

At 2-1 down we won a penalty. The tension was unbearable. It was one of those classic Wembley moments. This picture shows our keeper Jim Sanders not being able to even look as Ronnie Allen scores.

Captain Len Millard sits on my shoulders (fifth from right) to lift the trophy. The whole thing went by in a blur, but it was the most wonderful feeling.

VIC KEEBLE – 1955
NEWCASTLE UNITED 3 v MANCHESTER CITY 1

Jackie Milburn scores the incredibly early goal, heading in Bobby
Mitchell's corner, which settled our nerves.

Skipper Jimmy Scoular holds the Cup aloft. That's me on
the extreme left of the picture.

When Peter Murphy crashed into me, I had no idea of the damage that had been caused to my neck.

All I knew was that it hurt, but that I had to carry on to help win the FA Cup for Manchester City after the disappointment of the year before.

My clash with United's keeper Ray Wood has gone down in Wembley folklore, but I can honestly say that it was a pure accident.

My second goal came when I (extreme left) stole in behind Bill Foulkes and headed the ball into the net. We knew we'd won it then.

Lofty nets his first goal. He was the best centre-forward around and United had no answer to him, no matter what the emotions of the nation.

Manager Bill Ridding (left) helps our two goal hero
drink his fill from the Cup

Roy Dwight (extreme left) scores our opening goal. We scored both goals so early I think Luton didn't know what hit them.

Despite the one goal Luton did pull back, we managed to repel their attempts to score an equaliser. Here I fall on the ball to keep them at bay.

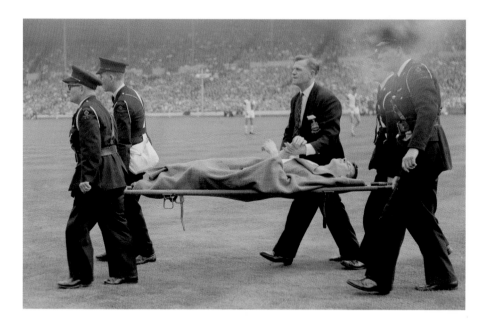

The big controversial incident saw Dave Whelan break his leg in a tackle with me. It left Blackburn down to ten men. But we were already in control

My second goal set the seal on a famous 3-0 triumph. I lashed it into the top corner after the ball rebounded around the area.

DAVE MACKAY – 1961 & 1962
TOTTENHAM HOTSPUR 2 v LEICESTER CITY 0
TOTTENHAM HOTSPUR 3 v BURNLEY 1

A rare colour phtograph from the 1962 FA Cup final shows the incredible
scene and how 100,000 fans, and a military band packed the stadium.

It felt like we passed everyone in north London on our
open top bus trip around Tottenham on both occasions.

The joy is written all over David Herd's face (third from left) as he puts us 2-0 ahead. He went on to put the game beyond doubt with his second goal.

(From left) Maurice Setters, captain Noel Cantwell and Paddy Crerand celebrate United's first trophy since the dark days of Munich.

A moment of ecstasy; Ronnie Boyce celebrates scoring our
dramatic last minute winner against Preston.

You can't beat showing off the FA Cup. I am standing on
the left of picture with my arm round keeper Jim Standen.

IAN CALLAGHAN – 1965
LIVERPOOL 2 v LEEDS UNITED 1

The scarf-wielding fan, who celebrated Roger Hunt's opening goal
by running onto the pitch, gets his come-uppance.

I managed to get to the bye-line and whip the ball into the middle where
Saint twisted in mid-air to nod the ball home for the winner.

Mike Trebilcock (dark shirt) fires the equaliser past Wednesday keeper
Ron Springett. His two goals in five minutes rocked the Owls.

The proudest moment of my life; receiving the FA Cup
as Everton captain from the Queen.

PAT JENNINGS – 1967
TOTTENHAM HOTSPUR 2 v CHELSEA 1

Manager Bill Nicholson (second left) hands out pre-match instruction to (from left) Frank Saul, Joe Kinnear, Terry Venables and myself.

Frank Saul's shot beats Peter Bonetti low to his left and we are 2-0 ahead and cruising towards a third FA Cup in six seasons.

The Everton net bulges as Jeff Astle's (second left) shot flies into the top corner for the only goal of the game.

Manager Alan Ashman proudly shows off the FA Cup to the thousands lining our route to the Town Hall for a reception.

My moment of Wembley glory. Scoring the winning goal past Peter Shilton fulfilled the dreams I'd had since the age of six.

Manager Joe Mercer shows off the Cup to the hordes of ecstatic City fans. What a magnificent feeling!

standing on the goal-line playing him onside and he jumped off the pitch backwards leaving Des technically offside. But the referee allowed play to continue. Quite rightly in my opinion as I scored!

At least we'd scored a goal ourselves, rather than just win the Cup with an own goal. No-one got over-excited. I just got a pat on the back and a couple of handshakes. I think a bit of the shine had been taken off the whole thing for a lot of the lads by Blackburn going down to ten men. And anyway, we were always of the opinion that it was a team effort. In those days it really was. None of these individualist stars. In fact if anything the real stars were the players who made goals rather than those that finished them off that won the plaudits.

Then I scored again. Des Horne played a short corner routine and crossed it into the box. He mishit it a bit and the ball actually hit the post and came out in front of goal. Woods tried to clear it, but he mishit it too. It fell to me perfectly on the volley. I timed it well and hit it.

I had spent hours in the "Dungeon" beneath the stands at Molineux banging balls off the rugged walls and practicing shooting on the volley. That paid off then as I turned and hit it cleanly. There was just that small delay while I saw the ball fly into the net and then I knew it was all over. 3-0 versus ten men. We'd won.

I actually should have scored at least twice more in the game, but I got over-excited about the chances that fell to me and snatched at them whilst not being balanced properly. I was a bit upset about that as no-one has scored four goals in a Wembley Cup final. I was getting so many chances, particularly once Dave had gone off and I should have done better really.

The next thing I knew the whistle went for the end of the game. It was a wonderful feeling. I was last up the steps to pick up my medal. My leg was still sore, although I'd managed to forget about it during the game. We then went on our lap of honour with the Cup and it was tremendous down at our supporters' end.

But when we reached the Blackburn fans' end they reacted very badly. They were throwing stuff. Apple cores, orange peel, money. They threw stuff at us, at the manager and at the referee, who I think they blamed for not sending me off after Dave broke his leg. We walked off and managed to avoid most of this hail of rubbish. The press called it the "Dustbin Final" because of that. And I think it really was the straw that broke the camel's back when it came to getting the authorities talking about substitutes. They didn't actually come in until some years later [1966], but I think that Cup final made them discuss it.

When we got down the tunnel I went to their dressing room and asked Ronnie Clayton, who I knew from the England tour I'd been on, how Dave was. There weren't a lot of press men around, but of course we had plenty of coverage in the papers, the Cup final being the football event of the year.

After a fantastic open top bus tour around the town on the Sunday, later that day I went to have an X-ray on my leg at the Wolverhampton Royal Hospital. Thankfully it was OK. In those days there wasn't much in terms of press aftermath to a big game like that. Not like nowadays when it all gets analysed to hell. I had a few questions about the incident with Dave Whelan, but generally it was accepted that it was an accident. Then we went on a family holiday – a fortnight golfing with my mate Peter Broadbent. He was a good golfer. He used to give me 14 shots and still beat me!

To think that Stan had accused me of throwing the semi-final and now I'd gone and won Wolves the final. He never let you get big-headed, though. That was one of his strengths.

I remember another occasion when he tried a spot of his 'motivation' on me. It was in 1957 and I'd scored 13 goals in 15 games early in the season, which isn't bad for a winger. Then I'd gone around ten games without finding the back of net. Stan had me into his office and said "Norman. Sit down. I have had a letter." He read out this letter from a fan which complained about me and the fact that I'd stopped scoring goals.

"What do you think of that?" Stan asked.

"Who wrote it?" I replied.

"It's anonymous," says Stan.

"He's stupid then," I said.

"So why aren't you scoring, Norman?" Stan continued.

And I told him that it was just one of those runs when every shot I struck seemed to hit defenders on the line, or hit the post, or the ball just flew wide and asked Stan what he thought was the reason. He looked at me and, without saying another word, he ripped the letter up.

I then scored in seven of the next eight games! Do you think a fan had written that letter?

DAVE MACKAY   1961/1962
MIDFIELD 1980–1984

BORN   14 November 1934, Edinburgh
SIGNED   March 1959 from Hearts
SPURS CAREER   318 appearances, 51 goals
HONOURS   Division One Champions 1961, FA Cup Winners 1961, 1962, 1967, European Cup Winner's Cup 1963, 22 full Scotland caps
LEFT   Transferred to Derby County, July 1968

The legendary Spurs midfielder of the 1960s, hardman Dave Mackay was an inspirational figure on and off the field with an insatiable desire for work and prodigious will to win; in 40 cup finals at all levels, he never finished on the losing side. Blessed with superb ball control, a sweet strike and sublime distribution skills, Mackay was a member of Spurs' 1960/61 double team and FA Cup winning side 12 months later. Recovering from a twice-broken left leg, Mackay captained Tottenham to a third FA Cup triumph of the sixties in 1967, before joining Derby County, where he became joint Footballer of the Year in 1968/69. As County manager, he won the First Division title in 1974/75. Prior to joining Spurs, Mackay won every domestic honour with his hometown club Hearts, including the League title in 1957/58.

Tottenham Hotspur 2 v Leicester City 0

FA Cup final
Saturday 6 May 1961

Wembley Stadium
Attendance 100,000
Gate Receipts £49,813

Spurs win the first double of the twentieth century

Teams

Bill Nicholson	**Managers**	Matt Gillies
Bill Brown	1	Gordon Banks
Peter Baker	2	Len Chalmers
Ron Henry	3	Richie Norman
Danny Blanchflower (capt.)	4	Frank McLintock
Maurice Norman	5	Ian King
Dave Mackay	6	Colin Appleton
Terry Medwin	7	Howard Riley
John White	8	Jimmy Walsh (capt.)
Bobby Smith	9	Hugh McIlmoyle
Jimmy Greaves	10	Ken Keyworth
Cliff Jones	11	Albert Cheesebrough
Smith 66, Dyson 75	**Scorers**	

Referee: J Kelly

Tottenham Hotspur 3 v Burnley 1

FA Cup final
Saturday 5 May 1962

Wembley Stadium
Attendance 100,000
Gate Receipts £53,837

Spurs win back-to-back FA Cups, becoming the first club to do so since Newcastle a decade earlier, and only the fourth to date

Teams

Bill Nicholson	**Managers**	Harry Potts
Bill Brown	1	Adam Blacklaw
Peter Baker	2	John Angus
Ron Henry	3	Alex Elder
Danny Blanchflower (capt.)	4	Jimmy Adamson (capt.)
Maurice Norman	5	Tommy Cummings
Dave Mackay	6	Brian Miller
Terry Medwin	7	John Connelly
John White	8	Jimmy McIlroy
Bobby Smith	9	Ray Pointer
Jimmy Greaves	10	Jimmy Robson
Cliff Jones	11	Gordon Harris
Greaves 3, Smith 51, Blanchflower (pen) 80	**Scorers**	Robson 50

Referee: J Finney

TOTTENHAM HOTSPUR in the 1960s was a wonderful place to be a professional footballer. We had great players, played with plenty of style and entertained supporters up and down the country. I also played against some of the greatest players to grace the game and, of course, we set a standard for other clubs to chase when we won the double in 1960/61. It was a tremendous achievement, but what is forgotten nowadays is how close we came to winning the double again the following season. No team has ever won back-to-back FA Cup and League doubles, but we came so close to achieving that in the middle of a golden era at White Hart Lane.

Growing up in Edinburgh, football was a major part of my life. Only a couple of years separated my elder brother Tommy, younger brother Frank and me. Another brother, Ronnie, was born after my dad came home from the war. Like lots of boys from our era, Tommy, Frank and I just had a tennis ball to practice with and did so at every opportunity. We didn't walk or run to school, we dribbled the ball to school along the pavement.

For as long as I can remember, I wanted to be a professional footballer. I would have joined any club to get my opportunity, but my number one choice was Hearts. All the family followed Hearts' fortunes every week and, from the age of eight, I stood on the terraces opposite the main stand at Tynecastle with Tommy and Frank.

The three of us were centre-halves for a local club called Saughton Park and it was a big story in local newspapers one year because the teacher in charge would not play us together in the Scottish Schoolboys' Cup, as he wasn't sure that we had a chance. The following year we faced King's Park in the final at Hampden Park and he did play us. It was every schoolboy's dream to play at Hampden and a marvellous moment for our family. All schools competed for the cup, as it was the most prestigious schoolboy trophy. We drew 0-0, which was incredible as many games could finish 5-0, 6-5, or even 10-0. We thought the replay might be at Hibernian's Easter Road ground, but for the three of us the perfect venue was Hearts' ground, Tynecastle. Incredibly, we got our wish and Tommy scored in a 2-1 win. It was a fantastic occasion.

In April 1952, when I was 17, Hibs manager Hugh Shaw arranged to see me. But Hearts groundsman Mattie Chalmers lived four doors from us and I'm sure my dad went to speak to him, because manager Tommy Walker asked me to come down to the club. I went to Tynecastle the day before I was due to see Hibs. I wanted to sign for Hearts more than any other team and got my wish. Tommy, who played semi-professional for Edinburgh City, and Frank both later signed for Hearts, but neither made the first team.

Hearts loaned me to Newton Grange Star Juniors to begin with, where I played wing-half in an open age League. We played the W-M formation, two full backs, a centre-back, two wing halves and five forwards. The back three were all over 30 years of age. I was one of two youngsters that did all the running for the older players. We had a great time and won five trophies. Hearts gave me an engraved watch to mark the achievement.

Hearts had not won a trophy for 49 years when I made my full debut against Clyde in November 1953, but we quickly developed and picked up four major honours during my years at the club. Alfie Conn, Jimmy Wardhaugh and Willie Bauld were dubbed the 'terrible trio' as they did the damage in attack. In fact, they scored so many goals we used to paralyse teams. Historically, Rangers and Celtic won the League every year. Hibernian and Aberdeen broke the domination only occasionally, so for Hearts fans it was fantastic to come from nowhere and challenge for major honours.

The breakthrough came in the Scottish League Cup when we defeated Motherwell 4-2 in the 1955 final, Willie Bauld getting a hat-trick. Then the following season we beat Celtic 3-1 to win the Scottish Cup. We let just one goal in during the run against Forfar Athletic, Stirling Albion, Rangers and Raith Rovers before Ian Crawford with two and Alfie Conn settled the final.

I was appointed captain for the 1956/57 campaign, which was a huge honour and we finished runners-up in the league to Rangers by two points. This was the second time we'd finished second, as Celtic edged the title in my first season at Hearts. In 1957/58, we made no mistake and won the First Division championship, finishing 13 points clear of Rangers. To lift the champion's flag was a very special moment. The season was also memorable because, having played for Scotland Schoolboys, I won my first full cap for Scotland against Spain and played in the 1958 World Cup finals.

The team did not have a manager in Sweden, but on our return, Manchester United manager Matt Busby was appointed and took charge when Scotland played Wales in Cardiff at the start of the new campaign. We trained at Reading's ground before travelling. Matt took me aside and said, "Davie, you take throw-ins, free kicks and penalty kicks. How do you take penalties?" We tried a few; it was only practice, so you could hardly miss. Matt said, "I don't like penalties being taken with the side of the foot because if a keeper guesses the right way he'll save it unless it's six inches from the post." I thought, "no problem," and battered a few straight in.

Come the match, in the opening minute, Mel Hopkins brings down Bobby Collins for a penalty. As Matt requested, I stepped up and whacked the ball as hard as I could. Jack Kelsey saved it! It was a bad penalty. Matt apologised afterwards, but thankfully it didn't matter because we won 3-0. Some years later I was talking to one our players from that day and he'd forgotten I'd missed, but only because we won. If we had drawn or lost, you can be sure he'd have remembered! Matt didn't last long as manager as he was rebuilding Manchester United after the Munich air disaster.

Every time that I played for Scotland, it was brilliant, though I wasn't selected as often as I'd have liked due to injuries. We had some great Scottish players playing in Scotland, but the strength in depth of Scottish players in England was far greater. Bill Shankly took Denis Law to Huddersfield, Don Revie took Billy Bremner to Leeds and many other great players made their names in England. It always puzzled me that they were not picked up first by a Scottish club.

In what would be my last season with Hearts I picked up another League Cup winner's medal when we defeated Partick Thistle 5-1 in 1959, Willie Bauld and Jimmy Murray grabbing two apiece. What pleased me about my Hearts career was that we competed at the highest level and finished in the top-four every season.

I was a combative player and always went in for hard tackles. This cost me during my time at Tynecastle because I broke my foot three times. When Tottenham Hotspur offered £32,000 before the transfer deadline in March 1959, Hearts accepted, deciding that if I got another bad injury I may be finished. Tommy Walker said I could think the move over, but there was nothing to think over for me. My transfer from Hearts to Tottenham was a record for a wing-half.

I have always been lucky, and looking back, the move was at the right time. Tottenham, under manager Arthur Rowe, had won the First Division title in the early 1950s, but after slipping down the league and climbing back into the top-three, had slipped back again. Bill Nicholson had replaced Jimmy Adamson as manager. Spurs were leaking goals and Bill Nick believed I could help them become tighter in defence and also score goals. He was also confident I could fit in alongside the likes of Tommy Harmer, Danny Blachflower, Maurice Norman and Bobby Smith.

When I first met Bill Nick in Edinburgh to discuss a move, I realised quickly that I wanted to sign for him. His team had just defeated Everton 10-4, which was a fantastic result, but they went through a terrible run. Tottenham were just above the relegation zone when we defeated Manchester City 3-1 on my debut. A 5-0 win over West Brom in our final home game saw us safe.

My dream as a kid, other than playing at Hampden Park, was to play at Wembley Stadium because I had never seen such a pitch in my life. Watching the FA Cup final on television every year in Scotland, it looked unbelievable, whereas Hampden Park was a wee bit lumpy and jumpy. I soon found out for myself because I represented Scotland Schoolboys against England Schoolboys at Wembley in 1950. Johnny Haynes was in the England side and I came up against Johnny in a full international a few weeks after I joined Tottenham. England edged a 1-0 win as Billy Wright won his 100th cap. Johnny broke a finger following a heavy challenge by me. Wembley was everything I imagined, but I was desperate to play in a Cup final there.

By New Year 1961, the double side-to-be was in place, with Bill Brown, Ron Henry, John White and Les Allen cementing first team spots. There were plenty of jokers in the dressing room, especially Bobby Smith, Terry Dyson and myself. Danny Blanchflower was the governor type and there was great camaraderie. After an early game that season, Terry said to me, "Davie, do you want to go for a drink?" I said, "I'll follow you in the car," but he explained that they drank around the corner at the Bell and Hare. At Hearts, you could not drink within a couple of miles of the ground after the game! Bill Nick didn't like us drinking, but we didn't have a game for a few days, so felt it was OK and it was great having room to relax.

Whatever Bill Nick said was always nice and sensible. On a Friday, after four days' hard training you could do whatever you wanted to do as long as you had a 15-minute five-a-side game in the gym. I had never experienced this. If you wanted to go out on the track that was OK, there would be nobody there demanding, "do five laps, three laps or two strong laps then sprints." Depending on how I felt, I'd do different things, which was fantastic.

Growing up in Scotland, every year we watched the FA Cup final. The first one I saw was the 'Matthews Final' in 1953 when Blackpool defeated Bolton Wanderers. I used to love wingers like Stan, Tom Finney and later Jimmy Johnstone of Celtic and Tommy Henderson of Rangers. They were all fantastic footballers.

Bill Nick's only selection decision in that team was whether to pick Cliff Jones or Terry Medwin on the right wing. You never knew which way Cliff was going to go as he could play on either wing, but mainly operated on the left during the 1960/61 campaign. Cliff was fast, tricky and brave. Often he'd make a late run to finish off a move with a neat header or strike.

Like Cliff, Terry played on both wings and also played occasionally at centre-forward. He was strong in the air and a very dangerous player. Bill Nick chose Cliff at the start of the campaign and he remained first choice apart from injuries.

On the left wing was Terry Dyson; he was some player. Terry was just over five foot tall, but caused problems for opponents with his skill and would score crucial goals during the coming season. I was disappointed when out-and-out wingers disappeared from the game. I loved having wingers in my team because, other than scoring goals, they offered the most entertainment you can get in football. There was no finer sight than a winger taking on an opponent; guys like Tom Finney and Stan Matthews were entertainment on their own.

At inside-forward were John White and Les Allen. John was slight, but gave us balance, had a great strike and was extremely dangerous because he used to drift in from the left flank in the main. Tragically, he was stuck by lightning during the summer of 1964 while sheltering under an oak tree during a round of golf with Cliff and died. He was such a popular guy, it was dreadful. Les was much stronger and an excellent player. Hard working, instinctive in the penalty area and unselfish, Les scored important goals for Tottenham.

Bobby Smith was a terrific leader of the line and a prolific goalscorer. I didn't mind playing against anyone, but one guy I would not have liked to face was Bobby because he was big, strong, powerful and awkward to mark. Bobby was excellent in the air, bustled past opponents and was a nightmare for goalkeepers at set-pieces.

I was confident we would make an impact during the season and was right because we made an excellent start to the 1960/61 campaign, winning our opening 11 league games. We began with an opening day 2-0 win against Everton and among our victories were four-goal triumphs over Blackburn Rovers and Manchester United, and a 6-2 thumping against Aston Villa, a match in which I scored my opening goal of the season.

Everything just clicked and we made it go right because the team knitted together so well. We had only just started together, but it worked out, which was fantastic and you must give credit to Bill Nick for changing what was a bottom-four team. Our initial target in 1959 was to escape relegation because that's where we were at that particular time. Now the target was to win a trophy.

Five consecutive wins in December, including a fine 3-1 win at rivals Everton when I scored our opening goal, meant we had won 22 out of 25 league games, which was incredible. We had a points cushion and talk now was of the double with the FA Cup coming up. We felt confident, but realised a lot of football had to be played.

I loved the competition and atmosphere of a big cup-tie because it was a one-off, so both teams had a chance on the day. It was that bit different for not only players, but also supporters and with us going so well in the League there was that extra feeling of anticipation at the club. The 1961 FA Cup run went relatively smoothly for us and with Leicester suffering an injury in the final, we won that game comfortably too, to add to the league title which we'd clinched with a 12 point margin.

At the final whistle, I was so happy. We all congratulated each other and really tried to take in the atmosphere. Then it was time for Danny to collect the trophy, before we posed for photographs and enjoyed the lap of honour. Bill Nicholson waited for us to shake us all by the hand before the celebrations continued in the dressing room where there was lots of singing.

We'd claimed the double, which is much more than just winning the FA Cup. Achieving the double was important, but I realised it would not sink in for some time. However, at the time, we were in cloud cuckoo land, away with the fairies. After a celebratory dinner at the Savoy Hotel the following day, we went on an open top bus to show off the trophy to supporters.

During the summer, I played plenty of golf and attended a number of functions. Up until 1961, we were earning £20 a week. This was the first season without the maximum wage and you were lucky if you could negotiate more then £100 a week. Spurs were now in the European Cup, so had an exciting season ahead of us. We knew that we would be the team to beat, but went into the campaign thinking we could win the double again.

Our title defence began slowly compared to the previous season as we collected just five wins in the opening ten games. I was in and out of the side due to injury, but managed a goal in a 1-0 win at home to Wolves. As we settled into the title race alongside Burnley and newly promoted Ipswich Town, managed by former Tottenham player Alf Ramsey, we played in the European Cup for the first time. It was brilliant to take part against the best European sides, but we did struggle to win league games immediately after midweek European fixtures.

We advanced into the quarter-finals, following aggregate wins over Gornik Zabrze and Feyenoord, but picked up only one League victory after the four ties and if you are not winning games after a European match, you will struggle to win the League. Without making excuses, playing in, say, Poland was not straightforward like it is today, with direct flights and motorway systems. We would play Wednesday, travel back Thursday then quite probably be off again on Friday for a domestic away match. We were also not eating as well, but I would not have missed the European adventure.

In early December, Bill Nick strengthened our side with the purchase of Jimmy Greaves. A prolific scorer of goals, I had faced Jimmy in his Chelsea days and he was a terrific goalscorer. After a spell in Italy with AC Milan, Jimmy joined Tottenham for just under £100,000, a huge amount of money in the early '60s. With Bobby Smith sidelined, Jimmy came straight into the side and would prove a great addition to the team.

I was still troubled with an injury, as was Terry Dyson, who was replaced by Terry Medwin. I came back into the first team and scored in a 3-1 win over Birmingham before Greavesie marked his debut with a hat-trick in a 5-2 win over Blackpool. Over the festive period, we enjoyed a double over Chelsea to send us into the New Year challenging for the title.

Our defence of the Cup was now upon us and we fancied our chances of doing well. There was a real sense that we had an opportunity of defending the trophy, but, naturally, we had to take each match as it came. The third round draw could have been kinder to us as we faced a trip to fellow First Division side Birmingham City.

The match proved far more difficult than we anticipated [Birmingham were fighting relegation at the time] and we had to dig deep to come from three goals behind to force a 3-3 draw. I remember that it was a windy day and the game was over by half-time, or so we thought, but as the wind advantage switched, Jimmy Greaves and Terry Dyson earned us an unlikely replay, which we won 4-2 in front of a packed house at White Hart Lane. Terry Medwin grabbed two goals.

We had a comfortable win in round four at lower league opposition. Facing Plymouth Argyle, we realised that the first game was their best opportunity of causing an upset, but the result was never really in doubt, as we ran out 5-1 winners. Jimmy scored two goals and was really beginning to make his mark with Tottenham supporters.

Before our fifth round clash at West Brom, we returned to European Cup action with a trip to Dukla Prague. It was a tiring journey, but we came home with a chance of progressing to the semi-finals following a narrow 1-0 defeat. We'd struggled on our return from European legs to date, but made no mistake this time with a 4-2 victory at The Hawthorns. Bobby Smith was back in the side for Les Allen, which could not have been an easy decision for Bill Nick, but Bobby and Jimmy Greaves leading the attack was some prospect. Bobby struck twice, as did Jimmy; one goal in particular being one of Jimmy's special goals.

Greavesie was without doubt the most natural goalscorer that I played with during my career. Jimmy had tremendous balance, anticipation in the penalty area and finished clinically. We knew that when Jimmy was one on one with a goalkeeper it was a goal. Other players, if they were through on a keeper six times would maybe score four. Jimmy would score all the time. If we were under pressure, often the ball would be knocked up to Jimmy 40 yards out; he'd take the defence on and score a great goal.

Although a great goalscorer, he was not a great trainer. During pre-season, Jimmy wouldn't come in from a road run until I'd be back and showered. He just couldn't do it... but come Saturday, he was one of the best players and every time you saw a picture of the six-yard box Jimmy was always there; he was match sharp.

It was great to be in the FA Cup quarter-finals, but there was no time to celebrate as we faced the return leg with Dukla Prague at White Hart Lane. I grabbed two goals in a terrific 4-1 win to set up a semi-final clash with Benfica, who had great players including Portuguese legend Eusebio. The matches were now coming thick and fast. Although I'd been ever-present in both cup competitions, I had missed a number of League games and all the big matches had affected our title defence. Since our Boxing Day win over Chelsea, we'd picked up just two victories, which allowed Burnley and Ipswich to build up a decisive-looking points advantage that we would struggle to claw back.

There was no time to feel sorry for ourselves though. We had to battle on and now faced Aston Villa in the Cup. At least we had a home draw and made it count in a 2-0 win; Danny Blanchflower and Cliff Jones grabbed the goals. Reaching the semi-finals gave us just the boost we needed before we travelled to Benfica and played vital League games. Against the Portuguese champions, we lost 3-1 at the Stadium of Light, but felt aggrieved as we had two goals disallowed that appeared fine. Bobby Smith's goal, however, kept us in the tie.

Back in the league, I missed a 3-1 win over Everton that kept us in the title hunt, but was fit for a glamour clash with Manchester United in the FA Cup semi-finals. Burnley played Fulham in the other semi-final, but our match was the one that generated massive interest. Playing United was always a special occasion as they had fanatical support and with players like Bobby Charlton in the team would be always dangerous. The match was played in an intense atmosphere and we played really well to win 3-1. Terry Medwin, Jimmy Greaves and Cliff Jones scored. Our dressing room was really buzzing with the prospect of playing either Burnley or Fulham in the final following their draw.

To defend the FA Cup was no mean feat. Only Newcastle United had achieved it at Wembley since the stadium's construction in 1923, so it was a huge target for us. Reaching the final could not have been better preparation for the return clash with Benfica, but we bowed out of the European Cup on aggregate 4-3, after winning 2-1 at White Hart Lane. We were unfortunate, though, because I hit the bar in the last minute. Had it gone in we'd have gone to extra time. Benfica's coach said that whoever won the semi-final would win the final and that proved to be true as Benfica beat Real Madrid 5-3 in Amsterdam. Eusebio said I was the best wing-half he'd ever faced, which was some accolade.

I missed the next few matches as our League campaign faltered again. Despite winning four of our five remaining games, we finished behind Ipswich Town, who won their first league title as they edged out Burnley after they slipped badly in the run-in. I scored in the last two games as we defeated both Birmingham and Leicester 3-2, but Ipswich finished four points ahead of us. Throughout the season few sports writers had given newly promoted Ipswich, under manager Alf Ramsey, a chance of lasting the distance, but with Ray Crawford and Ted Phillips leading the line they scored plenty of goals. Our away form had cost us, but we had come close to retaining our league title. If we'd not lost at home against Ipswich 3-1 between the FA Cup fifth and sixth rounds, and we'd beaten them instead, we'd have retained it on goal average. It was that tight.

It wasn't strange being back at Wembley, we expected to be there and looked forward to facing Burnley after they won their semi-final replay against Fulham. As always, we fancied our chances. All the team felt we were the best side around. Burnley was a team under pressure as they'd let the League slip from their grasp, whereas we'd been through the pressure of a Cup final just the year before and appeared more relaxed in the days leading to the game.

Come the big day, we didn't have any injury concerns. Since the fifth round, we'd played the same XI, so the team picked itself. The only changes from the Leicester final saw Terry Medwin and Jimmy Greaves line up instead of Terry Dyson and Les Allen. Our preparation was similar to the previous year and we knew what to expect. Bill Nick gave his last instructions before we got the call to line up in the tunnel. Tottenham supporters were in fine voice and we met the dignitaries that included the Queen, Duke of Edinburgh and Duke of Gloucester.

Determined to play well, we made the perfect start and caught Burnley by surprise with a goal inside three minutes. Bobby Smith created the opening for Jimmy Greaves from goalkeeper Bill Brown's long ball upfield. Jimmy didn't control the ball perfectly, but still had enough composure to beat Tommy Cummings and slide the ball home past keeper Adam Blacklaw.

Burnley had to come at us and did carve out openings, but their finishing was not clinical. If Jimmy had been in their attack, we'd have been in trouble. They did go close, though, and Bill Brown had to be alert to turn a Brian Miller strike over the bar. Jimmy nearly doubled our lead on 19 minutes when he burst through past Cummings and Miller to fire in a shot that Blacklaw did well to turn over the bar. Soon afterwards Bobby went close with an effort.

With Danny staying back, I was able to attack far more than I had against Leicester City and enjoyed the freedom to roam. Burnley, though, were a dangerous side with the likes of Jimmy McIlroy, Jimmy Robson and Miller, but there was no further score at half time. Bill Nick told us to be alert, but carry on playing the same way and more goals would come.

Five minutes after the break their pressure paid off when Gordon Harris found Robson with a left wing cross. Robson's low shot went through Bill Brown's legs. It was a blow, but we didn't panic. In fact, the goal pushed us on and we caught Burnley cold within a minute when John

White made ground on the left wing before finding Bobby near the penalty spot. A quick turn from Bobby past Miller and a clinical shot past Blacklaw put us back in front. It was a similar goal to the one he had scored in the Leicester final 12 months earlier, bringing the ball down, holding the player off, taking the ball on and volleying it into the back of the net. Bobby's strength got him his Cup final goals.

We urged each other on to get a third, but knew Burnley would not give in. Robson had an effort ruled out for offside before John Connelly went close with a snapshot. Ten minutes from time, Blacklaw dropped a cross and Cummings was forced to handle on the line. He'd have been sent off if that had happened now, of course, but back then a penalty was deemed enough. Danny made it 3-1 with a lovely spot-kick, right in the corner giving the keeper no chance.

In recent years, there was the Arsenal fiasco when Pires and Henry made a mess of passing between each other from a penalty. Danny and I were going to do the same in the Cup final because we'd practiced it on the training ground. It was all Danny's idea, but that was Danny, always think-ing about something a bit different. He was going to knock it to the side and I was to rush in and stick it in the back of the net. Bill Nick didn't know about it as he would not have allowed it, but if the score had been 3-0 or something like that we'd have done it. With the score being 2-1, though, I stayed back on the half-way line because if we'd tried it and I'd missed and we'd lost the FA Cup I'd have been shot! As it turned out Danny stuck it away no problem. There was quite a bit of pressure on him as it happens, because at that stage no-one had ever missed a Wembley Cup final penalty, but Danny tucked it away without showing it if he was feeling it.

The game was now over and at the final whistle; there were great scenes of celebration. I was particularly pleased for Terry Medwin, who'd missed out against Leicester and obviously Jimmy Greaves in his first final. Second time around you do tend to take more in, but the occa-sion does go by so quickly. Before we knew it, Danny had lifted the Cup again, the lap of honour was over and the celebrations were beginning. It was a fantastic feeling.

Again, we fancied our chances of performing well in the new season and eventually finished runners-up to Everton in the League, but we enter-tained, thumping West Ham 6-1, Nottingham Forest 9-2, Manchester

United 6-2 and Liverpool 7-2. Burnley avenged the Cup final defeat by knocking us out in the third round of the 1962/63 tournament, while in Europe we became the first British club to win a trophy when we hammered Atletico Madrid 5-1 in the Cup Winners' Cup final in Rotterdam. I played in every round, but missed the final after picking up a pelvic injury playing for Scotland against Austria. I received a medal, but felt sickened to miss out on the final.

A twice broken leg cost me much of the next two seasons as the double team began to break-up. The first fracture came in a European Cup Winners' Cup clash at Old Trafford, the second on my comeback against Shrewsbury Town reserves.

I succeeded Danny Blanchflower as Spurs skipper in 1965. It was a very hard job because of what Danny had achieved, but also easy because of my personality. I was one of those players that, when I crossed the line, was a captain anyway. It was my nature. Even at age ten, I'd been giving orders. If anyone ducked out of a tackle I'd be onto them, "Hey, get your foot in." Everyone hates losing, but I really hate losing. Really. I got so up tight, if anyone let a goal in for nothing I'd go crazy with them. Being skipper suited me and picking the FA Cup up myself when we won it again in 1967 was such a special moment.

In July 1968, Brian Clough persuaded me to sign for Derby County. As with my move to Tottenham, it was just the right time and in my first season, as captain, Derby won the Second Division championship. I also picked up the Footballer of the Year award jointly with Manchester City's captain Tony Book, which was a memorable moment. Following two seasons of top-flight football, I ended my career at Swindon Town.

Looking back, winning the double was a great achievement, but I've always felt that Tottenham should have won the League more than just the once during my time at the club. Our style of play was always to entertain whatever the score and it cost us some games, but we were competitive. On our day, we could and did beat every top team, often scoring bags of goals.

People have often asked me how I'd have adapted to the modern game and the answer is simple - brilliant. It would not have been a problem at all. Whether the current players would have got into our Tottenham side is another matter!

My years at White Hart Lane were special as I was fortunate to play with brilliant players and the camaraderie was excellent. I have so many fond memories, but high up on the list are the three occasions that

Tottenham lifted the FA Cup. All three were very special days and ones I will never forget.

BILL FOULKES
FULL-BACK 1949–1970

1963

BORN 5 January 1932, St. Helen's
SIGNED March 1950 as Amateur
UNITED CAREER 682 games, 9 goals
HONOURS 4 First Division championships, 1 FA Cup, 1 European Cup, 1 full England cap, 2 England U23 caps, Football League representative
LEFT Retired, June 1970

A resolute defender and backbone of United's defence, Foulkes survived the Munich air disaster in 1958 when eight of the Busby Babes died. Powerful in the air and a strong tackler, Foulkes won four League Championship medals in a top-flight career that lasted two decades. Twice an FA Cup runner-up, Foulkes captained United's decimated team against Bolton Wanderers in the 1958 final and was a member of Busby's rebuilt side that won the trophy in 1963. Ten years on from Munich, Foulkes helped United claim the ultimate club honour, the European Cup; another emotional Wembley occasion.

Manchester United 3 v Leicester City 1

FA Cup final
Saturday 25 May 1963

Wembley Stadium
Attendance 100,000
Gate Receipts £88,882

United rise from the ashes of Munich to win their first major trophy since the disaster which tore the club apart

Teams

Matt Busby	**Managers**	Matt Gillies
David Gaskell	1	Gordon Banks
Tony Dunne	2	John Sjoberg
Noel Cantwell (capt.)	3	Richie Norman
Paddy Crerand	4	Frank McLintock
Bill Foulkes	5	Ian King
Maurice Setters	6	Colin Appleton (capt.)
Johnny Giles	7	Howard Riley
Albert Quixall	8	Graham Cross
David Herd	9	Ken Keyworth
Denis Law	10	Dave Gibson
Bobby Charlton	11	Mike Stringfellow
Law 29, Herd 57, 85	**Scorers**	Keyworth 80

Referee: K Aston

I WILL ALWAYS BELIEVE that Manchester United's FA Cup victory in 1963 was the single most important trophy in the history of our great club. We'd been down and out after Munich. No club could recover quickly from the kind of devastation that the air disaster had caused. We lost so many players and so many friends, but incredibly, even though we battled against relegation all season in the league, in 1962/63 we had enough about us to fight our way to Wembley and win the FA Cup for United the first time in 15 years and several seasons of success followed.

Growing up in St. Helen's, everyone followed rugby league. I played full back locally, but was also making my way in football and joined St. Helen's Town, which is where Manchester City spotted the legendary Bert Trautmann. Bert played his last game for St. Helen's the year before I joined, but I was aware of his presence and went on to play against him many times. I played full back or centre half. Jimmy Murphy at Manchester United asked me to a trial. I saw Matt Busby with Jimmy on the sidelines and could not believe they had come to watch me play. Nothing happened initially, but Jimmy got back in touch and I signed as an amateur in 1949, while still working in the administration department at the local pit.

United won the League for the first time in 40 years in 1951/52, Johnny Carey was captain and Arthur Rowley top scorer. The following season I made my first team debut at right back just before Christmas at Liverpool. We won 2-1 and then defeated Chelsea 3-2. I came in for Tom McNulty, but didn't think I was good enough to displace him permanently.

Matt however, must have seen something, so I persevered and eventually left the colliery and signed professional. It was a hard decision because I had a good job and it was a risk, but a calculated one. United slipped down the league as the team which had won both the Championship and the 1948 FA Cup final broke up, so Matt brought a number of youngsters such as David Pegg, Tommy Taylor and Duncan Edwards and myself through in 1953/54 to join new captain Roger Byrne and Johnny Berry from the title team. We began to be known as the Busby Babes because of our tender ages.

In 1954/55 we continued to improve and enjoyed some terrific results, especially a 6-5 win at champions-elect Chelsea. Towards the end of the campaign, Mark Jones and Bill Whelan broke into the side as we finished the fifth. The Busby Babes side was developing.

During the season, I played for the Football League and gained selection for England. A number of players including Don Revie and Johnny Haynes made their full England debut and lining up alongside Billy Wright, Stan Matthews and Nat Lofthouse against Northern Ireland was great. I asked Walter Winterbottom what he wanted me to do. Walter told me to play as I did for United. I asked Stan Matthews the same as he was walking towards the halfway line before kick off. He said, "pass it to my feet, not in front, but to my feet." He was a tremendous player. We won 2-0, but it would be my only full England cap.

We'd made giant strides at United and knew we'd be a force in the coming season. We made a steady start and began to challenge the likes of Blackpool and Wolves at the top. Opponents took notice from December on as we collected 12 wins in 15 games. Among some great performances, we defeated Wolves 2-0 and clinched the title in our penultimate home game with a 2-1 victory over Blackpool in front of 62,000 fans. We won the league by 11 points. The Busby Babes had arrived.

Breaking into the team in 1955/56 was Eddie Colman. The average age of the side was 22 and most of us had been developed through the club's youth policy. The first team picked itself and our title defence began superbly as we collected ten wins from 12 games including a derby win over Manchester City. The Manchester derby was always special. It was a hard game because it didn't matter where the teams were in the League, it was always a battle. We were some side, though, and did not fear anyone home or away.

The title was our number one target; Matt made us aware of that, but the European Cup was in its second year and Matt convinced the directors that we should compete. Winning this trophy was Matt's dream. I enjoyed the standard of play and we learned a lot. Matt loved the challenge. There was no football on television like today, so it was an unknown quantity, but we were so confident in our ability. We played each game as it came and let the championship take care of itself.

Playing European football was a novelty, but we loved it. The style of play was different to domestic football and we had some fantastic games. We faced the likes of Eusebio of Benfica and Di Stefano at Real Madrid. We still meet occasionally, it's wonderful. We defeated Anderlecht 10-0 in the preliminary round; Tommy Taylor scored a hat-trick before we edged past Borussia Dortmand and Athletico Bilbao in thrilling fashion on aggregate.

By the time we faced Real Madrid in the semi-finals, I was looking forward to playing at Wembley in the FA Cup final. The League title was clinched and we enjoyed some fantastic results, thumping Newcastle United 6-1, Manchester City 4-2 and Charlton Athletic 5-1 in consecutive games. This time we finished 12 points clear of our nearest rivals Tottenham Hotspur, Preston and Blackpool, but we failed to overcome Madrid over two fantastic legs.

The season was far from over, though, and I was delighted to be playing at Wembley in the FA Cup final against Aston Villa. The FA Cup is such a special tournament, everyone watched it around the world and for a player it was great to play in. When I started out at United I never dreamed I'd play at Wembley and, of course, we were going for the double. No team had achieved it for years and we were such a young side. If we won, the sky was the limit for us.

Our Cup run had been eventful. Our third round opponents Hartlepools United gave us a fright before we scraped through 4-3. After a comfortable win at Wrexham, Duncan Edwards scored the only goal against Everton. Johnny Berry edged us past Bournemouth before striking again against Birmingham along with Bobby Charlton in the semi-finals.

The build up in Manchester was fantastic and the city was buzzing with excitement. I'd never played or even watched a game at Wembley, so the journey to the stadium was special. Matt geed us up and, waiting in the tunnel, I was ready, though obviously nervous. But once the game started it felt like just another match.

On the day, things did not work out. Our goalkeeper Ray Wood got injured following a challenge from Peter McParland after six minutes and Jackie Blanchflower, who was deputising for Mark Jones, went in goal. Duncan moved to centre-half. There were no substitutes then and we were down to ten men, but still, I feel, played the better football. McParland scored twice, though, before Tommy Taylor grabbed a late goal with a towering header from a corner. We were disappointed, but Johnny Byrne said, "don't worry, we'll be back next year."

During the close season, I looked forward to the new campaign because I really enjoyed playing in this team. It was an honour and we had so much in front of us. Ray Wood was a good keeper and commanded the penalty area. I was a steady player and was relied on for certain things, but if we got a penalty kick, they would not have given it to me!

Roger Byrne was quick, had strength bringing the ball out of defence and was a good captain. Mark Jones was a resolute central defender, nothing got passed him. Eddie Colman's movement in midfield made him a threat. He was nicknamed 'Snakehips' because of his propensity to sell dummies to players. Eddie dictated play and developed a fantastic midfield partnership with Duncan Edwards. Duncan was exceptionally strong and could play anywhere. Opponents feared him; he was a fantastic player.

On the flanks, Johnny Berry was a great little fellow, clever and quick. David Pegg was brilliant on the ground, a good winger; he would take on full backs that were hard to beat. Bill Whelan was dangerous as was Dennis Viollet, who was replaced by Bobby Charlton during the season. You could tell Bobby would be some player. He was a fantastic striker of the ball and dangerous. Bobby had stature even at an early age.

Tommy Taylor led the line and was simply unstoppable at times. Tommy was the player opponents most feared. His presence, height and strength made him a great centre forward. The team was at the start of something big and as players, we knew it.

Again we began the season well and, despite a few defeats, headed the table by Christmas. We played thrilling football and supporters flocked to see us home and away. We hit four goals in wins over Manchester City, Blackpool, Arsenal and Aston Villa, hammered Leeds United 5-0, and came out on the wrong end of 4-3 defeats against West Brom and Tottenham Hotspur. Every game was entertaining for supporters.

We were also making progress in the European Cup. Following aggregate wins over Shamrock Rovers and Dukla Prague, we earned a hard fought victory over Red Star Belgrade in a quarter-final first leg at Old Trafford. Before the return, we blitzed Bolton Wanderers 7-2 at home before claiming a 5-4 win at Arsenal. These would be the last games the Busby Babes would play together in England.

Following a superb 3-3 draw in Belgrade, we boarded a BEA Elizabethan aircraft and stopped at Munich airport to refuel on the way back to Manchester. On the third attempt to take off the plane crashed in a snow blizzard. The memories of that night have lived with me since. Matt Busby was fighting for his life, and among 23 fatalities, eight of my team-mates Roger Byrne, Geoff Bent, Eddie Colman, Mark Jones, Duncan Edwards, David Pegg, Billy Whelan and Tommy Taylor died.

The crash should not have happened. It was obvious that we would struggle to take off. Everybody was feeling really scared. The plane was bouncing along, not going fast enough, then suddenly there were three tremendous thuds and everything was spinning around. A second later, I was sitting in my seat with my feet in the snow. The aircraft had split in half directly underneath me.

I struggled out of my safety belt and ran before turning to see the plane's wreckage. Then I saw Matt Busby laying on one arm and Bobby Charlton, Dennis Viollet and Jackie Blanchflower lying unconscious in their seats. Harry Gregg came around the back of the aircraft with his face covered in blood and holding a baby. I ran over to Matt, we put an overcoat underneath him; he turned over, groaned and passed out. By this time, Bobby and Dennis were standing in shock.

Harry Gregg and I stayed in a hotel overnight and went to the hospital early in the morning. I saw Duncan, who at that stage was still alive. He half said something, but was rambling. I asked the nurse how he was and she said he was 50-50 and I felt relieved. If anybody could pull through it was Duncan, but he died ten days later. Johnny Berry was next to Duncan and the nurse shook her head. That's when I got worried. Johnny survived, but would never play again; neither would Jackie Blanchflower.

I then saw Dennis, Albert, Bobby and Ray Wood. I began thinking that it didn't look too bad, but then I asked where the rest of the team were. The nurse shook her head and said everybody else had died. It took me a long time to recover from that moment.

I don't feel guilty about surviving. I was lucky, so very lucky, but the crash wasn't necessary and that has always angered me. Families lost loved ones. As for the Busby Babes, we had a team that was youthful yet experienced, successful, and on the verge of dominating. It was such a tragedy.

We travelled home and had to prepare for an FA Cup fifth round clash against Sheffield Wednesday, having overcome Workington and Ipswich Town in earlier rounds. We had the sympathy of the nation behind us; everyone was talking about the disaster.

Jimmy Murphy took charge in Matt's absence and signed Ernie Taylor and Stan Crowther. Stan was given permission to play against Wednesday despite having played for Aston Villa earlier in the competition. I was appointed captain, and, along with Harry Gregg, Ernie and Stan, plus a number of youngsters including Shay Brennan and Alex Dawson, made up a makeshift side.

In the dressing room before the game, it was very emotional and all the younger players now had extra pressure. Of the Busby Babes squad, only Harry and I were playing; the others either had died or were injured. The atmosphere was incredible as we ran out. I've never kown such an emotion-packed occasion. The nation, everyone, wanted us to succeed. We felt this desperate need to win for our team-mates and got through. Shay and Alex scored the goals in a 3-0 win.

Against West Brom in the quarter-finals, Bobby Charlton was back in the side. Following a draw, we won the replay with a goal by Colin Webster. Our league form slipped, which was only natural after the disaster, and we only collected one more league victory during the remainder of the season, but the Cup was something else, the one-off games meant we could still compete at the highest level. We did reach Wembley again following victory over Fulham in a semi-final replay; Alex Dawson scored a hat-trick in a memorable 5-3 victory at Highbury. I felt that winning the FA Cup was the least I could do for my stricken comrades.

This was my second FA Cup final. In the dressing room, without the other players from the previous season being around me, it was hard. A year before we had all been together when we walked out. Walking out this time, I saw Matt for the first time since Munich. He was sitting on our bench. I could not believe it and had no idea that he had travelled to Wembley. He didn't look well. I tried to talk to him, but he looked in a trance, so I thought I'd better get on with the game.

It could not have been easy for Bolton's players because the whole country was behind us. It had been an emotional rollercoaster ride. Bolton was close to Manchester and all the players got on. They scored early, and then Nat Lofthouse barged Harry over the line when he appeared to have his hands on the ball. The referee gave the goal and there was no way back for us, but we received the nation's sympathy after we lost 2-0.

A few days after the final, we defeated AC Milan in the first leg of the semi-final of the European Cup, but there was to be no fairytale end to the season as we lost 4-0 in the return to go out 4-2 on aggregate. The legend of the club had taken on a new meaning though. Everyone knew about Manchester United and it built and has kept on building ever since.

Matt slowly recovered and began to rebuild a new club, although we all knew that it was going to be hard. Matt was determined, he really wanted to do something and had a taste for it. After we made a slow start in

1958/59, we recovered and a mid-season run of 16 wins in 18 games shot us up the table. We eventually finished runners-up to Wolves, but went out of the FA Cup in the third round at Norwich City. Albert Quixall joined from Sheffield Wednesday and made an immediate impact, but Bobby Charlton really came into his own and top scored.

The next couple of seasons saw us finish seventh and go out of the FA Cup to Sheffield Wednesday twice, including a 7-2 drubbing at home in 1960/61. I was still struggling emotionally and lost fitness and form, but Matt switched me to centre-half and I began to enjoy my football again. I was more comfortable at centre-half. I was quicker than I appeared, was strong in the air and had plenty of aggression and strength.

Playing for Manchester United there was a terrific atmosphere everywhere we played, especially at Old Trafford. I loved the dressing room banter and enjoyed training. Matt used to say that I did too much, but I would have run through a brick wall for him. Matt said I was the first name on the team sheet and if he had more Bill Foulkes's in the team, it would make things much easier. He could rely on what I was doing, which was a great compliment. On the field, timing was everything. People said I would go in fully committed, but I was a clinical tackler.

In 1961/62, we finished down the table, but reached the FA Cup semi-finals before going out to Tottenham Hotspur at Hillsborough. It was a big disappointment, but we were underdogs against the defending Cup holders. They had a terrific side and had Jimmy Greaves in attack. He was a great striker. On our day, though, we could take on any team, and the Cup demonstrated that as we beat Bolton, Arsenal and Sheffield Wednesday, who all finished above us in the League. Ipswich Town claimed the First Division title. We lost 4-1 at Ipswich, yet won 5-0 at home during their run-in to the title, which summed up our season.

The first team had changed with the arrival of full-backs Noel Cantwell, and Tony Dunne, striker David Herd, and defensive midfielders Maurice Setters, Nobby Stiles and Johnny Giles. I remember going to Ireland with Jimmy Murphy to watch Tony play before he signed. I don't know why, maybe it was to steady me down or something, but Jimmy took me and we watched Tony, who was quick. I remember telling Jimmy that he'd do fine. Noel succeeded me as captain. I was the senior player, but there were off the field distractions associated with the role. It was not a job for me and Noel found it easier.

Matt then signed Denis Law from Torino during the close season of 1962 and Pat Crerand would soon join us from Celtic. A new era at Old

Trafford was beginning, but it would take some time for the new players to settle into the side.

We got off to a dreadful start in the league, suffering numerous defeats. Relegation was a possibility, but, after 6-2 loss at White Hart Lane, we started our most consistent form of the campaign as Denis showed his class in wins over West Ham, Wolves and Nottingham Forest. Denis also scored four in a 5-3 at Ipswich Town, who were struggling alongside us. Bobby Charlton scored the only goal at Charlton Athletic on Boxing Day to send us into the New Year in better heart, but, due to an incredible freeze which swept across the country it would prove to be our last fixture until the end of February, when we drew at Blackburn Rovers.

The FA Cup had come around and it was strange to start our campaign in March once the country had thawed out. Even though we'd been struggling in the League, every team had a chance in the Cup. Each year I looked forward to the third round and like every professional footballer, the FA Cup was a trophy I was desperate to win. All the more so for me as I'd lost two finals. The draw took place on a Monday lunchtime and was something all players looked forward to hearing. As usual, we hoped for a slice of luck with our opponents.

We had a good third round draw as we faced Division Two side Huddersfield Town at home and ran out comfortable 5-0 winners with Denis grabbing a hat-trick against his former club. An Albert Quixall strike accounted for Aston Villa before Albert and Denis struck in a great win over Chelsea.

Following three home ties, our good fortune continued in the quarter-final draw when we faced the only Third Division outfit left in the competition, Coventry City. It would be tricky, however, as it would take place at Highfield Road in front of a capacity crowd looking for a major upset. As things turned out, we put in a professional display to win 3-1. Bobby scored twice and Albert hit the target for a fourth consecutive round.

We were through to another semi-final and naturally wanted to go one better than the previous season. We were drawn to face the winners of Nottingham Forest v Sheffield United, which had gone to a replay. When Second Division United came through after a second replay, I really began to think that this might just be our year; after all, we had faced only one First Division side. Liverpool faced Leicester City in the other semi-final.

It was now time to concentrate on avoiding relegation. Our league form throughout that Cup run was terrible. We had lost four consecutive games and hovered around the relegation zone. Victories over Aston Villa and Sheffield United were welcome, but we suffered losses against both potential Cup final opponents Liverpool and Leicester City.

Come semi-final day at Villa Park, it was something of a relief to get away from the pressure of trying to avoid relegation, but we knew that we would have a battle on our hands. True to form, we were a shade lucky to get past Sheffield, but Denis saw us through to Wembley. I was delighted and it was a day to look forward to.

Back in the League, there were a few more points to gain. With Denis scoring freely, I felt confident we would avert disaster and we eventually made sure with a hard-earned draw at fellow strugglers Manchester City and a 3-1 win at home to Leyton Orient. We were mathematically safe with a match to go. Despite losing our last game at Nottingham Forest, City and Orient went down.

As everyone breathed a huge sigh of relief, we looked ahead to the Cup final where we would face Leicester City. It took place three weeks later than scheduled due to the mid-winter freeze. Outside Manchester, few pundits tipped us, but although Leicester finished fourth in the League, I fancied our chances as I knew that on its day our side could perform.

David Gaskell was not first choice keeper, but came in over the years when Ray Wood or Harry Gregg was injured. David was strong and did well whenever called upon. Our full backs Tony Dunne and Noel Cantwell were both solid players. Tony would be a stalwart for many years while Noel was inspiring to the younger players in the squad and a good captain.

I was always going to be steady in defence, while Maurice Setters was the type of player we needed at the time and Matt knew it. Maurice had great authority and added steel to the midfield. Johnny Giles was very skilful, supplying the strikers with opportunities and alongside them was Pat Crerand, who would dominate midfield. A robust player, Pat distributed the ball superbly and could switch play with ease. Albert Quixall supported the attack with crucial goals, while Bobby Charlton quite simply had everything; balance, strength, and packed a terrific shot in either foot.

The partnership in attack between the two forwards David Herd and Denis Law was terrific and they complemented each other. David was a great striker. I remember when he'd played for Arsenal, I was marking him and he came in from the side on me with his knee into my ribs. I thought, "you so and so." I was pleased we signed him. David's attitude was good; he was strong and had a great strike on him.

Denis was a brilliant player. I'd faced Denis when he played for Manchester City and Huddersfield Town and you could see he was going to be a star. Denis was so quick mentally and his ability to control the ball was fantastic. Denis saw opportunities other forwards could not take and put them away in a flash. He was brave and went to places others forwards wouldn't go. Denis made things happen and for me was one of the best players in the country.

Leicester had lost a final to Spurs in 1961, so desperately wanted to win. During Easter, we played them twice, losing 4-3 and drawing 2-2. They finished fourth in the League and had fine players, especially Gordon Banks in goal, while David Gibson and Mike Stringfellow were dangerous attackers. Leicester had a reputation for making sudden breaks to score and manager Matt Gillies had welded them into a compact well-drilled team.

We stayed at the Hendon Hall hotel where Matt Busby gave his main team talk. The journey to Wembley was quick and it was great seeing the fans all dressed up for the occasion. The Cup final meant so much to fans and they made a big effort. Arriving at Wembley, we checked the pitch before getting changed. All the players had particular routines and Matt had a final word with us all to encourage us.

We may have been underdogs, but we settled quickly and it was clear early on that the occasion had affected Leicester because a number of their players seemed unnerved. Maybe the pressure of being favourites had got to them. My nerves soon cleared, especially when our keeper David Gaskell dropped a cross to David Gibson right in front of goal. I sensed the danger, instantly went in to clear the ball and that felt great.

I was marking Ken Keyworth. He was quite good in the air, but didn't really give me problems in the opening exchanges. Defensively we looked sound, while Denis Law and David Herd were giving the Leicester defenders a torrid time. Despite being on top, we nearly gifted Leicester the lead on 14 minutes with an own goal, when Noel Cantwell deflected Stringfellow's goal-bound shot just past our post. It was a key moment, but we rode our luck and escaped.

That would prove to be Leicester's best chance of the half as we began to dominate, especially in midfield where Pat Crerand was dictating play. Maurice Setters was also looking solid and Bobby Charlton was on form. Our opening goal came on 29 minutes with a Denis Law special and it was a great moment. Pat set up the chance with a neat pass to Denis, a quick feint and shot gave Gordon Banks no chance. It was a typical Denis Law goal; his reactions were electric. A second goal before half time would have been terrific, but our promptings came to nothing.

Matt told us to carry on playing the same and more goals would come. He warned us to keep tight, though, because Leicester would attack more as they had nothing to lose. Leicester did come at us in the opening minutes of the second half, but failed to trouble us and just before the hour mark, David Herd was on hand to score when Banks, who had looked jittery, only half saved a Bobby Charlton special. I thought, "that's it, now let's keep in tight."

Leicester had to push on, and to their credit, got back into the match when Keyworth equalised ten minutes from time from a twice taken free kick. It was disappointing because we had controlled the match, but we were not to be denied. Denis almost scored with a header, but hit a post before Banks spilled a Johnny Giles cross and David was on hand to clinch the game five minutes from time. There was no way back for Leicester.

At the final whistle, the initial feeling was one of relief. I was delighted, and so was Matt. We had played the better, more stylish football and deserved to win. Receiving my medal was a special moment and the fans sang throughout the lap of honour. Back in the dressing room, there were great celebrations. It was the first trophy we'd won in a number of years - and obviously the first since Munich - so was a really great feeling.

In the evening, the celebrations continued at the Savoy Hotel. We had a comedian, who was perfect. He knew all the players, knew football and had us rolling in the aisles. We travelled back to Manchester by train and went on an open top bus to the town hall where thousands came to greet us, which was fantastic.

This was the start of a successful period for us. The team developed and we played some great football. The Cup win was a springboard for us, but I would not enjoy any more FA Cup success. In fact, during my final years at Old Trafford we'd reach the semi-final in three consecutive years between 1964 and 1966 before going out in the semi-finals to West Ham, Leeds United and Everton. All three defeats were huge disappointments and the difference in the dressing room was enormous. Everything you had been working for was gone. Losing in the semi-final was terrible and far worse than in a final, when at least you have reached Wembley, although it is so disappointing to lose on the big day.

The 1963/64 season would see Nobby Stiles break into the first team and, of course, George Best would made his mark. George was a fantastic player, he was blessed with so much skill and tormented defenders. We went on to clinch two further League titles in 1965 and 1967. Both were memorable, but the way we clinched the championship in '67 was special because we defeated West Ham 6-1 in the penultimate match of the season and I scored one of my rare goals. I always saved them for special occasions!

Manchester City pipped us to the title in 1967/68, but at the same time, we were going well in the European Cup. We were so determined to win the trophy not only for the current side, but also for the Busby Babes that died. In 1965/66, we had defeated Benfica 3-2 at Old Trafford when I grabbed the winner before claiming a brilliant 5-1 win in the return when George played one of his best-ever games for us, but we went out in the semi-finals to Partizan Belgrade.

By 1967/68, I knew this may be my last opportunity to win the trophy. We defeated Hibernians (Malta) and FK Sarajevo before easing past Gornik Zabrze in the quarterfinals. George gave us a slender lead against Real Madrid in the semi-final first leg at Old Trafford before a titanic battle in Spain. I scored our third goal in a 3-3 draw to take us through to the final. It's a goal I'll never forget. I only got nine in my United career. This was my last goal for the club and the most important by far.

In the final against Benfica at Wembley, we deserved to win. Everything went well, every player did his part and we played fantastic football. Bobby gave us the lead before they equalised and nearly won it at the end, but Alex Stepney, who'd come into the side in 1966, made a great save from Eusebio. Matt said before extra time, "come on lads let's go again." George scored a wonderful goal and we murdered them in the end with further goals from Brian Kidd and Bobby. We had to win this match and I had this feeling behind me for the players who died in Munich. I was relieved and it was the highlight of my career, but there were mixed emotions.

The Busby years can never be eclipsed and to have built two great teams shows the character of Matt. Before the crash, Manchester United belonged to Manchester, but afterwards it captured the imagination of the world. I played in two of the greatest post-war teams created by Matt Busby and was privileged to be a part of those years. The European Cup was certainly the highlight, but the league titles were also special.

As for the 1963 FA Cup win, it was a real thrill and so important to the club's rehabilitation because it is such a great competition that has so much history and I'm just so glad I was able to win it the once.

JOHN BOND 1964
FULL-BACK 1950–1965

BORN   17 December 1932, Colchester
SIGNED March 1950 from Colchester Casuals
WEST HAM CAREER   428 games, 35 goals
HONOURS   1 FA Cup, 1 Second Division Championship 1957/58,
Football League representative
LEFT   Transferred to Torquay United, January 1966

John Bond was an unsung hero for West Ham United during a 16-year playing career at Upton Park. Predominantly a full back, Bond made his debut under Ted Fenton in a 2-1 win at Coventry City in February 1952. A stalwart in defence, Bond also enjoyed brief spells at centre-forward, scoring a hat-trick against Chelsea in 1960. One of only four players to feature in at least 40 matches as the Hammers won the Division Two title in 1957/58, Bond was a key member of the team that won the FA Cup in 1964. He ended his playing days at Torquay United before being offered his first managerial post at Bournemouth and then taking the hot seat at various clubs, including Norwich City and Manchester City, whom he led to Wembley finals.

West Ham United 3 v Preston North End 2

FA Cup final
Saturday 2 May 1962

Wembley Stadium
Attendance 100,000
Gate Receipts £89,289

*West Ham United win their first ever FA Cup in a thrilling,
record-breaking final*

Teams

Ron Greenwood	**Managers**	Jimmy Milne
Jim Standen	1	Alan Kelly
John Bond	2	George Ross
Jack Burkett	3	Nobby Lawton (capt.)
Eddie Bovington	4	Jim Smith
Ken Brown	5	Tony Singleton
Bobby Moore (capt.)	6	Howard Kendall
Peter Brabrook	7	David Wilson
Ronnie Boyce	8	Alec Ashworth
Johnny Byrne	9	Alex Dawson
Geoff Hurst	10	Alan Spavin
John Sissons	11	Doug Holden
Sissons 11, Hurst 52, Boyce 90	**Scorers**	Holden 10, Dawson 40

Referee: A Holland

LIKE ALL PROFESSIONAL FOOTBALLERS, I hoped to play in an FA Cup final at Wembley Stadium. It seemed not to be destined for me as year after year West Ham went out of the Cup in the early rounds. But late in my career, the opportunity arose when West Ham United twice came from behind to defeat Preston North End in a classic final. The occasion was everything I imagined, as there is nothing like winning the FA Cup.

It was strange how I came into football. I lived in Stanway, just outside Colchester when I left the senior amateur club in the town, Colchester Casuals, because I was not doing my stuff at centre-forward. I was a big lazy so and so. I played for the Army Cadet Force and joined a village team called Stanway Rovers as it was the only way to get a game.

Then Colchester United manager Ted Fenton was appointed manager at West Ham. One morning in March 1950, while delivering pies for a local firm, I got a message from my brother to go to West Ham. They wanted me to sign professional forms. I was amazed. I was 17. I handed in my notice, borrowed my brother's overcoat, went to London and signed for West Ham. I found out later that Ted, who was a keen army man, had seen me play for the Army Cadet team. He saw something in me. I was a big lad and could kick the ball, but never thought about being a professional footballer. I got a £20 signing on fee and £7 a week. I felt a rich feller as it was more than the average person earned.

Every day the squad walked out of the tunnel at West Ham and around the pitch, then Billy Moore, who doubled as both our physiotherapist and trainer, came over. We'd run around the perimeter of the pitch a couple of times and then he'd just say, "have a walk, then have another run." After 45 minutes, he would throw a couple of balls on the pitch for us to do what we wanted. That was training. It was amateurish.

I made my debut at left back against Coventry City in February 1952. I played well and Ted said he was pleased, but I had to wait until another opportunity came along. I got more run outs over the next couple of years as we failed to make an impact in Division Two. We did have our moments, though, and showed we could battle when fighting back from 3-0 down to win 4-3 at Fulham in 1953/54. During the season I switched to right back and remained there throughout my career apart from the occasional game as an emergency centre-forward.

We were terribly inconsistent. In 1954/55, we shipped five goals to Swansea Town, Blackburn Rovers twice and Notts County before winning eight in ten games. There was no real coaching as such, but we were keen to learn. I joined a group including club captain Malcolm Allison, Noel Cantwell, Frank O'Farrell and Dave Sexton that met regularly at Cassettari's cafe to talk football. Ted arranged for us to receive vouchers from the club. Malcolm was the driving force and we picked his brains about the way the game should be played. While some of the lads went to the snooker club and pictures after training, Malcolm demonstrated things to us and worked us hard. We all became managers and I will be forever thankful to him.

W e started the 1957/58 campaign poorly, but ended up as Division Two champions. In our side, Ernie Gregory was a steady keeper; Ken Brown a pivotal figure in defence, while Andy Malcolm was a key player at right half. John Dick partnered Billy Dare in attack. Vic Keeble from Newcastle United soon joined them and the trio were tremendous, scoring over half of our 101 League goals. Billy missed the latter part of the season, but John and Vic scored regularly. Among many notable displays, they scored in an 8-0 win over Rotherham United and hit the target when we clinched the title in the final game at Middlesbrough.

I missed just one league match and got in on the scoring action with eight goals. This was something of a surprise to me as I'd only scored three since breaking into the first team. Among my memorable moments were winners against Middlesbrough and Derby, a brace during an Easter victory against Notts County and a crucial strike in the penultimate match at home to Liverpool that earned us a draw.

I really looked forward to taking on the likes of Wolves, Manchester United, Bolton and Burnley in Division One. Not knowing what to expect, we got off to a tremendous start winning our first six league matches at home, including a 2-0 win against Wolves, who would go on to claim a second consecutive title, before hammering Aston Villa 7-2 and Blackburn Rovers 6-3.

Teenager Bobby Moore had made his debut against Manchester United; we won 3-2, then he played against Nottingham Forest, but was dreadful in a heavy defeat. Ted dropped Bobby, who at the time was far from the world star that he would become. Bobby was slow, neither a great tackler nor a fabulous header of the ball, but he wanted to play and wanted to be somebody. Within a couple of seasons, Bobby had replaced Malcolm Allison, who was struggling to come back from tuberculosis. Following an operation to remove a lung, Malcolm retired and began his coaching career in which he would make his name at Manchester City.

After a poor run, seven wins in eight games over Christmas and New Year pushed us up the table. They included a 6-0 victory over Portsmouth and a double over Tottenham Hotspur. Spurs knocked us out of the FA Cup, but we recovered to finish in a sixth place. Towards the end of the campaign, an injury to Vic Keeble saw me play as a striker and I found that I still had the instinct, scoring twice in a 4-3 win over Bolton and the opener in a 3-2 victory against Everton.

Vic was back leading the line by the start 1959/60, which was fine by me. Sides were wary of us, but, after a good start, by the New Year, results were not going our way as a 7-0 loss at Sheffield Wednesday and 6-2 defeat at Blackburn Rovers illustrated. Five-goal losses in the FA Cup to Huddersfield and Burnley, then Newcastle, Wolves and Manchester United in the league completed a miserable campaign in which we only finished four points clear of relegation. I did however, enjoy a spell in attack with Vic injured and scored my only career hat-trick in a 4-2 win against Chelsea.

The 1960/61 campaign saw me back in defence and followed a similar path with big home wins over Aston Villa, Preston, Arsenal and Wolves cancelled out by many defeats including a 6-1 drubbing at Old Trafford. There was an amazing 5-5 draw at Newcastle, but all in all it was another poor season.

Towards the end of the campaign, Ted Fenton mysteriously resigned. Arsenal assistant manager and England U23 coach Ron Greenwood, who bless him died recently, became manager. In 1961/62, results both on and off the park improved as we finished eighth. Record signing Johnny Byrne from Crystal Palace had arrived and some of our youngsters showed a lot of potential.

From the youth academy, Geoff Hurst and Martin Peters broke into the first team. The fabulous thing about Geoff was that when Ron arrived, Geoff was a very ordinary wing half, but Ron eventually made him into a striker and he became one of the top strikers in the world. To be honest Ron was a revelation. I had not seen anything like him. He made the lads want to improve and the club began to be more competitive.

Bobby Moore was also making progress. His thirst for knowledge and natural leadership made him an obvious captain. Bobby's ability to intake information was tremendous, he wanted to learn and allowed nothing to interfere with his football. People used to tell him things and he would learn very quickly. He kept things simple in everything he did on the field; he never held the ball if he didn't need to, never touched the ball twice if he could touch it once, never touched it three times if he had to touch it twice. And, of course, one of his great strengths was his anticipation, that was always there. How to time a tackle came instinctively to him.

I was his room-mate for away games and everything about Bobby was methodical. If Bobby had pound notes in his hand, they would be folded over neatly. He folded his handkerchief neatly and items by his bed would be laid out perfectly. He was a tidy and meticulous person. When you worked with Bobby, you realised football was a simple game. People thought he couldn't play and that there were better players, but he had something special. Bobby's belief in sportsmanship as well as his leadership and playing skills set him apart.

Ron's arrival helped Bobby develop. Walter Winterbottom gave him his England debut before the 1962 World Cup finals and he never looked back. It was incredible. Alf Ramsey made him England captain within a year of becoming manager in autumn 1962 because he sensed Bobby could lead by example and he was absolutely right.

Come the 1962/63 season, I fell out with Ron over an incident and, bar a three game run due to an injury to Joe Kirkup, would not regain my first team place for a year. Ron had me up in his office with the chairman about being left out. He said to me at the time, "don't think I have never been left out when I was a player." But I was the senior player at the football club and playing in the A team every week as the first team finished mid-table made it a depressing time.

By the start of the 1963/64 campaign, Ronnie Boyce, Johnny Byrne and Geoff Hurst were leading an exciting forward line. The first team had made a poor start and I was still out of favour. Three months into the campaign, I was walking down the passageway after training, when I suddenly realised that being out of the first team set up was my own stupid fault. It was as if someone had tapped me on the head and knocked sense into me. I told myself to sort myself out.

A few days later, I was in the treatment room before the first team played Aston Villa in the League Cup. Ron asked if I wanted to come to

Villa as Joe Kirkup was injured. I said, "are you kidding, I'd love to." It was unfortunate for Joe, but in football, you must take your opportunities. We won 2-0 and I scored the opening goal. I was back.

It was great to be playing in the first team again. We defeated defending champions Everton 4-2, Manchester United 1-0 at Old Trafford and West Brom 4-2 in the next three games, but our form dipped and hit rock bottom on Boxing Day when Blackburn Rovers thumped us 8-2 at Upton Park. The result was a record defeat in a first-class game for the club. We got changed and immediately went to get a train to travel up to play at Blackburn the next day. The papers were full of stories saying how many Rovers would win by. One paper predicted 16-0. Blackburn's manager, Jack Marshall added fuel to the fire by saying that he'd be pleased just to win 4-0!

We'd taken a hammering, but that made us all the more determined to get a result. Ron made one change; he left Martin Peters out and brought Eddie Bovington back. We won 3-1. It was unfortunate for Martin, who would, of course, go on to become a world class player. Martin was a classic midfielder, blessed with delicate touches and became renowned for making late runs to get on the end of crosses with a flicked header or shot.

Things clicked. Ron had not panicked; he'd assessed the situation and made the right tactical changes. The previous day when I marked Michael Harrison, he gave me the roasting of all roastings. He ran my legs off, so in the team talk, Ron said to me, "if you can't get to him, don't tackle him, jockey him, make him think." It worked; Harrison didn't create much trouble and we beat Blackburn handsomely.

The result gave us confidence as we looked ahead to an FA Cup third round clash at home to Charlton Athletic. I always enjoyed playing in the FA Cup, but had not enjoyed much success at West Ham. In Division Two, we'd caused a couple of shocks by defeating First Division Preston and Cardiff on our way to the quarter-finals in 1956 before losing to Tottenham Hotspur after a replay. Since promotion though, we'd only reached the quarter-finals once, and that was the previous season when I was out of favour. Liverpool had defeated us at Upton Park.

You never really target a Cup run; you listen to the draw, hope for a home tie and go from there. We got our campaign off to a comfortable start with a 3-0 win against Charlton. Geoff Hurst, Peter Brabrook and John Sissons scored to set up another derby, this time at Leyton Orient. This was the second time we had been drawn against them during the season because we had already overcome them in the League Cup. The League

Cup was in its days when most top sides opted out and the final was a two-legged affair, not even at Wembley, but played on the home grounds of the two competing clubs. We'd reached the semi-finals following further wins over Aston Villa, Swindon Town and Workington Town. Of those, only Villa was a top-flight team, but we were not complaining as we now faced Leicester City in the last four.

Orient gave us a real fright and we were delighted to get away with a 1-1 draw, courtesy of Peter Brabrook. The return four days later at Upton Park was far more straightforward as we again ran out 3-0 winners; Geoff scored two goals and Johnny Byrne one. Next up was Leicester in the League Cup and we were satisfied after a 4-3 defeat in the away leg, but the second game would not take place until after the FA Cup semi-finals, so we refocused on the FA Cup again.

Incredibly, we drew Swindon again. In the League Cup we had come through after a replay, but inspired by Peter Brabrook, this time we won at the first time of asking 3-1. Again Geoff scored two goals and Johnny Byrne got the other. We had reached the FA Cup quarter-finals and Cup fever gripped the club. We had a home draw, but faced a tough tie against Burnley, who'd lost the 1962 final.

In a thrilling game, we came through 3-2; Ronnie with two goals and Geoff scored to keep our hopes of glory alive. We were in our first FA Cup semi-final since 1933 and throughout the cup run, had been in a rich vein of form with league wins over champions-elect Liverpool, Tottenham, Wolves and Sheffield Wednesday.

Following the Cup win over Burnley, though, we had lost at Turf Moor and at home to our possible semi-final opponents at Hillsborough, Manchester United. Matt Busby's side had a second quarter-final replay with Sunderland to overcome first, while Division Two sides Preston North End and Swansea faced each other in the other semi-final.

Losing at home to United was not the best preparation a week before a potential semi-final. David Herd and David Sadler scored and, as we walked off the pitch, United's keeper David Gaskell, was clearly confident they would get past Sunderland, because he said to Bobby Moore, "don't bother turning up next week." In the dressing room, Bobby mentioned what Gaskell had said to him. United did defeat Sunderland at the third time of asking two days later and we were determined to make Gaskell regret his words.

Apart from the FA Cup, United were going well in League and due to return to European Cup Winners' Cup action a few days after the semi-final.

They were Cup holders, too, and rightly favourites with the likes of Bobby Charlton, Denis Law, Paddy Crerand and so on in their side. They were more than a decent team and I was up against a new talent breaking through, George Best. He was only 17, but clearly a terrific prospect.

George was the new kid on the block. I had played against all the great wingers including Stan Matthews of Blackpool and Tom Finney of Preston. They were a nightmare to mark. Stan never used to say anything; he would just get out there and play. He'd get the ball and take you on, if you stopped him he would get up and take you on again. Stan was relentless. It was a never-ending thing, every time he got the ball you knew he was going to come at you.

Tottenham's Cliff Jones was another one who would frighten the living daylights out of a defender because he would come in on crosses to head home at the far post. As a technical player, George would prove the hardest; he had so much ability. I faced him in the coming season and he ran the life off me, ran me ragged.

Despite being underdogs, we were up for the challenge. The FA Cup is such a great leveller; it's what happens on the day and we had an advantage because there was thick mud as there had been a lot of rain. The conditions were not good for United because it slowed down their quick passing game, and for me especially, the conditions would help me more than they would Bestie, that's for sure.

In driving rain, after a goalless first half we built up a 2-0 lead with two goals by Ronnie Boyce. All of a sudden, though, 15 minutes from time, our keeper Jim Standen was in trouble after getting mud in his eyes and was still having difficulty focusing when a quick cross came in, Denis Law said thank you very much and the score was 2-1. It was game on again, but we were not to be denied our victory. Bobby went down the pitch, nipped a cross in to Geoff Hurst just before the ball went out of play, and Hursty smashed it into the back of the net to make it 3-1. On the day we played superbly, adapted better to the heavy conditions and deserved our victory.

Our dressing room was a great place to be following the win. There was a great sense of achievement. For the club, apart from a wartime Cup final this was West Ham's first appearance at the Twin Towers since the famous 'White Horse' final in 1923 when they lost to Bolton in the first match played at the stadium. For the players, it was a first FA Cup final and for most a first appearance of any kind at Wembley. To play in a final had been such an ambition for me; I was delighted.

We had a six-week build up to the final where we would go in as favourites against Second Division Preston after they had overcome Swansea. It didn't go particularly well. We lost 2-0 to Leicester in the second leg of the League Cup semi-final, which was a blow because we fancied our chances. We ended the league campaign with three more wins to finish fourteenth, but all thoughts were on the Cup final.

I had seen many games at Wembley, but not played there, so it was an exciting time. Whenever England played at Wembley, the club hired a coach to take the team, so I knew what it was like as a spectator, but not as a player. The FA Cup final was the big game each year. No games were covered live on television during a season apart from the final and *Match of the Day* was still some months away from providing highlights of even just a couple of matches. All football fans looked forward to watching this one live game of the year.

I could remember the classic 1948 final when Matt Busby's first great Manchester United side beat Blackpool 4-2; it was some game. Johnny Haynes of Fulham once said to me that he'd played 50 odd games for England, but he would have given up all his caps to play once at Wembley in the FA Cup final. That told me what playing in a Cup final meant to players - even greats like Johnny.

Our Cup final line up was settled as the same XI that had played throughout the competition. Jim Standen was an experienced goalkeeper. There was nothing flashy about Jim. He would make the save and get on with it. Jim was reliable. Jackie Burkett was a good left back, a physical player and dangerous on the overlap. Jackie had a good left foot, was a useful tackler, honest as the day was long and would give you everything. Playing on the opposite flank to Jackie, I offered experience and gave balance to the defence.

Eddie Bovington was a workhorse, a good tackler, honest, won the ball and moved it on. He did not have a great range of passes, but Eddie could stop an opponent playing. He was also a good man-marker. Kenny Brown was a solid centre half, a fine header, strong and a good distributor of the ball. Bobby Moore was skipper and an inspiration to us all; you knew he wanted to win. He was going to put his best foot forward all the time. Bobby was a winner, simple as that.

Peter Brabrook was quick as lightning. Peter could take people on and take them out of the game. He was a danger against any team he played. I played behind Peter at full back and knew that he could run the ball out of trouble. Ronnie Boyce was an unsung hero in the team. He was nicknamed

'Ticker' because of his work rate. Ronnie never stopped and we appreciated his efforts. The players rated Ronnie; he was a player's player.

Johnny Byrne was nicknamed 'Budgie' because he was always talking on and off the pitch. He fitted in well to our pattern of play. Johnny was an instinctive player. Teams would try to wrap him up, but he would do something different to get to the byline and deliver a cross. Johnny was also a real character. I remember one game, after I'd given a goal away, he promptly scored and on his way back for the restart said to me with a grin, "don't worry Bondy, I'll get you out of trouble!"

Geoff Hurst was a magnificent player to have playing up front for you. He came into his own when he converted to striker. It was fantastic to witness and he did become something special. Johnny Sissons was terrific for such a young lad. He was only 18, but had a magnificent left foot, and could strike a ball with power and accuracy. Johnny was a danger to anyone that marked him and he could win you a game on his own.

Of course, the press coverage built up as the match approached, although not like today's blanket coverage. We organised a player's pool that generated funds for the squad from ventures that included a colour booklet and a commemorative tie. We also had around 100 tickets each for family and friends. We stayed at a hotel the night before the game. As usual, I roomed with Bobby. We chatted about how we'd do the next day against Preston and tried to relax. We looked forward to the occasion immensely. Ron gave a team talk in the morning to stir us up. He kept it simple, telling us to just play our normal game.

Then we headed off to Wembley alongside a police escort. Seeing all the supporters and especially going down Wembley Way was great. I remember walking around the pitch and taking in the atmosphere, then we made our way to the dressing room before the match. I put my shirt on then took it off, then put it on again. Ron asked, "what are you doing?" It was just nerves. I just wanted to get at it. We all had our superstitions, the order we went out in and so on. When Ron said, "right, let's go," for home games, Bobby would always tap the top and both sides of the door leading out of the dressing room, then put his shorts on and that would be him ready.

I had thought this day would never come, and for me this was the moment I got edgy and nervy. I wanted to get on with it. The noise walking out was something else. Hearing 100,000 fans cheering really hits you. I was used to a cheer running out around the country, but this was a one-off. You try taking everything in when you look around, but all I could do was think, "I hope I play well."

After introductions to dignitaries, at last it was time for the kick off. That was some relief. We were heavy bookies' favourites because we were a First Division side, but Preston settled quickly and Bobby had to be sharp to clear dangerous balls from Alan Spavin and Howard Kendall, who was becoming officially the youngest player to appear in an FA Cup final, just edging out our own Johnny Sissons to the record, although it's been beaten twice since. Nobby Lawton in particular was creating us problems with his incisive passing. Strikers Alan Ashworth and Alex Dawson were also giving us a tough time. Being underdogs suited Preston and being favourites seemed to be affecting us.

We struggled to find rhythm and our counter-attacking game was not slick. We had a let off when Ashworth shot wide from close range, but then Preston deservedly opened the scoring on nine minutes when Jim Standen could only parry Dawson's shot and Doug Holden reacted first to prod the ball over the line. It was a shock, but probably one we needed. We bounced straight back within a minute to equalise. Bobby started the move when he dispossessed Ashworth before laying a neat ball to Johnny Sissons. Sizing up the moment, Johnny flicked the ball to Johnny Byrne, raced ahead for the return, burst past two defenders before firing home a left foot shot past Alan Kelly. It was a great moment for us and made Johnny the youngest player to score in a Cup final.

Our supporters were now in fine voice, singing *I'm Forever Blowing Bubbles*, but Preston picked up the tempo again. With Lawton dictating play, they dominated, but missed a great chance when Ken Brown made a terrific last-ditch challenge to deny Ashworth. For all Preston's possession, we should have edged ahead, but Johnny Byrne blazed over and Kelly made a brilliant stop to deny Geoff Hurst.

Five minutes from half time, Preston scored again when big Alex Dawson came charging in to convert a David Wilson corner. I remember him shouting "yeh" before heading the ball in the back of the net. It's funny what sticks with you, but I remember that as clear as day. On the balance of play, it was coming, but we were unfortunate because both Jim Standen and Ken Brown slipped while going for the cross.

We may have been favourites, but with Holden, Ashworth, Kendall and Dawson impressing, it was tough going as Preston were showing they were worthy of a place in the final. We were relieved to be only a goal down and knew we had to change things during the interval if we were to win. Ron was not panicking, and made three tactical changes because we'd given them far too much room in midield. Ronnie Boyce was told to track Lawton, Eddie Bovington had to watch Spavin, while Bobby Moore was to tighten up on Ashworth.

We came out and looked a different side. Our equaliser came on 52 minutes, but to be honest it was a bit lucky. Ken Brown joined the attack and rose above Dawson to head a Peter Brabrook corner goalwards. Alan Kelly could only parry the ball out to Geoff, whose header against the crossbar bounced down and hit the unfortunate Kelly on the back of the head before ricocheting into the net. It was lucky for us, but we were not complaining. I didn't go charging off after Geoff, I felt I had to conserve energy, so simply went back to my position feeling good. I fancied our chances now.

We were back in the game and Preston were not dominating anymore. I think being pegged back a second time hit them mentally. I almost set up a goal for Johnny Byrne, but he failed to control my long pass. Geoff then went close from a Johnny Byrne cross and Johnny Sissons fizzed a shot wide. Our approach play was fine, but we lacked a clinical finish. Preston were now playing on the break and I got in on the action again towards the end when I managed to just stop Holden breaking through.

Tiredness and cramp was creeping in for some of the players on the lush Wembley turf. Extra time looked on when Geoff took the Preston defence on again, stumbled and recovered before sweeping the ball to Peter Brabrook on the right wing. Peter floated a great ball over the Preston defence; and then it all went into slow motion. As the ball floated across, everyone seemed to stop and watch it. Everyone except Ronnie Boyce that is, who came racing in unmarked to head past Kelly before running around the back of the goal celebrating like a maniac! Fantastic, we're up 3-2. It was an unforgettable moment.

Little time now remained, but Preston had one last chance from a free kick. Dawson lined up and fired just wide before the referee signalled the final whistle. It was an unbelievable moment. Bobby came over to me; he was so delighted that we had performed, as he was the captain. I was near the front when we went up for the FA Cup. Bobby wiped his hands on his shirt as he would when he lifted the World Cup at Wembley two years later and bowed perfectly as the Earl of Harewood presented the Cup to him. The lap of honour and celebrations in the dressing room were unforgettable.

We went back to the hotel before attending an official club banquet and I woke up next morning feeling like nothing on earth, having had a few too many drinks. Then we had the victory parade in an open top coach. We knew supporters would come out in droves, but never dreamed that the tens of thousands that did turn up would. The crowds were incredible to welcome the Cup back to the East End as we crawled though Aldgate, Whitechapel Road, Mile End Road on route to the Town Hall. After all it was their first ever FA Cup win - and if it's one thing East Enders know about, it's how to celebrate!

The following season I played in a 2-2 draw against Liverpool in the Charity Shield, but lost my first team place part-way through the season. It was time to move on. Apart from playing matches, the best part of being a footballer was the dressing room banter. The Mickey taking, the training, everything, it wasn't all about playing on a Saturday. Football was all I knew, so I joined Torquay United for a spell as a player and then went on into management, firstly with Bournemouth, as I seemed destined to after those sessions in Cassettari's cafe with Malcolm Allison and the other boys who went on to good careers as managers.

The day I left West Ham for Torquay, Ron said to me, "just remember that all you need to get on in the game is a good memory. Everything we have done will hold you in good stead wherever you go." That is exactly what I did and made an awful lot of silk purses out of sow's ears. Ron was everything in the world to me; he was a terrific man manager.

Ron is still a million miles better than anyone else I have seen in football in terms of coaching. Ron was in a different world. He was quiet, unassuming and so simplistic in everything he did. His whole concept of playing the game was simple, using space on the football pitch. The things he taught me as a footballer held me in good stead as a manager. It was unbelievable. Ron never did the same thing two days running; he would stimulate your brain. He also gave great team talks to motivate us. You could not wait to get out and play.

As a manager, I was the first one in and the last to leave. I loved being involved. I did the coaching and then watched games every day of the week, it was fabulous. I taught Ted MacDougall how to use space and in two seasons, he scored nearly 100 goals, including his famous nine in an 11-0 win over Margate in the FA Cup. After a spell as Gillingham coach, I was appointed Norwich City manager.

Signing Martin Peters was the best signing I made at Carrow Road. Martin never let me down, and every player tried to live up to him. We won promotion and made the League Cup final in 1975, but lost to Aston

Villa. When I moved to Manchester City we reached the FA Cup final in 1981, but lost to Tottenham. Wembley is the worst place in the world when you lose. If you go to Wembley, you must win and I would not return in my other managerial posts.

Both those defeats made the win against Preston even more special because you experience such different emotions. Recent finals have taken place at the Millennium Stadium, which is a fabulous venue, but it doesn't have the name or history of Wembley. There is something special about Wembley and when the final reverts, it will make a significant difference to the competition. Just the word Wembley is special. To say we are going to play at Wembley, not the Millennium, Old Trafford, White Hart Lane, Anfield or Highbury is special. Fans sing it during the early rounds of the Cup. Wembley is the FA Cup final. It may look different after the rebuild, but it will have that magical name.

When I look back at my playing days, we played in front of massive crowds everywhere we went. It was such a great time to be a professional footballer. As a team, the players gelled, got on and we still keep in touch, which is fabulous. I still see a number of the lads, but bless their hearts; Bobby died a number of years ago and Noel in 2005.

As players, we saw each other every day. We trained and almost lived together. There was such an affinity and such a feeling amongst all of us; it was fabulous. The 1964 final was my only game as a player at Wembley and winning the FA Cup was the highlight of my career. I was so fortunate to play in a Wembley final, let alone win it, because so many great players didn't. The memories of that day in May will live with me forever.

IAN CALLAGHAN 1965
RIGHT-WING 1960–1978

BORN   10 April 1942, Toxteth, Liverpool

SIGNED   March 1960 as apprentice

LIVERPOOL CAREER   856 games, 69 goals

HONOURS   5 League Championships, 1 Second Division Championship, 2 FA Cups, 1 European Cup, 2 UEFA Cups, 4 full England caps, 4 U23 caps

LEFT   Free transfer to Swansea City, September 1978

No-one has played more times in Liverpool's famous red jersey than Ian Callaghan. As a flying winger and later a cultured central midfielder he was a constant in the sides which won promotion from Division Two in 1962 through to the club's first European Cup triumph in 1977. Today he remains a popular figure at the club he helped make famous. Ian was a part of Alf Ramsey's 1966 World Cup winning squad, voted as the Football Writer's Footballer of the Year in 1974 and later that year was deservedly awarded an MBE for his services to the game.

Liverpool 2 v Leeds United 1

(after extra time)

FA Cup final
Saturday 1 May 1965

Wembley Stadium
Attendance 100,000
Gate Receipts £89,103

*Callaghan provides the cross for the winning goal as Liverpool
lift the FA Cup for the first time in their history*

Teams

Bill Shankly	**Managers**	Don Revie
Tommy Lawrence	1	Gary Sprake
Chris Lawler	2	Paul Reaney
Gerry Byrne	3	Willie Bell
Geoff Strong	4	Billy Bremner
Ron Yeats (capt.)	5	Jack Charlton
Willie Stevenson	6	Norman Hunter
Ian Callaghan	7	Johnny Giles
Roger Hunt	8	Jim Storrie
Ian St. John	9	Alan Peacock
Tommy Smith	10	Bobby Collins (capt.)
Peter Thompson	11	Albert Johanneson
Hunt 93, St. John 111	**Scorers**	Bremner 101

Referee: W Clements

WHEN I LOOK BACK at my career at Liverpool, there were so many highlights. We won many honours domestically and in Europe, but for me two triumphs will always stand out; our FA Cup final win in 1965 against Leeds United 1965 and the European Cup final triumph over Borussia Mönchengladbach in 1977 because they were the first occasions Liverpool had won either trophy.

For me the FA Cup win was very special and supporters still talk about that final today, even with all the triumphs Liverpool have had, because it was at the true start of the Shankly era. To reach Wembley and win was incredible. It's such a special place, a magic place and every footballer wanted to play there. Many didn't achieve it.

For all kids, the FA Cup final was the big game of the season as there was all the ballyhoo surrounding it. The first one that sticks out for me was in 1953. I was 11 years-old at the time growing up in Toxteth and I remember watching it on television. Stan Matthews was, of course, the central figure, laying on the winning goal for Bill Perry. Stan Mortenson also starred by scoring a hat-trick. That game simply captured me, the drama, the passion, with almost the entire nation willing Stan to finally win his Cup medal. Over the next few years, I always looked forward to the Cup final. It was so exciting and the whole thing caught my imagination.

I came into the Liverpool first team towards the end of Bill Shankly's first season in charge and made my debut aged 17 against Bristol Rovers in 1960. Shanks was a larger than life character and made you believe in yourself. I remember when he first came to meet my parents to tell them he wanted to sign me as a professional. He convinced them I'd make it and said he'd look after me. He'd seen me play as an amateur and I was soon training twice a week after work. I can't praise him highly enough. I never asked for a rise, but he always gave me one. He was a fantastic man and broke the mould. I'll never meet anyone like him again.

Winning an FA Cup winner's medal was a major target for me, but first I had to hold down a first team place. It was a surprise that honours came so quickly, but you could see that something was happening at Anfield because of Shanks. He bought new players in for a lot of money at the time. Buying both Ian St John and Ron Yeats was inspirational. Then Roger Hunt arrived and things came together. Within four years, I had a Second and First Division championship medal. It was a great time to make my way as a professional footballer, but I still had yet to play in a Cup final.

Being part of that squad was special, we all got on well from the start, and that helps. We bonded as a unit and created the special togetherness that helped bring the club their initial success. Our strengths as a team lay in the basics. We had a decent goalkeeper in Tommy Lawrence, big Yeatsie at centre-half, and Ian St. John at centre-forward. That was our basic spine; those three players and the rest just took shape around that.

Our full-backs complemented each other brilliantly. On the left Gerry Byrne was very hard and almost impossible to get by, whilst Chris Lawler was a wonderful footballer, who scored an incredible amount of goals from right-back. He scored 70 odd in his Liverpool career, which is amazing, especially as he never took penalties or free-kicks. It worked well because, whilst Peter Thompson over on the left wing liked to get going to the by-line, I was that bit more of a deep-lying winger. I had no problem sitting back or coming inside and that allowed Chris the opportunities to bomb forward. It was very hard for teams to defend against.

There was a great balance because we had other players like Gordon Milne, Willie Stevenson and Geoff Strong, who were fantastic. It was the age-old adage at Anfield, good players playing to a very easy system. Shanks had us so well organised and we all knew our jobs. It was all so simple. Having won the League in 1964, we were on top of the world, but Shanks wasn't going to stop there. He blooded new youngsters, the pick being Tommy Smith.

What struck you about Tommy was his instant confidence. It is hard to recall Smithy as anything but a man, but he came into the squad as a mere teenager. Mind you, Shaks once said: "Tommy Smith wasn't born. He was quarried". He was a hardman all right, tough as granite, and Smithy had all the confidence in the world. He was a fantastic player for the club. A real inspirational leader.

We had so many characters in the team, so many leaders, but we all looked up to one man, Bill Shankly. He revolutionised Liverpool Football Club. I still get such a buzz when I go back to Anfield today. It's such an incredible club. The ground is fantastic, the supporters are the very best in the land, the trophy cabinet is bulging with history and silverware and when I walk in through those Shankly Gates I always have a smile as I think about the great man. This guy started this all off. He took the bull by the horns and fashioned what was a plodding Second Division side into simply the best.

Shanks seemed to know exactly what the place needed and everything he did seemed to work. Even the little things; the details. Having won the league in 1964, during the summer Shanks had a notion to change our kit that was, at the time, the traditional Liverpool red shirts with white shorts and white socks. There had been talk for a while about a kit change and Admiral had been designing some alternatives, but Shanks said "no" as he felt the new kits were simply too up-market. Instead, he just changed the colours from white shorts to an all red. I didn't think about it at the time, but it was a massive change from years of the red and white kit. Shanks got the gigantic Ron Yeats to model them and both of them loved the fact that the all-red kit made Yeatsie look even bigger.

We were defending League champions when the 1964/65 season kicked off, so were a confident squad, but with Shanks, Bob Paisley and Joe Fagan around, we weren't allowed to become over confident or arrogant about our new success. If anyone was seen to be getting too cocky, they were quickly brought down to earth. With our opening day 3-2 win over Arsenal being televised on the new weekly *Match of the Day* programme on the BBC it really was the beginning of a new era, but our league campaign did not get off to a great start.

By January, we were off the pace in the league, which would be ultimately disputed between Manchester United, Leeds United and Chelsea. As we embarked on our FA Cup run, we had also reached the quarter-finals of the European Cup and were waiting to play FC Cologne, having already defeated KR Reykjavik and Anderlecht in earlier rounds.

Shanks loved everything about Europe. He would send Reuben Bennett to scout opposition and he enjoyed having to come to terms with new systems and new players. The players thought the same. It was a break from the normal routine and the same opposition where you knew everybody. There was no squad rotation, no new foreign players in British football at the time. You knew everybody, week in and week out and it did become a little monotonous. So the European games were exciting. We quickly learnt about European football and that made us a better outfit.

My own game was coming along. You couldn't help but learn and improve in the winning atmosphere that Shanks had created. He had put together a wonderful backroom staff and that rubbed off on us all. We had

Bob Paisley and Joe Fagan, who was fantastic, and they all complemented each other. Joe was always there for us players. Rueben Bennett was too. If Shanks wasn't speaking to you for one reason or another, usually if you were injured, which he hated, then Rueben would put his arm around you and say, "come on lad, don't worry, you'll get over this soon." It was a joy to be there.

For 73 years, Liverpool had never won the FA Cup, and that's what it was back then The Cup. Older fans talked about the loss to Burnley in 1914 and, of course, we had been beaten by Arsenal in 1950. The Cup had become something of a Holy Grail for the club and its supporters. From my first season at the club, when the third round draw was made, I hoped it would be our turn. Since making my FA Cup debut in a 4-3 win over Chelsea in 1962, every campaign had ended in disappointment. The closest we'd come was the semi-finals in 1963 when Leicester City knocked us out 1-0. Mike Stringfellow scored, but Gordon Banks played superbly. It was so disappointing; you'd sooner get to the final and enjoy the excitement of getting to Wembley and at least have a day out than lose a semi-final after getting through all the preceding hard games; it was shattering really.

After our poor start to the league campaign, we had enjoyed a bit of form when we overcame a tough West Brom side 2-1. Roger Hunt and Ian St. John eased us 2-0 ahead, but we had a stroke of good fortune when Bobby Cram, uncle of top athlete Steve Cram, shot wide from a penalty. Jeff Astle grabbed a late goal for the Baggies, but we were through.

The fourth round draw gave us a home tie against the team which would eventually finish bottom of the entire league, Stockport County. Games against lower league teams are always tricky as they have nothing to lose, but we should have won comfortably, especially as the match was played at Anfield. Shanks was away for the game watching Cologne, so left Bob Paisley in charge. The week before we had been due to play Everton, but it was postponed due to snowstorms, which didn't help.

The cup-tie took place in front of a packed Anfield, but most of the country was watching the funeral of Sir Winston Churchill and we observed a minute's silence before kick off. Our pitch was not in particularly great condition with the bad weather, but that was no excuse for allowing Stockport to settle and they took a shock early lead. We equalised through Gordon Milne just after half time, but Stockport were inspired and created chances. After they had a penalty appeal turned down, Gerry Byrne saved us in the dying moments when he kicked a shot off the line. We were lucky and could easily have gone out. That was our lucky game.

Shanks rollicked us on the Monday, he thought we should have won easily and we made sure in the replay. Stockport's pitch was in a terrible state, but they made a mistake by sanding the pitch. We had a special ridge put on our boots and that helped. They had a real go, but after Roger Hunt scored in the first half it was over. They lost confidence and Roger scored again for a 2-0 win.

With Everton knocked out of the competition, local interest centred on ourselves. Our league form was improving and we played well in the European Cup quarter-final first leg to draw 0-0 in Cologne. Cup fever was gripping Merseyside when we travelled to Second Division Bolton Wanderers for the fifth round. It was a tight game, but the match will always stand out for me because I scored the winner with a rare headed goal past Eddie Hopkinson from a Peter Thompson cross five minutes from time. We were in the quarter-finals.

When we drew Leicester City away, we knew that it would be a battle as we always struggled against them. I don't know why, but we always did. We had only won one of our last six league meetings and had lost that semi-final clash at Hillsborough in 1963.

It proved to be another tight game. Stringfellow missed a couple of opportunities and I missed a great one in the dying minutes from close range, but we were satisfied to take them back to Anfield for the replay. When we ran out we knew the prize was a semi-final clash with Chelsea. The other semi would see Manchester United take on Leeds United. It was some line up and guaranteed a great final. Gordon Banks played superbly that night, but we were not going to be denied and Roger Hunt grabbed the winner in the second half.

Before the semi-final against Chelsea, we faced Cologne in a quarter-final play-off after the second leg also finished 0-0. The match was played in Rotterdam three days before the Villa Park clash. We were trying to become the first British club to reach the European Cup final and went 2-0 up before they forced a draw. We got through to the semi-finals on the toss of a disc. So, although tired, we were in great spirits for the Chelsea clash. The Blues were a classy, young side run by a young manager, Tommy Docherty. "Docherty's Diamonds", as they were known, were top of the First Division and in Peter Bonetti, Bobby Tambling and Terry Venables they had some of the brightest talent around.

Chelsea were favourites because of our fixture pile up, but Shanks got us going in the dressing room when he brought in this Cup final brochure that Chelsea had already had produced. Shanks didn't need a team talk after that. We were raring to go after the indignation and temerity of that brochure, and in a tense match came through 2-0. Peter Thompson scored the first before Willie Stevenson slotted home a penalty. The scenes in the dressing room were fantastic. It was a sweet, sweet victory.

Reaching my first Cup final was magic and the build up was great. The hype and the interest has waned so much now, which is a real shame. There was an old wife's tale that stated that if Liverpool ever won the FA Cup then the Liver Birds would fly away from the city. We didn't believe that, or the cynical belief that the club was destined never to win the FA Cup. We had to get the players' pool together, give extra interviews and it seemed the fans wanted to chat about nothing else.

The final took over really. We had our Cup final suits fitted. None of us bought suits off the peg back then. We would have them tailor-made. Shanks had put us on to a tailor who did suits for the comedian Jimmy Tarbuck. For the final though, a local fella, Louis, got the job. He was a real character and came down to Anfield to measure us up. But when the suits arrived some didn't fit, so there we were exchanging jackets. They had the club badge on and were lovely.

There was such a buzz about the city. The expectation was enormous and you realised that you had a chance to make history. You got caught up with the razzamatazz. Of course, the main talk among fans surrounded Cup final tickets. Being a scouser, all the 100 or so tickets we were allocated were taken up with friends and family; we could have done with a lot more.

Before the final there were a few more League matches to play and we eventually finished seventh. I was injured in a 4-0 defeat at Chelsea along with Ian St. John and Gordon Milne. I had a bad ankle and had to have my foot in a bucket on the train journey home. I was still living with my parents at the time and they called a doctor out as the pain was so bad and this Hungarian doctor gave me an injection to ease the pain. The three of us missed the last four league games and had intensive treatment. Our trainer Bob Paisley worked on my ankle. He had no formal training with injuries, but had this amazing knack of diagnosing a problem. I was in good hands. We had all the new machines, all the new gadgets, but Bob didn't really know what he was doing.

I was very concerned and it was only a couple of days before the match that I knew I was going to be OK. It was a worrying time. I agonised over my fitness, but finally got the all clear and I was overjoyed. It took a lot of treatment though. Mornings, evenings and nights with Bob. Ian was also passed fit, but Gordon wasn't so fortunate, so Geoff Strong came in. I felt sorry for Gordon. Even today when I see old footage of the game I feel for him and it reminds me that I was so close to also missing out.

Our opponents in the final would be Leeds United, who'd beaten Manchester United in a replay. Matt Busby's team edged Leeds for the title, though, on goal average. We had great respect for Leeds and manager Don Revie. No team finishes runner-up after just gaining promotion without having something special about them, so we knew it would tough. We'd lost 4-2 at Elland Road in the league, but gained a 2-1 win at Anfield. They were clearly going to be a top club and over the coming decade would become our greatest rivals. Apart from veteran skipper Bobby Collins, who picked up the Footballer of the Year award, and centre-forward Alan Peacock, Leeds were a young side with the likes of Billy Bremner, Jack Charlton, Norman Hunter and Johnny Giles key players. All would become world class. Many bookies had Leeds as favourites.

The staff tried to keep the routine the same as usual, but it was hard amidst the blaze of publicity. We were constantly doing interviews about the final. Shanks arranged for the reserves to play to Leeds' system at Melwood in our final training session before we departed by train on the Thursday for our base at the Oatlands Park Hotel in Weybridge.

Shanks took us to the Palladium that night for a show. That helped relax the lads and take our minds off what we had to do. On Friday, it was train-ing and the normal routine as he would do at Anfield, but it's tricky. You are training in a different place and you know what is around the corner, so you can't help but be aware and feel the nerves.

I roomed with Gerry Byrne and we both woke up early on the big day, turned on the television and there was the build up. I could not eat much breakfast, so we both went for a walk. You try to do anything to keep calm, but it's bloody hard. We managed some lunch and then the last team meeting. Shanks never talked much about the opposition and that day he didn't need to. We knew what to expect. It was Leeds and as players, we had a lot of respect for them and their strengths. We went in knowing what sort of game we were in for, we didn't need Shanks telling us.

It seems strange now, as we went on to win trophy after trophy, but that day it was all new. This was an occasion like no other, this was the FA Cup final and none of us had ever been involved in anything like this. As we drew closer to the stadium the crowds began to swell and then for the first time you see those famous Twin Towers. It was magic, it really was. Then the bus goes into the tunnel and the fans are banging on the windows. The Liverpool fans were great and the song that day was *Ee-ay-adio, We're going to see the Queen!* It was incredible and you knew you were involved in something special.

The first thing we did was check the pitch. The old stadium was massive, the pitch looked enormous. You take it all in for ten or fifteen minutes and then it's off to the dressing rooms. Ours was a very relaxed dressing room and Shanks loved that. We had both Tarby and Frankie Vaughn come in cracking jokes. It took our minds off the seriousness of the situation. I think you'll find the Leeds dressing room was a far tenser place. They had a young team and maybe we could relax that bit more.

With about ten minutes to go before the game, Shanks told Jimmy and Frankie to leave and it was down to business. Shanks trusted us all to our own routines and that helped. He then got the eleven together and gave us an inspirational speech: "You're going to win because you're the best team," he said, "Leeds are honoured to be on the same field as you. AND you're not going to disappoint the greatest supporters in the world. If necessary, and it won't be, you should be prepared to die for them." We were.

We completed our own pre-match preparations, then we lined up with the Leeds players in the tunnel. Everybody has their own little superstitions. Smithy always followed me out the tunnel. When you start to walk out it is like nothing you have experienced before. The buzz, the atmosphere that was the best I have ever heard, the noise, the colour, lining up looking for your relatives. It's special, it really is.

There was no Cup final sunshine, it was very grey and raining heavily. You don't think about that too much as the nerves were jangling. You just have to get on with it. After winning the toss, we began with the wind behind us. The match began dourly with lots of broken play. Defensively, Leeds were solid, but the Collins-Bremner midfield duo was not firing, so they posed little threat in attack where Peacock made little impact against Yeatsie. On the wing, they had South African Albert Johanneson, who made history by becoming the first black player in a Cup final, but he had a poor game.

Tackles flew in during the opening period and trainers Les Cocker and Bob Paisley were called on numerous times. It was competitive stuff, not nasty, as both sides looked to take control. Bremner needed treatment after being sandwiched in a heavy challenge by Gerry Byrne and Tommy Smith, but soon recovered. Ian St. John received a lecture after a challenge on Johanneson and Leeds striker Jim Storrie was clearly not fit and moved out to the wing.

It wasn't one way, though. We also took our share of knocks as Bobby Collins and Norman Hunter made their presence felt. Geoff Strong needed treatment and Gerry Byrne, following a Collins challenge, had, totally unbeknownst to us all, dislocated a collarbone. But Gerry carried on as if nothing had happened. He showed tremendous courage and if you watch the final now on video, Gerry plays the whole game with his arm limp and down. It was a remarkable feat, but you either soldiered on or departed as substitutes were still not allowed.

We had the better of those opening exchanges. Ian St. John and Roger Hunt looked dangerous going forward, but were well marshalled by Jack Charlton. Tommy Smith and Willie Stevenson dominated midfield, I also got the chance to run at Willie Bell, but we failed to take any of the half chances we created.

At half-time, there was no score. As we walked off the Leeds players looked at Gerry in disbelief that he was still playing. I think they knew how bad he was, but we didn't know the extent of his injury until later. We could see he was in pain, but the management kept it from us. Shanks was content and told us we were the better team. We were to carry on playing our way and he felt we would eventually break them down. They couldn't defend forever, gaps would soon arrive.

The rain became heavier as the second half kicked off. We began brightly, but Leeds held as Ian and Roger went close again. I almost grabbed a goal with a strike that went into the side netting and then Charlton blocked another effort by me from close range. Leeds, playing deep, hoped to break quickly. We were wary of the likes of Bremner, who could turn a game in moments. The Liverpool fans reserved some jeers for Billy, who kicked the ball into the crowd in one moment of frustration. To be fair though, our defence wasn't being tested and Big Tommy in our goal was a spectator. Leeds held mainly through keeper Gary Sprake, who made three great saves from Peter Thompson. He also denied Geoff and Roger.

We had controlled the 90 minutes, but still the score remained 0-0 and now faced extra-time; the first final to reach extra time since 1947. Again, Shanks urged us to keep going. Wembley was a huge pitch and he just kept saying that they would wilt soon. We were always told not to sit down, not to let the opposition see that we were tired, but some players simply couldn't help it. "Up on your feet", they'd say. I was shattered going into that last half hour.

You could sense the tension around the ground, but our supporters drowned the Leeds fans with numerous chants including "Ee-aye-addio", "Liv-er-pool" and "You'll Never Walk Alone".

Leeds moved Bremner into the attack, but he was up against Yeatsie, who looked a giant next to him. The first goal was always going to be crucial and three minutes in we finally broke the deadlock. Peter began the move by evading two tackles before slipping the ball to Gerry. A quick centre and Roger headed home. I recall being so elated. The stadium erupted and one exuberant Liverpool fan joined in the celebrations on the pitch, but was ejected by five coppers. He departed waving his Liverpool scarf confident we had won.

We were ecstatic and had dominated the game, but we all took our eye off the ball and a few minutes later Bremner equalised with a great strike. I was guilty of standing off Giles out on the wing. He found Norman Hunter in acres of space and his chip was headed down by Peacock for Billy to rocket a half-volley into the far corner.

Shanks must have been livid with us as we'd dropped our concentration. How many times did that happen? Not many and we wouldn't make the same mistake twice. Leeds must have felt they had grabbed a draw and packed the defence looking for a replay, but I was confident we could win. We had 19 minutes to make sure all the effort was worth it. The equaliser had been a blow, but we were strong both mentally and physically. I think we were the fittest team in the league and, despite the equaliser still looked the stronger side.

Geoff Strong went close with a shot before eventually the winning goal came nine minutes from time and it's a moment I'll never forget. Wembley had a reputation that the pitch sapped your legs and pulled your muscles, but I felt great. I got the ball on the right from Tommy and took on Leeds left back Bell, who was a little isolated. I knew I could beat him for speed; I pushed it past him and raced after it. I was concerned the ball was going over the by-line but whipped it across. The ball was a few feet off the turf and actuallyslightly behind Ian St. John, but he twisted in mid-air and turned the ball in with a glancing flick.

Once we went 2-1 up, we weren't going to make the same mistake as before. We had to keep switched on. Shanks would never have forgiven us giving up a lead twice in such a big game, but you could see Leeds were spent. Big Yeatsie was Shanks' voice on the pitch and made sure we all knew what we had to do. We had a few vocal players. Ian would be doing it from the front. Smithy was also giving it to us as well, of course. I was quiet and knackered at the end. In fact, the right side of our team was like a monastery. Chris Lawler was the quietest man you've ever met. It was a great combination of different personalities though. That's what made us gel so well. That's what made us tick.

Peter almost grabbed a third for us, but we saw the remaining minutes out with no major scares - however they seemed to last ages. At last, the final whistle went. The feeling was pure relief and joy mixed together. We celebrated on the pitch and Shanks congratulated us all. It's different from winning the title. That's a great feeling, but the Cup is such a one off. It's a bigger instant buzz. We made history that day and that can't be eclipsed. We won it again in 1974, which was great, but nothing could better that feeling in '65. Nothing.

It's all a blur after the game. I have looked back at the footage, but it all seems like a dream. We went up and got our medals. I couldn't say anything to the Queen, I couldn't say much to anyone. I shook hands with our chairman and then it was down the steps and off around the pitch for the lap of honour. Going back to the dressing rooms, "We've Won The Cup, We've Won The Cup, Ee-aye-addio We've Won The Cup" was ringing in our ears. Then the champagne came out as the celebrations continued.

It was only then that we heard Gerry had broken his collarbone. We were full of admiration. You played for Shanks. He hated injuries anyway. He wouldn't stand for them. If you could play, you would, but what Gerry did was to me the bravest thing I had ever encountered in all my days playing the game.

We had a few beers and then had a great banquet at the Grosvenor House Hotel. I remember the menu with the Liverpool badge printed on it and going around getting my team-mates to sign it. Shanks was never one to show his emotion, but, he was elated and came around to us all individually and you could see what it meant to him. He had brought the title and now the FA Cup to Liverpool. He was back to normal soon, though, and went to bed early saying he was off to plan for the next few seasons and reminding us that we had a massive European Cup semi-final against Inter Milan on the Tuesday. We had to take Gerry to hospital and I helped him on with his jacket. It had been an unforgettable day in so many ways.

The train was full of fans on the Sunday as we travelled back to Lime Street Station in Liverpool. We were in our own compartment and had to put up a sign saying that Gerry was feeling very comfortable, but he won't be playing on Tuesday. There were thousands and thousands waiting for us in the city centre. The reaction was unbelievable from the supporters. I had never seen anything like it; the streets were lined with a quarter of a million fans as we made our way slowly to the Liverpool City Hall. The sea of red showed what winning the Cup meant to the people of Liverpool. In typical style, while we were on the bus after the Lord Mayor's banquet, Shanks let us all know that it was training as usual the following morning as we had to prepare for Milan. There were still plenty of Liver Birds in evidence, so we'd scotched that fallacy as well as the thought that Liverpool would never win the FA Cup.

Nothing can take away the glory of winning the FA Cup. It was my first game at Wembley and I was involved in the winning goal. The city of Liverpool is football crazy. It's mad and so when you contribute to it in some way and make history at the same time, it is a marvellous feeling.

BRIAN LABONE 1966

CENTRE-HALF 1957–1972

BORN 23 January 1940, Liiverpool
SIGNED July 1957 as apprentice
EVERTON CAREER 530 games, 2 goals
HONOURS 2 League Championships, 1 FA Cup, 26 England caps,
7 England U23 caps, Football League representative
LEFT Retired, July 1972

A one-club player and Everton legend, from watching his boyhood heroes on the terraces, Brian Labone became a stalwart in the Everton defence. A model professional, Labone was a stylish defender, solid tackler and outstanding in the air. Booked just twice in an illustrious career that saw him win League Championship and FA Cup honours, Labone represented England on 26 occasions and was a key figure in the 1970 World Cup team. A stopper centre-half, Labone was skipper in Everton's two FA Cup finals of the 1960s.

Everton 3 v Sheffield Wednesday 2

FA Cup final
Saturday 14 May 1966

Wembley Stadium
Attendance 100,000
Gate Receipts £109,691

*Brian Labone lifts Everton's first FA Cup for 33 years after one of the
greatest Cup final comebacks of all time*

Teams

Harry Catterick	**Managers**	Alan Brown
Gordon West	1	Ron Springett
Tommy Wright	2	Wilf Smith
Ray Wilson	3	Don Megson (capt.)
Jimmy Gabriel	4	Peter Eustace
Brian Labone (capt.)	5	Sam Ellis
Brian Harris	6	Gerry Young
Alex Scott	7	Graham Pugh
Mike Trebilcock	8	Johnny Fantham
Alex Young	9	Jim McCalliog
Colin Harvey	10	David Ford
Derek Temple	11	Johnny Quinn
Trebilcock 58, 63, Temple 80	**Scorers**	McCalliog 4, Ford 57

Referee: J Taylor

OF COURSE, ALL ENGLAND supporters remember '66 as the year when Bobby Moore lifted the World Cup, but for Evertonians it was also the year when we enjoyed one of the great Cup final triumphs. Incredibly, we are still the last team to come from two goals behind to win the FA Cup. It was a wonderful occasion at Wembley when our never-say-die spirit shone brightly. Being captain was an honour and made it particularly special for me.

I've always been a very biased Evertonian. As a kid, I watched Everton play every home game. I went to a secondary modern school before passing a scholarship exam, which meant I could go to Liverpool Collegiate. Unfortunately, when you went to a grammar school you could not play for Liverpool Schoolboys, so I just played football for the school team.

I must have made an impression as I gained selection for a Merseyside Grammar School XI to face a combined team from Oxford and Cambridge called Oxford Centrals. We played at Everton's Bellefield training ground. Afterwards, Everton scouts invited me to train Tuesday and Thursday nights. I lived close by, so it was only a five-minute walk. I played a few practice games before signing professional forms three days after leaving school in 1957.

During a public practice match, the first team attack faced the reserve team defence with me at centre-half and I had a blinder against Everton favourite Dave Hickson. He was probably not fully match fit! Dave was every supporter's hero and as a kid, I used to watch him from the boys' pen. My performance that day got me into the reserves, but the first team still seemed a million miles away.

There was no manager at Everton when I joined. Ian Buchan was coach, but Johnny Carey soon took up the managerial post. I watched the first team from the stands and hoped for an opportunity, but didn't want to get in through an injury to another player. One day though, centre-half Tommy Jones went down and didn't get up, so I made my debut against Birmingham City in March 1958. We lost 2-1 and I played a handful of games during the remainder of the season. A few more first team games came my way until finally I got my opportunity to claim a regular first team place a few games into the 1959/60 season.

All of a sudden, I was playing with the likes of Dave Hickson, but he controversially joined Liverpool just after I'd broken into the side, which did not amuse the Everton faithful. It was great being in the first team, although I played a few stinkers. We had some good players including Brian Harris and Derek Temple. The star of the side, though, was Scottish international midfielder Bobby Collins, who arrived from Celtic after the 1958 World Cup finals. Bobby was five foot nothing, but put me on my backside a few times in training. I remember being flattened by Bobby during a five-a-side game. I went in like a big pansy. The following week I made up my mind to hit him hard. I did and afterwards, as he picked himself up, Bobby quipped, "you're learning son!" Bobby was a great influence on me in my early days.

We played the old 2-3-5 system and stamina training was the main thing initially. That changed because Bobby arrived with a pair of running shoes. We used to run in pumps; Bobby was grease lighting over ten yards. It rubbed off on us and transformed part of our training regime. We all got running shoes, marked out sprint areas and developed our speed off the mark. We trained at Goodison on the Friday before a game and sprinted at the side of the pitch. We rarely touched a ball during the week, later more ball work came in, which sounds incredible today.

Pitches could be a quagmire unlike today's that are like a carpet. Everton were one of the first teams to install underground heating, but there were wires near to the surface, so when the groundsman aerated the pitch with forks, the pitch went like a morass. Our stamina won many games at home, as opponents ran out of steam on this dreadful pitch. It was impossible to play attractive football at times, but we were not the only ones, even grounds like Old Trafford were boggy.

As a team, we were inconsistent. During the season, we thumped Leicester 6-1 before losing 8-2 at Newcastle United. Then we defeated Chelsea 6-1 prior to a 6-2 defeat at West Brom. Our chairman John Moores, an Everton fan and a member of the family that founded the Littlewoods Pools company, began signing players like Welsh international inside-forward Roy Vernon, Frank Wignall and attacking midfielder Alex Young. Pundits dubbed us the 'Millionairos' – although we weren't quite like Abramovich's Chelsea today! With the end of the maximum wage around the corner, it was a bit rich with us earning £25 a week!

Results improved and soon Jimmy Gabriel and Irish winger Billy Bingham joined us. The 1960/61 campaign saw us make a great start and we were quickly challenging at the top as Tottenham Hotspur led the way. The improvement brought packed crowds to Goodison, but the majority of a capacity attendance went home disappointed when Tottenham defeated us 3-1 just before Christmas.

We faded in the New Year, but a late run brought a fifth place finish, our highest post-war placing. The dip in form cost Johnny Carey his job as Mr Moores appointed former Everton centre-forward Harry Catterick manager during the close season. Following a shaky start in 1961/62, results picked up. Gordon West joined for a goalkeeping record fee of £27,000 and we ended the campaign on a high with an 8-3 win over Cardiff City and 3-2 victory at Arsenal to finish fourth behind champions Ipswich Town.

Harry Catterick always wanted a solid defence, but that didn't stop him wanting us to play attractive football. Harry was a disciplinarian. You had to be at Bellefield at 9am every morning. If you had a puncture or anything else he would say, "what time did the game finish Saturday? You've had plenty of time since to get here." We'd get fined a fiver, which was a lot from our wages.

The 1962/63 season would see us going for the title alongside Spurs. Our opening games included a double over Manchester United, a 5-0 win against Blackpool and thrilling 4-3 victory at Nottingham Forest. By Christmas, we had lost just three games and had drawn 0-0 at White Hart Lane. It was the year of the big freeze and we did not play again until mid-February. Liverpool were back in the top-flight after winning promotion as Second Division Champions and it was great to play in a derby clash. Bill Shankly was building a good team at Anfield. He was the opposite of Harry in personality; Bill was a real character. The clashes were the first derby games in 12 years. We drew 2-2 at Goodison and 0-0 at Anfield before capacity crowds. The atmosphere was electric.

In the title race Tottenham, double winners in 1960/61 and FA Cup holders, were favourites, but it went our way in the run-in as we enjoyed a 12-match unbeaten run. Among eight victories, an Alex Young strike defeated Tottenham, while Roy Vernon grabbed a hat-trick on the final day as we celebrated the championship in style with a 4-1 win over Fulham at Goodison. Winning the title was a great achievement because you play in all conditions, so the best team comes out on top.

In the 1963/64 pre-season curtain raiser, we enjoyed a 4-0 Charity Shield win over FA Cup holders Manchester United, but playing in the European Cup for the first time we went out immediately to Inter Milan on aggregate, which was frustrating. In the league, I experienced my first derby win and defeat. Losing was a nightmare. A poor run-in saw us finish in third spot some five points adrift of champions Liverpool. Losing our title to them hurt.

We slipped a place in 1964/65 as Manchester United, who knocked us out of the Fairs Cup, edged out a new force, Leeds, on goal average to win the title. To compound a poor campaign, Leeds knocked us out of the FA Cup at Goodison before losing to Liverpool in the final. Liverpool had not enjoyed the best of form in the League, finishing below us. We thumped them 4-0 at Anfield and 2-1 at Goodison to record a league double, the only one in my Everton career, which pleased all Evertonians.

As professional footballers, we could walk around town, unlike modern players, and if fans lost a fiver on a derby, they let you know until they had a chance to get it back in the next derby clash. A lot of pride was at stake. Employers at the Ford factory in Liverpool reckoned that half the workers supported Liverpool, half Everton. If either won a derby, absenteeism saw the factory shut down, so they always hoped for a draw! That said, there was tremendous banter between players and supporters. Liverpool fans enjoyed the bragging rights over that summer after winning the Cup.

Leeds United would become a great side, but never got the credit they deserved. My old mate Bobby Collins was now their captain and he was helping bring on the likes of Billy Bremner, Johnny Giles and Norman Hunter. Leeds went over the top sometimes and we had some ding-dong physical battles. During that season, Sandy Brown was sent off after I gave him a hospital pass and he clattered into Giles. Willie Bell then clashed with Derek Temple. While both were being treated, the referee took both teams off to cool down. Willie scored the winner that day and the coming years would bring more good-natured skirmishes!

By 1965/66, Everton's first team line up included Alex Scott from Rangers, Ray Wilson from Huddersfield Town, Fred Pickering from Blackburn Rovers and local lads Tommy Wright and Colin Harvey. I was now club captain, which was a huge honour. I'd taken over from Tony Kay, who joined during the title-winning season, but was banned from football for life in 1965 after a much-publicised bribery and match-fixing scandal. We had a great mix of youth and experience.

Training was by now more intense and imaginative, which was not before time, and we were more diet conscious. But we had a poor start to the 1965/66 season in the league and supporters made their frustrations known. By Christmas, we were well off the pace and out of the Fairs Cup, having lost to Ujpest Dozsa. Our only chance of silverware was the FA Cup. As a kid, I remember the Matthews final in 1953 when Blackpool beat Bolton 4-3; I also watched Jackie Milburn star when Newcastle United beat Manchester City in 1955, before Bert Trautmann broke his neck as City defeated Birmingham City 12 months later. That was the history which made me feel so special about this great competition. I loved it and I was desperate to play at Wembley in the final.

But since I'd turned professional Everton had only reached the fifth round, so I probably didn't think much of our chances. It was always a thrill listening out for the draw on a Monday lunchtime. You can't be too choosy about who you want to be paired with in the draw. Normally anybody at home would do us, but we'd come unstuck in my first cup-tie in 1960 when Division Three side Bradford City caused a shock by winning 3-0. It was very embarrassing. A year later Division Two outfit Sheffield United knocked us out at Goodison and I was on the wrong end of another Goodison shock in 1964 when Sunderland, also from Division Two, sent us packing in a fifth round clash.

Come the third round draw in 1966 we were happy to receive a home tie against Sunderland, now a Division One outfit. We had defeated them 2-0 a few weeks earlier in the league, but expected a tough match. For a cup-tie, there was always that extra sense of anticipation in the build up during the week. We had a main team talk on a Friday and then there would be a livener immediately before the match. We had a black board to illustrate set pieces and tactics. Playing at home, I got down to the ground early. All the players had different routines. Some got dressed in a particular order; others had a massage or swift cigarette.

The week before the Sunderland cup clash, we lost at Blackpool 2-0 and there was an unsavoury incident when some Everton fans made their views known to Harry Catterick, which received a good deal of publicity, but we responded by winning comfortably 3-0. Derek Temple gave us an early lead before Fred Pickering and Alex Young secured a victory. With Cup holders Liverpool knocked out, focus centred on ourselves in the local media. We had few complaints with the fourth round draw as we faced Southern League giant-killers Bedford Town. Of course, Bedford had nothing to lose, but we were determined to put on a professional display.

We turned our attention back to the League and gained welcome league wins against Northampton and Stoke to boost our confidence. In the days leading to the Bedford match, the media bandwagon built up their centre-forward. Arriving at their ground, we were pleasantly surprised the pitch was in good condition, though a bit heavy. Non-league grounds had a reputation for proving a problem to Division One sides, so it was a relief not to be in that position.

On the day, Derek Temple converted two crosses by Alex Scott to quieten the crowd. Fred Pickering sealed a 3-0 victory. The fifth round brought Coventry City to Goodison, which was fine. Alex Young swept us ahead early on before Coventry came back into the match and we were indebted to Westy for some tremendous saves. Coventry centre-forward Bobby Gould had a goal ruled out for handball, but we eased through 3-0 with Derek Temple and Fred Pickering scoring for a third successive round.

This was the first time that I had reached the FA Cup quarter-finals and the excitement was building among supporters. The sixth round draw took us to either Leicester or Manchester City. Eventually, Manchester City somewhat surprisingly overcame Leicester to begin an epic struggle with ourselves. Although a Division Two side, City under Joe Mercer and Malcolm Allison were amongst the favourites for promotion and were desperate to show how they would fare against a Division One side.

Our success in the Cup was having a knock-on effect in the League as our unbeaten run continued with wins over Chelsea, Arsenal and Nottingham Forest. After going down to an embarrassing 5-0 defeat at Anfield earlier in the season, a match I went off injured in, we held the champions-elect to a 0-0 draw at Goodison. Our thoughts now centred on Cup football again. With Fred Pickering and Jimmy Gabriel injured, the majority of a capacity Maine Road crowd sensed an upset in the offing. In awful conditions, City did give us a real fright on a greasy surface cut up by persistent rain, but we settled for a draw and felt very confident of progressing at Goodison.

Another bumper crowd watched a tight game three days later. Gordon West was phenomenal and pulled off a brilliant stop after a dreadful back pass by me. Mike Summerbee was going through, I was just ahead of him and hit the ball back far too quickly. It was flying into the top left-hand corner until Westy pulled off in my estimation the best save in his career. The match ended 0-0 after extra-time. But for Westy we would have been knocked out.

A week on and we met again at Molineux. Once more, it was a tough encounter and Westy kept us in it early on. City were growing in confidence, but a defensive mix-up saw Derek Temple smash a volley home before Fred Pickering sealed the win to see us through to a semi-final clash with Manchester United. We were now just one match from Wembley.

In the other semi-final, Sheffield Wednesday took on Chelsea and pundits selected their preferred final as United versus Chelsea, but both Wednesday and ourselves would have a major say in that prediction.

City went on to gain promotion as Division Two champions and I'd face on many occasionsthem over the coming years. With the likes of Colin Bell in the team and Francis Lee joining them soon, every domestic honour would come their way. Franny was some character. He was a bundle of energy, who was brilliant at winning penalties. I once tackled him on the halfway line and the referee awarded him a penalty! Joking apart, City developed into a fantastic attacking side with a sublime forward line of Colman, Young, Lee, Bell and Summerbee.

Our focus was very much now on the FA Cup and our League form dipped over Easter. A 1-0 win over Newcastle United would be our sole victory during three matches in four days. Before the semi-final, we played Leeds United at Elland Road. Harry rang the changes. Only Sandy Brown and reserve striker Mike Trebilcock would face Don Revie's team and Manchester United a week later at Burnden Park. United on the other hand faced a European semi-final clash against Partizan Belgrade before our FA Cup tie.

While we enjoyed a 12-day break from first team action, United played their first choice XI. Three days before our semi-final clash, they lost to Partizan Belgrade on aggregate, which was a crushing blow for them. With George Best sidelined, we arrived at Burnden Park confident. George was brilliant; he had so much skill and caused trouble for defenders. With no Bestie they would not be able to tear our backsides off, but we still had to be on our guard with Bobby Charlton, Denis Law, John Connelly and David Herd leading the line. Psychologically we were fresher and Mike Trebilcock kept his place for the injured Fred Pickering.

The match was a dour clash. United came at us early on and Law was a handful. I remember Sandy Brown kicking one off the line as we suffered a torrid time. We held on and knew with them coming back off a European match they would tire. Towards the end, Colin Harvey scored a tremendous 25-yarder. There was pure elation when the goal went in.

Relief was the main emotion at the end, but that soon disappeared because we knew Wembley beckoned. It was an incredible feeling. The match was hard going because the anticipation is enormous and for the loser it is dreadful. It's only during a break in play that you realise there are 60,000 people watching, and then the action resumes and you get back to concentrating on the game.

Two days later, we faced United again, this time in the league, and drew 0-0 before losing our last league games of the season to finish eleventh. It was disappointing, but would be the only time in my Everton first team career that we'd finish outside the top ten. Our attention was firmly on the FA Cup final where we would face Sheffield Wednesday, something of a surprise as Wednesday finished just above the relegation zone, while Chelsea finished fifth. The result illustrated what can happen in Cup football as the form book often goes out of the window.

We had a players' pool and the Milk Marketing Board sponsored us. It wasn't a vast pot, but we each made a few hundred pounds. At the time, the two main boot companies were Adidas and Puma. Some of the lads switched from their favourite boot. Ray Wilson was having none of it. He was not prepared to take his favourite slipper off in a Cup final just to earn a few quid. We got tickets for family and friends, but, of course, it was not enough, as all of a sudden, everyone was your best friend. The letters and phone calls were unbelievable.

We trained at a nearby works ground, as the turf was the closest Harry Catterick could find to Wembley conditions. Then during Cup final week there were interviews and pictures taken as we settled into Selsdon Park Hotel, which had a golf course, swimming pool and indoor facilities. Golf was banned in case we pulled muscles, but we did have a putting competition during a tight schedule of activities. Nobody could compete with Brian Harris.

Harry gave us a final team talk. There was one enforced change to our final line up. Fred Pickering would have been an automatic choice but, Harry made the tough choice to omit him the day before the final. Mike Trebilcock keeping his place from the semi-final, even though he had been dropped again for the league games once Fred had returned to fitness. Mike was a nobody really to supporters as he had only played a few games. It was a surprise and we did feel very sorry for Fred. Harry told him the news before announcing the team. He decided not to take a risk on Fred's injury as it was still the days when no substitutes were allowed. Fred was very unlucky because the following season one substitute was allowed.

One other injury scare was our keeper, Gordon West, who had a damaged thigh muscle, so would not kick the ball out, but he could throw a ball over halfway. Westy strapped his leg as a precaution. A quiz question that has gone around Liverpool ever since is, name the player who never kicked a ball in the '66 cup final at Wembley. The answer is Gordon West because apart from me, Ray Wilson, Tommy Wright and Brian Harris took the goal kicks. However, we watched the match again during a reunion at the Adelphi Hotel and Westy did take one, so we have been living a false paradise for 40 years! I was confident that we had the team to win.

Gordon West represented England when the likes of Gordon Banks and Peter Shilton played regularly. Gordon was much underrated. He was a great goalkeeper, athletic and won many a game for Everton. Tommy Wright was nerveless. Tommy was quick, he started out as a forward before moving back to midfield and then full back. He was mainly right-footed; nothing fazed him. Our left-back Ray Wilson was the player I'd give the ball to if I was in trouble. Ray was brilliant, just brilliant. Commanding, great anticipation, quick, a sound tackler, Ray had everything. He was world class in every sense.

Jimmy Gabriel and I formed quite a young central partnership. Jimmy was an aggressive wing half, fiery, brash and had a terrific right foot. Jimmy got stuck into opponents. Brian Harris was a good all-rounder, he played on the left wing, so had plenty of skill on the ball. Brian was a real character. Jimmy, Brian and I worked as a defensive unit with the full backs. We played a swivel system. If the ball was up the left, I'd cover Ray and Tommy would cover me. If the ball went to the right, I'd cover Tommy and Ray would move over. We really only played with three at the back because Jimmy didn't play as a true centre half. While I stayed back, Jimmy and Brian pushed up towards midfield to support the attackers.

Alex Scott was called 'Chico' because he looked Mexican. He was red-hot fast and did exactly as wingers should do, get down the flank and get the ball over. On the other flank was Derek Temple. Derek was very quick and had a great shot. He was all right foot, would cut in from the left and score wonderful goals. Derek was very cool, modest and a perfect professional. Mike Trebilcock was an unknown quantity and came in so late his name didn't appear in the match programme. Mike would play just 14 games for Everton, including those two in the FA Cup when he replaced Fred in the semi-final and final. Being thrust into the biggest stage of all, to Mike was like manna from heaven and he would made his mark.

Alex Young was dubbed the 'Golden Vision' and is still revered at Everton. He was a very skilful player. Alex wasn't outstanding on muddy pitches and suffered with blisters. Supporters used to send in all kinds of remedies, but they never worked. Mainly right-footed, Alex was deceptively good in the air. Colin Harvey was some player. Colin could keep going and had a tank that was phenomenal. Colin didn't score as many goals as he should have, but was quick, skilful and a marvellous asset to the team.

Under police escort, the drive to Wembley was memorable. Supporters were wishing they could be with us on the bus and the nerves almost made us want to be outside with them drinking a pint! Of course, there were nerves, but as you approached the stadium, you knew it was time to get on with things. We had the usual walk around the pitch and it was good to be back at the Twin Towers because the last time I'd played there was for England in the Home Internationals in 1962. It was a big day and there were thousands of Everton fans willing us on, with many more watching on TV. We knew that the match was being screened around the world, but all that disappears as you focus on the match in hand.

We went into the match as favourites because we had not let a goal in throughout the cup run, a total of 660 minutes, and had finished higher in the League. During the regular season, we'd played both encounters in the opening month, which was no guide. Wednesday won at Hillsborough 3-1, while we'd claimed a 5-1 victory at Goodison.

We won the toss to be in the North dressing room and there was a tense atmosphere. Many of the team had not played at Wembley before and there were nerves etched on players' faces, even the practical jokers in our team. After our final instructions, lining up in the tunnel and walking out was a special moment. The roar from the crowd is amazing and after the introductions to dignitaries, it was game on.

Wednesday came right at us from the kick off, playing confident, direct football. Having not let a goal in during the cup run, our so-called impregnable Everton defence was breached in the opening minutes. From a throw-in, David Ford pulled the ball across our penalty area, Jim McCalliog picked it up and cut inside before trying his luck with a shot that Westy had covered, only to be wrong-footed by a deflection off Ray Wilson.

The goal put their tails up and was a shock to us, but we quickly got into the game. Alex Young appeared to have equalised only for the referee to disallow his effort. Then when Wednesday keeper Ron Springett pulled

Alex down our appeals for a penalty were turned down by Mr Taylor. No matter how much possession we had, the Wednesday defenders played well and kept us away from creating a clear opening. It was disappointing, but we were not too disheartened at half time in the dressing room. Harry told us play to our strengths and the goals would come.

On the resumption, however, we were soon in deep trouble when four Everton defenders, myself included, made a poor attempt at tackling Johnny Fantham. Westy parried Fantham's shot, but the ball rebounded off his chest for David Ford to knock in a simple goal for a 2-0 lead. It was a gift from our part and we now had a mountain to climb if were to win the Cup.

Only 33 minutes remained and I remember actually thinking, "we are going to have to win the Cup next year," because you should never lose when you are 2-0 up. However, we had to keep going because it is never over until the final whistle. Psychologically I think Wednesday also thought they'd won the game because their concentration lapsed and we pulled a goal back immediately. Suddenly it was game on again.

I didn't always go up for corners. I only scored twice in over 500 games and was a better header in our area, but with us being two behind we pushed men forward. I remember looking over my shoulder when Derek Temple's cross came over and then I tumbled onto the floor in a heap with a couple of Wednesday defenders. I was on my hands and knees as Mike Trebilcock fired home a great right-foot half volley past Springett. I've often joked that if I had not gone up we may not have scored!

Now we had the ascendancy. Within five minutes, we were level when Sam Ellis headed an Alex Scott free kick out to Mike, who again smashed the ball home with his lethal right foot. Our supporters went crazy. Two diehard supporters could not contain their joy and congratulated Mike on the pitch. One was Eddie Kavanagh, who, cheered on by 100,000 supporters, and, no doubt, millions on television, left a number of policeman in his wake as he ran across the Wembley pitch in jubilant celebration.

Eddie was eventually caught minus his jacket by a policeman with a flying rugby tackle before being escorted from the ground by six officers. I collected a discarded policeman's helmet and handed it back, but could not resist wearing it briefly. I'd actually played with Eddie in the Everton youth team in 1957 and recognised him and I tried to inform the referee of that fact as the police chased him round Wembley. Eddie told me later that he actually got back in to the stadium in time to witness the crowning moments of the match. Eddie died some years ago. His run across the Wembley pitch is his claim to fame and in many ways is as memorable to Everton supporters as the game itself.

Mike's goals justified Harry's decision to play him and now we scented victory. Wednesday were shell-shocked; we could see they had gone. Mike almost grabbed a third goal before, ten minutes from time, our comeback was complete when one of Wednesday's best players, Gerry Young, failed to trap a punt up field by Westy. Derek Temple, cool as a cucumber, picked up the loose ball, and raced 35 yards unopposed before slotting it into the corner of the net past Springett.

It was a magical moment for us, but a cruel one for Gerry. As a defender, you could not help but feel some sympathy, but not at that moment. It was an amazing feeling to be ahead and have one hand on the Cup. In my mind there was no way back for Wednesday. We urged each other not to let the game slip, but we did not need to worry as Derek's goal proved to be the match winner.

Because of our comeback, there was a mixture of relief, elation and shock at the final whistle. Before the final, pundits argued that we were lucky to get to Wembley and wondered how we'd react to going a goal down. We gave them the perfect answer. There was a group of ecstatic players behind me when it was time to collect the FA Cup from Princess Margaret. It was a real honour captaining the team in the final and it was a thrill to go up the Royal Box steps. I remember thinking at the time, "don't drop the Cup!"

Despite his disappointment at missing the final, I was delighted that Fred Pickering joined us on the lap of honour because he'd scored crucial goals during the run. It was important he shared our moment of triumph. Harry joined in the celebrations and we carried him off the pitch at the end. We drank champagne out of the Cup, but not until we'd been pictured drinking a pint of milk due to our sponsors. We celebrated at an official banquet at the Grosvener House and travelled back the following day by train. Arriving in Liverpool was murder with all the fans, but you felt the bee's knees on the open-top coach showing off the trophy to supporters decked out in blue and white and then meeting the Lord Mayor.

With Liverpool winning the Cup a year earlier, there had been an added pressure on us to win, especially as they won the Championship that season. The rivalry was intense, we won a title, then they won it; they won the Cup, then we won it. It's sad at the moment that Everton can't compete because in the '60s, it was tit for tat and the town was buzzing.

The World Cup was about to start in England. I wasn't selected for the original 28 that toured Scandinavia from which the final 22 would be chosen, but after the final, Harry rang me to ask if I wanted to join the squad because they only had one centre-half, Jack Charlton. Ron Flowers was going to double up as a wing half and centre-half. However, I'd arranged to get married so declined.

Of course, with England winning the World Cup, players and supporters alike could not wait for the new season. We played Liverpool in the Charity Shield; Roger Hunt scored the only goal. During the close season, we signed Alan Ball, so had two World Cup winners in our side as Ray Wilson also played in the famous win over West Germany. During the season we improved our League position to finish sixth. I remember a cracker at home to West Brom that we won 5-4 and a packed Goodison saw a thriller against Liverpool when we came out on top 3-1. We also defeated Liverpool in an FA Cup fifth round clash before falling at Nottingham Forest in the quarter-finals, which was a big disappointment.

In 1967/68, we finished fifth and enjoyed another thumping win over West Brom, this time 6-2, but they got their revenge in the FA Cup final. It was fantastic to be back at Wembley after overcoming Southport, Carlisle, Tranmere, Leicester and Leeds. We always changed tactics for teams when necessary and in the semi-final against Leeds, our centre-forward Joe Royle made sure Leeds' keeper Gary Sprake cleared a ball whenever possible with his weaker left foot. Gary fluffed a kick, Jack Charlton handled Jimmy Husband's goalbound shot on the line and Johnny Morrisey stuck away the penalty for a 1-0 win.

How we lost the final, I'll never know. We were heavy favourites after defeating West Brom at the Hawthorns in the March on a day when Alan Ball scored four goals, yet Jeff Astle hit a great shot home in extra time at Wembley after his first effort ricocheted off Colin Harvey. We had enough chances to have buried them in the ninety minutes, but unfortunately, none of our headed chances fell to big Joe.

The following season, we finished third behind champions Leeds United and played some terrific football. I remember hammering Leicester City 7-1. Leicester went on to reach the FA final, defeating holders West Brom in the semi-finals, while we went out in the other semi at Villa Park to a last minute goal against Manchester City. Losing at Wembley is dreadful, but going out in a semi-final is far worse. Losing semi-finals, you appreciated winning all the more.

In 1969/70, we lost in the FA Cup fourth round to Manchester City again, but had the Division One title on our minds again with the season compacted due to the impending World Cup finals. We wrapped up the title, while Leeds finished runners-up in both the League and FA Cup. By now, Colin Harvey had formed a great partnership with Howard Kendall and Alan Ball. The media made out that they were the reason we won the Championship. We used to joke with them by asking what the other eight of us were doing!

As with Manchester United the year we won the FA Cup, a backlog of fixtures proved too much for Leeds, which was something we experienced in the coming season when Liverpool caught us on the rebound of a European Cup semi-final clash with Panathanikos. We'd battered Panathanikos at Goodison, but only drew 1-1 and then drew 0-0 in Greece to exit on away goals, which was heart breaking. The 1970/71 campaign would be my last for Everton as Roger Kenyon started to gain selection and an Achilles tendon injury in September 1972 would ulti-mately end my career.

Looking back, I was very fortunate because I achieved all my ambi-tions. I played for my local team and won both the Division One title and FA Cup in addition to representing England in the 1970 World Cup finals. Every team had great strikers such as Denis Law, Jimmy Greaves, Wyn Davies, John Radford, Ian St. John, Mick Jones, Ron Davies and Derek Dougan, who tested your skills every week. There was far more competi-tion in our day. Up to ten teams could win the League in any one season and the FA Cup was basically a bit of a lottery, which only served to make it more magical as anthing could happen.

Winning the Cup was a marvellous memory, but it all happened so quickly. Supporters still ask me what is was like to skipper Everton to the FA Cup triumph, but you are so euphoric, everything just flashes by. There is no time to take it in at the time. You want to, but it's not possi-ble. Thirty years on, Ray Wilson, Derek Temple and I attended a Cup final reunion and it was great meeting all the Wednesday lads again. We had a great night. The camaraderie has not disappeared and that summed up the era in which we all played.

PAT JENNINGS   1967
GOALKEEPER 1964–1977

BORN 12 June 1945, Newry, Northern Ireland
SIGNED May 1964 from Watford
SPURS CAREER 676 games, 1goal
HONOURS FA Cup Winner 1967, 1979, League Cup winner 1971, 1973,
UEFA Cup 1972, 119 Northern Ireland caps
LEFT Transferred to Arsenal, August 1977

One of the world's great goalkeepers, Pat Jennings played over 1,000 games
in a glittering 22-year career. At Spurs, Jennings claimed FA Cup, League
Cup and UEFA Cup winner's medals; he also famously scored in a 1967
Charity Shield thriller against Manchester United and was a UEFA Cup
finalist in 1974, before joining North London rivals Arsenal. Footballer of the
Year in 1973, Jennings was PFA Player of the Year in 1976, the same year he
received an MBE for services to football. Northern Ireland's most celebrated
international with 119 caps, Jennings was outstanding in the 1982 and 1986
World Cup finals. A goalkeeping coach at Tottenham since 1993, Jennings
was inducted to the English Football Hall of Fame in 2003.

Tottenham Hotspur 2 v Chelsea 1

FA Cup final
Saturday 20 May 1967

Wembley Stadium
Attendance 100,000
Gate Receipts £109,649

Spurs win the first all-London final and their own third of the Sixties

Teams

Bill Nicholson	**Managers**	Tommy Docherty
Pat Jennings	1	Peter Bonetti
Joe Kinnear	2	Alan Harris
Cyril Knowles	3	Eddie McCreadie
Alan Mullery	4	John Hollins
Mike England	5	Marvin Hinton
Dave Mackay (capt.)	6	Ron Harris (capt.)
Jimmy Robertson	7	Charlie Cooke
Jimmy Greaves	8	Tommy Baldwin
Alan Gilzean	9	Tony Hateley
Terry Venables	10	Bobby Tambling
Frank Saul	11	John Boyle
Robertson 45, Saul 67	**Scorers**	Tambling 86

Referee: K Dagnall

I ENJOYED MANY HIGHLIGHTS during my professional football career in both the domestic and international arenas, and among the great stadiums I played at was Wembley. As a one-off, appearing in a cup final or for Northern Ireland in an international was always special. In six finals at the Twin Towers for Tottenham Hotspur and Arsenal, I came away as a winner on four occasions, which was fantastic.

Growing up in Newry, I didn't dream about becoming a professional footballer because Gaelic football was the main sport. At Abbeycrombie Junior School, then St. Joseph Intermediate School, I played midfield, which would in the future benefit me as I was jumping, challenging players and catching the ball continually. Like lots of kids, I enjoyed football and after school, we would throw down a couple of coats for goals. I went in goal, probably because I enjoyed throwing myself about and if we didn't have enough players for an 11-a-side or five-a-side match, a few mates would try and score goals past me. I quickly developed my skills.

I played in a U-19 League when I was 11, but it only ran for one season before reverting to Gaelic football. They were street teams and around 1,000 people watched the matches. The next day at school, I knew that all my mates had seen me playing with the big boys. I returned to playing Gaelic football for my school until I left at 15 when I began work at a timber mine.

My brother played football for Newry Town. We'd played together in the U-19 League, so he suggested I trained with the team because I might get a game. After a month, I was selected to play. We won the Irish Junior Cup. I moved onto Newry United, who were playing in the Irish B League in Northern Ireland. It went well and the chairman told me that he had forwarded my name to try out for the Irish Youth team that was competing in a European tournament in England. A trial match between players from the North and South of Ireland was taking place in Dublin. The best would represent Ireland.

I was 17, and my first reaction was that I'd never been away from home. In fact, I'd never been further south than Dublin or north than Derry. I played in the trials and must have impressed because I was soon on my way to England where we were based at a Butlin's holiday camp in Bognor Regis. It was incredible; I'd been playing only a few weeks, everything happened so quickly. We played well and met England in the final at Wembley.

I'd heard about Wembley and seen it on television because we watched the FA Cup final every year. We didn't own a set ourselves, so crowded around my aunt's. Cup final day was a highlight of the year. All the kids supported British teams, but we also followed the fortunes of Northern Ireland international Peter McParland because he lived down the road in Chapel Street. Peter starred for Aston Villa and scored two goals when they won the FA Cup in the 1957 final against Manchester United. There was nothing like a big match. When Northern Ireland played at home, my dad somehow always got tickets. I loved the atmosphere.

Arriving at Wembley was unbelievable and although we lost the final, it was a tremendous experience. The tournament was a shop window for many players. Of the Irish team, Dave Clements played for Everton, while Sammy Todd went to Burnley. England had John Hollins and Ron Harris on Chelsea's books, Tommy Smith at Liverpool, John Sissons at West Ham and Jon Sammels at Arsenal. Only one English player wasn't signed up.

Playing at Wembley gave me an opportunity because when I got home, Watford and Coventry City from Division Three approached Newry Town. Jimmy Hill was Coventry manager and Professional Footballers Association chairman, but a deal was done with Watford.

There were four games left in the 1962/63 season. Watford were in trouble, but managed to finish two points clear of the relegated teams. I played the final two games and then for most of the next season when we developed into promotion candidates. It was a tremendous battle, but we finished just two points behind Coventry and Crystal Palace. It was bitterly disappointing, but more for the established players. I was starting my career and felt an opportunity would arrive.

I didn't have to wait long because our manager, Bill McGarry, who was just starting out in management and went on to be successful at Wolves, told me that Tottenham Hotspur manager Bill Nicholson had enquired about me. I was delighted because Spurs were a top side. Tottenham had won the double in 1960/61, the FA Cup the following year and then the European Cup Winners Cup in 1963, so for me this was the team. I joined in a £27,000 deal.

Bill Nicholson gave me my debut in the opening game of the 1964/65 season. We defeated Sheffield United 2-0 and I kept my place until the New Year when Bill Brown in the main played. I was pleased how things had gone and particularly enjoyed a 3-1 win against Arsenal in my first derby match against our North London rivals.

I arrived at an exciting time because Tottenham was developing a new team. Cyril Knowles arrived just before me and a number of younger players such as Alan Mullery, Jimmy Robertson, Phil Beal, Alan Gilzean and Frank Saul were making their mark. Jimmy Greaves had signed a few years earlier and was a fantastic striker. Club captain Dave Mackay missed that season with a broken leg, but was inspirational behind the scenes. Crowds were massive and football was booming. I went with the flow because a couple of years earlier I was playing in the Irish B League. It was a great set up at Tottenham and there was tremendous banter.

Bill Nick and Eddie Baily were the management team and made sure we were a well-disciplined club. Bill was so professional, the training sessions were always enjoyable and he put together training programmes that still occur 40 years on. Bill Nick was way ahead of his counterparts. I have not heard much new from any manager since, but one major improvement is that there are now specialist goalkeeping coaches, a role I enjoy.

At Tottenham, I had no goalkeeping coach. When I joined Arsenal in 1977, double-winning keeper Bob Wilson came in twice a week. That was the first time I had specialist coaching and I was in my early 30s. Arsenal was one of the first top flight clubs to go down that route. Today all clubs have followed suit. At Tottenham, now Hans Segers is full time; I assist and love the involvement. Training has improved handling, catching, angles, kicking, in fact everything a goalkeeper does in a match.

In the early part of my career, goalkeepers were only used for practice matches or shooting practice, but it was never what we wanted, it was what the forwards wanted. All players did the same training. Nowadays when outfield players go off to develop skills, goalkeepers do specialist exercises. It may sound amazing, but the three goalkeepers in Tottenham's squad in the sixties went to a corner of the field, knocked the ball to one another and just worked on a few things.

Back in the summer of 1965, it was an exciting time for me because not only was I playing professional football at the highest level for one of the best sides in the country, but I was earning great money in comparison to what I was earning when cutting timber in the mines. I went from £5 a week to £25 at Watford and £40 at Tottenham, which was far higher than the average working wage. It was fantastic, but we knew how lucky we were because not so long before, footballers were earning a maximum weekly wage of £20.

By now, I had gained my first full cap for Northern Ireland, which was a great honour. I made my debut alongside George Best against Wales in 1964. We had the likes of George and also Derek Dougan, but there was little strength in depth, so we struggled against big nations. I was busy, which pushed my skills to the limit, but maybe I was too busy at times.

During the 1965/66 campaign, again I shared the goalkeeping duties with Bill Brown. Bill began the season in goal before I played in a televised match on *Match of the Day*, which was in its second season and proving popular with supporters. We thumped defending champions Manchester United who had the likes of Bobby Charlton, Denis Law and George Best in their side 5-1. It was a brilliant performance and we got rave reviews. I also played a few weeks later when they hammered us 5-1 at Old Trafford, a match also televised.

These games, a 4-3 win over Fulham and 5-5 draw with Aston Villa in consecutive home matches summed up attacking football in the mid-60s, but it also illustrated Tottenham's inconsistency. However, we always played football if possible. That was our style, Spurs supporters expected it, but we were shipping goals and had to tighten up.

The draw at home to Villa was particularly frustrating because we were 5-1 up at half time and would have lost in the last minute if Alan Mullery had not stopped a shot on the line. I also played in the FA Cup for the first time and after wins over Middlesbrough and Burnley, Preston knocked us out, which was particularly disappointing as they were in Division Two. It was an upset and illustrated how unpredictable the competition could be.

Following the World Cup, we returned for pre-season training. England's success created tremendous excitement for the new campaign. Every pre-season I never had a problem. I was always in the top six in sprinting and exercises. I was about to cement my place in the first team, while Mike England and Joe Kinnear would become regulars in defence alongside skipper Dave Mackay, now fully fit again and Terry Venables, newly arrived from Chelsea, in midfield. Because of the 1961 double team, expectations among supporters were always high. There was pressure on the players and Bill Nick to win a trophy or finish in the top three. Although no honours had come our way since the 1963 Cup Winners' Cup triumph, we felt confident and Bill expected us to be challenging.

We began the 1966/67 season well and enjoyed our best opening to a League campaign since my arrival. Among eight victories in the opening 11 League fixtures we defeated Leeds United 3-1 on the opening day, Manchester United and Manchester City 2-1, and Fulham 4-3. Jimmy Greaves, despite his bitter disappointment in missing the World Cup final due to injury, was on fire, scoring in seven successive games. Our first home defeat came against Blackpool, a match I missed through injury, and it proved the start of a worrying spell when we lost five games in the next six matches, but we soon bounced back and sent Tottenham supporters into the New Year on a high following a 4-0 victory over Newcastle United.

We played 4-4-2 with wingers. After the 1966 World Cup we were the first team to use Cyril and Joe as attacking full backs. Bill Nick encouraged us to play one and two-touch football. He preached this week in and week out in training. Joe would be playing like a right-winger, Cyril as a left-winger, but that was Bill Nick; if there was space on the wing, he expected us to exploit it. We had to find and play in space. We also had to strive to be entertaining; it was not good enough to just win.

This season was the first time Spurs played in the League Cup. We lost at West Ham, which was disappointing because, although the competition did not have the history of the FA Cup, it was a way into Europe. For players, it was great facing foreign teams. It was different tactically and a challenge. The final was also at Wembley for the first time, so now our only route was in the FA Cup.

During January 1967, I married Eleanor Toner, like me from Newry, and following a 2-0 win over Arsenal,, we lost at title-favourites Manchester United. It was a blow, but we were riding high in the League and looked forward to the FA Cup where we were among the favourites. Playing in a cup match, the atmosphere always had an edge and travelling to lower and non-league clubs in particular was not easy. In the FA Cup, it was tough in early rounds because often pitches were rock hard. It was like playing on the road, the bounce was uneven. The dangerous thing about a hard or dry pitch for a goalkeeper was coming out for a cross, especially if you had to get off the ground. People could easily take your legs away and coming down with a bump onto a hard or frozen pitch was pretty hazardous. I preferred to punch a ball rather than catch it and try hanging on. Pitches were also watered to make the ball skip along the ground, so I wore 'Bonetti' or 'Banks' gloves. They were more or less cotton; there were no 'Super' gloves with plastic grips, which only came in towards the end of my career.

We were reasonably happy with a third round tie at Division Two Millwall. It would be tough, though, and Millwall supporters were sure to be vocal. It was their cup final. We warmed up for the match with a 2-0 league win over Burnley and went to the Den in confident mood. We drew 0-0, which was a satisfactory result. Every team needs a bit of luck in a cup competition and we were fortunate. In fact, if Cyril Knowles had not cleared an effort off the line late on, we would have been knocked out. We scraped through the replay a few days later with an Alan Gilzean goal after a mistake by Tom Wilson.

Before the replay, we knew our fourth round opponents and did not complain at having to face Division Two outfit Portsmouth at home. A draw at title-chasing Nottingham Forest and win over Fulham kept our spirits up and we came through comfortably against Portsmouth 3-1. Alan Gilzean scored two goals, while Jimmy Greaves notched his first goal of the cup run.

The fifth round gave us a home tie against our third consecutive Division Two opponents. The clash with Bristol City came in the middle of a spell of three draws in the League. Jimmy Greaves saw us into the quarter-finals with two goals, one a penalty in a 2-0 win. Reaching the quarter-finals, you know that Wembley is only two matches away and the excitement builds up within the club and among fans. We had played in front of capacity crowds for all three home games and the atmosphere was tremendous.

Incredibly, the sixth round draw gave us another Division Two team, and our luck was certainly holding to miss the likes of Leeds United, Chelsea and Manchester City. Birmingham City now stood in our way and, although we knew it would be a tough battle, as we had to travel, we fancied our chances.

Away from the Cup, we were going well in Division One. The weeks leading to the Birmingham clash saw us pick up four consecutive victories including a double over FA Cup holders Everton and defending champions Liverpool. If you are winning, confidence builds for the next game. Our form was no surprise to me as we were developing into a cracking team and we needed to, having to face the likes of Manchester United, Liverpool, Leeds, Arsenal, Chelsea, Everton and Manchester City every week.

A bumper crowd was guaranteed for the trip to St. Andrew's and as expected, we had to battle hard, but were satisfied with a 0-0 draw. We ran away with the replay 6-0. Jimmy Greaves and Terry Venables scored two goals each, while Alan Gilzean and Frank Saul also found the target. Birmingham had their best chance in the first game, but failed to take it.

We knew that, whomever we drew in the semi-finals, it was going to be a cracking tie. It turned out to be Nottingham Forest, who alongside Leeds United and ourselves were chasing Manchester United at the top of the table. Forest had fine players in Frank Wignall, Ian Storey-Moore and Terry Hennessey, but we felt confident of winning as we were in the midst of an unbeaten run. In the other clash, Chelsea faced Leeds. The expectation among Tottenham supporters was enormous because we had not been in a semi-final for five years. Two more League victories came our way as our winning sequence stretched to six before the semi-final at Hillsborough.

The pressure was intense on match day. Nobody wants to lose a semi-final because of all the effort in previous ties. Early on, Forest striker Frank Wignall had to be replaced following a rugged Dave Mackay challenge. Frank was a key player for Forest, so it was a big loss for them. Jimmy Greaves and Frank Saul scored, which proved enough as we reached Wembley with a 2-1 victory. Terry Hennessey scored late on for Forest, but it was too late.

There was both relief and joy at reaching Wembley. This would be the first major final for most of our team, including me of course. For the first time in modern history, there would be an all-London final as Chelsea edged out Leeds United 1-0 in the other semi-final.

Talk among fans was now about the final and we ended the league season superbly with three victories from four games to finish third and qualify for the Fairs Cup [the predecessor of the UEFA Cup]. Jimmy Greaves scored in wins over Sunderland, West Ham and Sheffield United, but not even a run of nine wins from our final ten games was enough to catch champions Manchester United, who finished four points clear. Nottingham Forest edged us out of second spot on goal average. I was surprised Forest did so well because they'd just avoided relegation a year before, but credit to them.

We now had a week to prepare for the final against Chelsea, who, in the league, had defeated us 3-0 at Stamford Bridge before drawing 1-1 at White Hart Lane. Managed by Tommy Docherty, Chelsea had terrific players like midfielder John Hollins and fearsome defenders Ron 'Chopper' Harris and Eddie McCreadie and could beat anyone on their day. Nevertheless, we were in great form and fancied our chances. The local media analysed every possible angle and supporters were desperate for tickets. Everywhere we went; fans asked how we thought the game would go. As Peter McParland had experienced with Aston Villa in 1957 there was plenty of encouragement from my hometown Newry in letters, which was a great boost.

During the week, training was kept the same as in previous rounds. Our schedule went well at Cheshunt as we kept sharp before staying on the Friday night at a West End Hotel. We went to see *The Professionals* at a local cinema and Bill Nick gave the main team talk. Chelsea also had a great goalkeeper in Peter Bonetti. Then there was winger Charlie Cooke, who could cause a lot of trouble, while in attack Tony Hateley and Bobby Tambling would have to be tightly marked.

For all Chelsea had to offer, I was confident because we had a great side. Joe Kinnear was very steady, a good tackler and passer of the ball. Joe was one of those lucky lads who never lost a final and used to brag about it! Joe was a cocky Jack-the-Lad. Cyril Knowles had a brilliant left peg and could run all day. Cyril's tackling frightened the life out of the best wingers and he would be the one who would have to keep Charlie Cooke quiet.

There was no better centre-half around than Mike England. He could tackle, pass, score headed goals and was one of those players that was first on the team sheet. Mike was a born leader and captained his country Wales, as well as later managing them. As for Dave Mackay, he was a fantastic captain. Dave had moved back into defence by the time I arrived at Spurs. He inspired us to perform and drove us on. Dave was a tremendous tackler, a fearsome competitor and simply did not know the meaning of defeat.

Alan Mullery was a great player. We called him the Tank; he was such a strong tackler, and got up and down the field. Terry Venables had good ball control and was a nice passer. Terry liked to get it, look around, then pass it but when we needed to take the heat out of a game, he also played that role brilliantly. Terry was also the Mickey taker, a real Jack-the-Lad and had begun his career at Chelsea, only moving to White Hart Lane the previous summer, so there was a bit of needle there.

Winger Jimmy Robertson was unbelievably quick. When Jimmy got the ball, he had strength and pace to beat defenders and create chances.

Jimmy reduced pressure towards the end of a match by keeping the ball away from our goal. On the left wing, during the Cup run Frank Saul had replaced Cliff Jones, who'd played in Tottenham's FA Cup wins in the early 1960s along with Dave Mackay. I thought Frank was an unsung hero. At another club, Frank would have been a real superstar.

As a strike partnership, Alan Gilzean and Jimmy Greaves were among the best around. Dubbed the G-Men, they led the line brilliantly. Alan was a superb target man. For me it was brilliant because I could always pick him out with my clearances up field. Alan was a clever player, strong in the air, on the ground and was a good all round forward.

Jimmy Greaves was the most clinical finisher I played with during my career and I've not seen anyone since better. He had a great finishing technique. When Jimmy was one on one with a goalkeeper, he would not shoot immediately, he would let the keeper commit himself then slide it by him on the other side. Jimmy never hammered them in; he would pass them in to the net. Many times also, he would pick up a knockdown from Alan on the halfway line, set off on a dribble and score a great solo goal. Jimmy had everything, he was superb at scoring overhead kicks and was a great header of the ball; people often forget that. Jimmy was a complete natural and not just a goal scorer, often he'd link up play. People thought of him as brilliant only in the penalty box, but he could score from anywhere. Nobody could touch Jimmy Greaves.

On the morning of the match, I went for a walk with Alan Mullery, thinking through some of the points from our team talk. After a pre-match meal, it was time to depart for Wembley. At the ground, we walked around the stadium before changing in the enormous dressing rooms. I was only 21, but luckily I'd already played internationals at Wembley, so knew what the atmosphere and noise would be like. For others it was a first experience and it does hit you.

In the dressing room, I looked around and felt confident. Dave Mackay knew what it took to win. Bill Nick also had seen it all before. He came around each player with a reminder of what he expected and words of encouragement. For me it concerned Chelsea's wingers, when they liked to get crosses in and whether they would cut inside to get shots in. I also had to watch out for the centre-forward, Tony Hateley, who was strong in the air and the midfield men coming through the middle.

Thirty minutes before kick-off there was a heavy shower, but conditions were perfect on a sunny day. Walking out on to the pitch, I reflected on seeing players enjoying the moment and thought how lucky I was, but I was also conscious that we had to perform. I could not wait for the game to get started.

We were most pundits' favourites, but knew it would be a tough match. During the opening period, our plan to utilise Alan Gilzean's aerial strength worked well and we gained the early initiative. Facing Marvin Hinton, Alan's flicks caused Chelsea all sorts of problems. Ron Harris marked Jimmy Greaves tightly, but that brought opportunities for others and we went close to scoring several times. Alan and Jimmy sent Joe Kinnear clear, but his cross was too deep. Frank Saul then went close with a half volley from a great cross by Alan Mullery before Peter Bonetti had to be at his best to keep out a left-foot shot by Jimmy Robertson. Frank then headed wide when well placed.

Chelsea had a reputation as a physical side, but failed to get at us and, in Wembley's open spaces, Jimmy Robertson and Frank Saul had room to cause damage. The way the teams were set up, Chelsea had a man advantage in midfield, but early on Charlie Cooke was unable to get in a telling cross, while Tony Hateley found it impossible to shake off Mike England.

John Hollins was Chelsea's best player and I had to dive at two players' feet when he put in a great cross-shot from 25 yards. Jimmy Greaves then went close, before I was back in action after a great dribble by Charlie Cooke and just managed to push to his shot past the post. Jimmy again almost broke the deadlock with a terrific free-kick, bending the ball around the wall only to see it go inches wide. Late in the half, I tipped another Cooke effort over the bar. The score was 0-0, so it was an important stop because the first goal is crucial in any cup final.

Just before half time, we finally made the breakthrough after John Boyle was penalised. From the free-kick, Alan Mullery swept forward and had a strike at goal from distance. The ball struck Chelsea skipper Ron Harris and fell to Jimmy Robertson, who made no mistake with a low half-volley into the corner past Bonetti. The goal could not have come at a better time and we went into the interval feeling great. For Chelsea, it must have been a bitter blow.

We started the second half in confident mood and Chelsea struggled to break us down. They did go close when Hateley headed just over, but I felt another goal would come for us. Jimmy Greaves was just wide with a snap shot that almost caught Bonetti out before Frank Saul doubled our lead on 67 minutes. Dave Mackay floated a long throw in towards the danger area. Jimmy Robertson flicked the ball across the penalty area to Frank Saul, who swivelled brilliantly 15 yards out before hooking the ball past a surprised Bonetti in one movement. It was a fantastic goal worthy of winning the Cup.

In control, we nearly added a third, but Joe Kinnear's cross failed to reach Frank at the far post. Chelsea tried to hit back, but we slowed the game down then until, after Hateley headed over, I misjudged a long cross by Boyle with four minutes remaining. I could have left the ball to our defenders, but didn't. I got a nick on the cross, only diverting the ball to Bobby Tambling, who headed in a soft goal to give Chelsea hope. It was a blow, but we were in no mood to let them back into the game.

I knew that there was not long remaining. It was a matter of keeping concentration and we comfortably played the remaining minutes out without too many problems. At the final whistle, there was sheer joy to have won. For the club it was a third triumph of the '60s. No side was more successful in the competition during the decade and we'd matched the achievement of the legenndary Newcastle side of the 1950s. For me it was my first FA Cup winner's medal. It was an unbelievable moment; I was so delighted. We were the better team on the day and played within ourselves. Chelsea caused occasional problems, we weren't at our most fluent and it may not have been a classic final, but we thoroughly deserved the win.

After we all congratulated each other, it was time to go up the famous steps to receive the trophy and collect our winner's medals. Over the years, I'd seen so many players go up on television, now it was my turn. It was a marvellous moment when Dave lifted the Cup. Then we passed the trophy around on the lap of honour as supporters sang their hearts out.

In the evening, we attended a banquet and then the following day over 100,000 supporters lined the route as we went on an open top bus along Tottenham High Road for a civic reception to Tottenham Town Hall. It was an incredible few days. In the summer, I headed back to Ireland to show everyone at home my winner's medal.

We shared the Charity Shield with League Champions Manchester United following a memorable curtain raiser to the 1967/68 campaign, when I scored my only goal for Tottenham with a massive clearance that bounced over Alex Stepney's head in a 3-3 draw. We actually felt confident of further trophy success. I hoped to return to Wembley when our FA Cup defence started and was delighted when we overcame Manchester

United in a third round replay, but Liverpool then knocked us out in the fifth round. Sadly, we only reached the FA Cup quarter-finals a couple of times over the coming years.

We did win the League Cup at Wembley against Aston Villa in 1971 and Norwich City in 1973. Both were memorable events, but neither was the same as winning the FA Cup. The League Cup was less glamorous; the final was not live on television, but playing at Wembley was always special. We won the UEFA Cup in 1972, which was great, but some glamour was taken away because we played Wolves in the final. It wasn't quite the same playing against an English club as the two legs just felt like a couple of normal league games. We defeated fashionable European teams on the way and reached the final again in 1974, but lost to Feyenoord.

At the end of 1976/77, my contract was up. I had an ankle injury and Barry Daines had done well in my place, but I was hopeful of being offered a new contract. I would carry on because fitness was not a problem. When a contract was not offered, it was a shock. Although Spurs meant a lot to me, it was time to move on. During the close season, I more or less accepted an offer to join Bobby Robson at Ipswich Town, who were one of the best club sides around at that time. Bobby saw me as the missing part to a good team that included Mick Mills, Brian Talbot, Alan Brazil, Paul Mariner and Clive Woods, but the deal fell through when striker Trevor Wymark broke a leg, as they had to strengthen the attack instead.

While I considered options from a number of clubs, it was made clear to me that I was not wanted at Tottenham - even to train - as it would be an embarrassment to other goalkeepers. So I said "cheerio" to the players and staff. The Tottenham directors ignored me, which was some thanks after 14 years' service. At that point, I decided to join Arsenal as it would cause most embarrassment to directors. If any of them had rung to wish me luck, I'd have gone to another club, maybe a London club, but not Arsenal. The directors could not have hurt me more and even insisted on selling me for a profit when other long-serving players like Mike England and Ralph Coates had been allowed to leave on free transfers. I felt very let down by the club, but especially sad for Spurs supporters, who obviously weren't pleased that I'd moved to Highbury.

On the international scene, representing Northern Ireland, we enjoyed some fantastic results, especially at Wembley when we defeated England in the Home Internationals in 1972 and drew to qualify for the 1986 World Cup finals. I was 36 at my first World Cup in 1982 when we beat host nation Spain to qualify for the second round. I chose to bow out at the highest level against Brazil on my 41st birthday in the 1986 finals. I could have carried on, but decided that there was no further to go.

Looking back at my career, I was very fortunate because I had a fantastic rapport with fans at every club, but particularly at Tottenham. That was probably because, being a goalkeeper, I was so near to them. If you are doing the business then you are the hero, if not then you are in trouble. I remember going to Highbury after winning the Footballer of the Year award in 1973 and receiving a terrific ovation, which was unheard of for a Tottenham player.

Personal awards were special, but for players it was all about winning major honours. I collected five winners' medals and the FA Cup triumphs were particularly special.

The win with Tottenham in 1967 still means so much to me, as it was my first. I was so fortunate as many players never had that opportunity. Winning the FA Cup was fantastic. I was so lucky to have done it twice and it is a competition that for me will always have that touch of glamour. I would not swap my winner's medals for anything.

TONY BROWN 1968

MIDFIELD 1961–1981

BORN 3 October 1945, Oldham
SIGNED April 1961 as apprentice
WEST BROM CAREER 819 games, 312 goals
HONOURS   1 FA Cup, 1 League Cup, I England cap, England Youth
international caps, Football League representative
LEFT Transferred to Torquay United, October 1981

Tony Brown has scored the most goals and made the most appearances in West Brom's history. A stalwart for the Baggies, Brown scored a hat-trick in every competition, striking a total of nine. Blessed with a lethal strike, 'Bomber' played a pivotal role when the club battled its way to four major finals between 1966 and 1970, winning the League Cup in 1966 and FA Cup in '68. An England Youth international, Brown gained a full cap against Wales in 1971 and represented the Football League. A three-time Midlands Footballer of the Year, after brief spells at Torquay United and Stafford Rangers, Brown ended his playing days with NASL clubs New England and Jacksonville Teamen before coaching both West Brom and Birmingham City.

West Bromwich Albion 1 v Everton 0

(after extra time)

FA Cup final
Saturday 18 May 1968

Wembley Stadium
Attendance 100,000
Gate Receipts £110,064

*Jeff Astle nets a splendid winner with his weaker left foot
to settle an attritional final*

Teams

Alan Ashman	**Managers**	Harry Catterick
John Osborne	1	Gordon West
Doug Fraser	2	Tommy Wright
Graham Williams (capt.)	3	Ray Wilson
Tony Brown	4	Howard Kendall
John Talbut	5	Brian Labone (capt.)
John Kaye	6	Colin Harvey
(Sub. Dennis Clarke)		
Graham Lovett	7	Jimmy Husband
Ian Collard	8	Alan Ball
Jeff Astle	9	Joe Royle
Bobby Hope	10	John Hurst
Clive Clark	11	Johnny Morrissey
Astle 93	**Scorer**	

Referee: L Callaghan

OVER A 20-YEAR period at West Brom I experienced the ups and downs of life as a professional footballer. There were many highlights, but top of my list was the day we won the FA Cup at Wembley in 1968. Almost 40 years on, the memories are still clear of the drama we went through to reach Wembley before defeating Everton with a great strike by Jeff Astle.

As a kid, I watched the Busby Babes from the Stretford End. I was a crazy Manchester United supporter and went down to Old Trafford two hours before kick off to get behind a particular barrier for a good view. I liked all the Busby Babes, especially Eddie Colman and Bobby Charlton. United played great football, but tragically, eight died in the Munich air disaster. I remember coming home from school and bursting into tears when I heard the news. I was only a kid and did not really understand the long-term implications. All I knew was that the Busby Babes were my heroes and now they were gone.

Of course, I still followed United, but as my football career developed, watching United stopped. I played football for Columba Roman Catholic School (Manchester), St. Peter's (Wythenshawe) and St. Clare's (Blakeley) Schools, and represented Manchester and District Boys, and Lancashire Boys. When I left school at 15, I was all set to join Manchester City when West Brom's northern scout, Johnny Shaw, asked if I'd visit the club over a weekend. I had nothing to lose. I went down with my father and was impressed with the club and surrounding area. I signed for West Brom in April 1961.

Gordon Clark was then manager, but Archie Macaulay replaced him. Jimmy Hagan took over in April 1963. As apprentices, we arrived before the professionals and had all the dirty jobs such as painting the stands, cleaning the dressing rooms, terraces and boots. We didn't mix with the first team squad, but all worked hard and hoped for a first team opportunity.

Jimmy gave me my debut at Ipswich Town a few games into the 1963/64 season due to injuries. I barely slept the night before the game, but it went well and to cap a great day, I scored in a 2-1 win. I was just outside the six-yard box near the by-line, dragged the ball back and struck it from an acute angle into the roof of the net. It was a great feeling, one I'll never forget. As a kid, this is what I'd dreamt about, playing professionally and scoring. I was immediately dropped as players returned to fitness, but I'd made my mark. When I was next given an opportunity, I came in against Aston Villa and scored in a 4-3 victory at the Hawthorns. It was a great moment winning my first derby clash and I was rewarded for my early efforts with a first professional contract.

In the early days, training was stamina-based. Manager Jimmy Hagan was a sergeant major-type. The routine was lap, lap, lap. We'd have a couple of practice matches each week, but the rest of the time was spent physical training. During practice games, Jimmy would drag people off if they did something wrong and he'd replace them. Jimmy was the best player on the pitch every time. He must have been a brilliant player in his heyday because he was great in his 40s. Over the coming years, more of the tactical side came in where we practiced set pieces and the like, but there was still plenty of stamina work, especially in pre-season.

The 1964/65 campaign started well for me because I scored in a 2-2 draw with Manchester United before grabbing my first career hat-trick in a 4-1 win over Sunderland. But then a slipped disc sidelined me until the last couple of games. It was great to get on the scoresheet against West Ham in a 4-2 win. We had a useful team with the likes of Graham Williams, Doug Fraser, John Kaye, Bobby Hope and Clive Clark in the side. The campaign had also seen centre-forward Jeff Astle make an immediate impact following his arrival from Notts County.

In 1965/66, I at last had a clear run in the first team and began to develop a formidable partnership with Jeff and John Kaye. We enjoyed some terrific displays as we thumped Stoke City and Fulham 6-2. I scored in both games and found the target again in five-goal wins over Sunderland and Nottingham Forest. We also defeated the champions-elect Liverpool 3-0; I scored our opening goal, and drew 2-2 at Anfield, which was some achievement. We ended the campaign in sixth place, which was a big improvement on recent seasons.

Winning silverware was so important to every footballer, it was a major goal and we came up trumps when I had my first taste of League Cup and FA Cup action. The League Cup did not have the FA Cup's glamour and not all big teams entered the competition, but the tournament was a passage into European football, which would be a first for West Brom.

During our run to the 1966 final, I scored in every round as we beat Walsall, Leeds, Coventry, Aston Villa and Peterborough. Before the two-legged final against West Ham, as it was then, I made my FA Cup debut in the third round, but we lost to Bolton. Our attention switched to West Ham, who had won the FA Cup and European Cup Winners' Cup in recent seasons, so were a renowned cup team. They also had Bobby Moore, Martin Peters and Geoff Hurst playing. All three would shine in the forthcoming World Cup triumph.

We lost the first leg 2-1 at Upton Park, but the lads were pumped up for the return. They were banging on the dressing room door to get out on to the pitch and finish the job. We brushed the Hammers aside with a brilliant first half display, scoring four goals. I grabbed the second, and, although Peters scored a late goal, we won 5-3 on aggregate. Our per-formance was the best I was ever involved at Albion. It was my first major honour and the feeling in the dressing room afterwards was pure elation.

With England winning the World Cup, playing in Division One was the place to be. There was an amazing buzz in the country. Following the summer break, it was great seeing the lads for pre-season training, but it was tough. Roadwork was the routine in the first week and it was really punishing, especially if you had let yourself go. Over the rbeak I always kept myself reasonably fit, so it was not too bad. Each season we didn't set a target, we played our football and saw what developed.

When I'd first got into the team, we played five up front in the old W-M formation, now we had a flexible 4-3-3 system. Jeff Astle led the attack with Clive Clark and me coming in or supplying crosses. Midfielders Bobby Hope and Graham Lovett switched to wing or attack. Opponents and fans admired us because we played attractive football, especially at home. If opponents scored, we felt that we could score more, but the opening months in 1966/67 were tough.

Scoring goals was fine, leaking goals was the problem, though I doubt neutral supporters complained. Among several defeats, Manchester United, who would win the title, claimed an opening day 5-3 win before completing the double over us at Old Trafford with a 4-3 victory. Dick Shepherd replaced Ray Potter in goal, but we still struggled. I missed a 5-4 defeat at Everton and 3-2 loss at Aston Villa, but scored in welcome wins over Liverpool and Tottenham. Our Boxing Day triumph against Spurs was also memorable as I grabbed a hat-trick.

Away from league action, our first taste of European football had lasted three rounds. After a bye, I notched a treble as we defeated DOS Utrecht before Bologna outclassed us. In our League Cup defence, we progressed to the final. The format had changed now though, as the final was a showpiece event at Wembley, which was a real bonus. During the run, we thumped Aston Villa 6-1 and in the semi-finals played superbly to overcome West Ham on aggregate. They must have hated the sight of us!

The lure of Wembley attracted more Division One teams, so it was quite a surprise that we faced Queen's Park Rangers, even though they were runaway leaders of Division Three. Credit to Rangers however, they'd eliminated top-flight outfits Sheffield United and Leicester then stopped an all-Midlands final by overcoming Birmingham City in the semi-finals. Nevertheless, we were overwhelming favourites, despite our poor league form that saw us near the bottom.

Our league position was cause for concern, but we went into the match confident and could not see ourselves losing. We were massive favourites; everyone tipped us to win. To play at Wembley in a cup final was a major ambition for me and I enjoyed the build up and journey to the stadium. Unlike the FA Cup final, there was no mass media coverage and the final was not live on television, but it was still a great thrill to be playing at the 'Twin Towers'.

Going down Wembley Way was incredible, seeing our supporters in blue and white shouting and waving. I thought, "this is it." Walking out, the roar was incredible. We got off to the perfect start, Clive Clark had scored in every round and continued with two first half goals. At 2-0, we were cruising. A story went out afterwards that Jimmy Hagan said things at half-time that disrupted us, but that did not happen. Roger Morgan scored early on to make it 2-1 and for some reason we collapsed. Rodney Marsh turned on the magic with a solo goal to equalise and eight minutes from time Mark Lazarus scored the winning goal, but we felt our keeper Dick Shepherd had been fouled.

We threw the game away really because we murdered them in the first half. It was a massive disappointment and in the dressing room, nobody said a word. Everybody sat disconsolate. There was gloom, tears; we just sat on the benches stunned and dejected with our heads down. It was the biggest disappointment I experienced in football. We'd let the supporters down big time and they let us know how they felt as we went back up Wembley Way. We had a reception of some sort after the game, but every-one was crestfallen.

There was no time to be despondent, though, because we had to pick up our form and credit to the lads, we won eight of our final ten matches to finish in mid-table. One new arrival was goalkeeper John Osborne and he impressed with some assured keeping. I was also pleased to rediscover my scoring touch and enjoyed a scoring spree in the last three games in wins over West Ham, Blackpool and Newcastle United. The 6-1 victory over Newcastle was particularly memorable as I scored a hat-trick. Off the field, though, Alan Ashman replaced Jimmy Hagan as manager.

When we gathered for pre-season training, anticipation was high in the Midlands, especially for a new derby clash. Aston Villa had been the big game as Wolves and Birmingham were in Division Two, but with Wolves promoted and Villa relegated, Wolves was now the big game. Playing in a derby always had that extra spice, but we also geed ourselves up when facing the likes of Manchester United, Manchester City, Leeds United, Liverpool or Tottenham Hotspur as we faced star players such as George Best, Roger Hunt, Colin Bell, Billy Bremner and Jimmy Greaves. Because of the strength in depth across clubs, no team dominated the league or cup competitions and few star players requested transfers.

There was a real family atmosphere at West Brom, all the lads got on and visited supporter's club branches to play darts and dominoes. It sounds crazy now, but we mixed freely with fans back then and it was wonderful. We had a good night out and accepted it as part of our role. We also had a drink with opponents after a game and I knocked about with the Aston Villa lads. There was not the same animosity that has developed over recent years, which is sad. There was rivalry between supporters, but it was the era before segregation. There was good-natured banter. It was a tremendous time to play football.

We started the 1967/68 campaign poorly, but did get the better of derby clashes with Wolves, drawing 3-3 at Molineux and winning 4-1 at the Hawthorns. After exiting the League Cup in the second round at Reading, we bounced back. I found the target in a 4-1 win over Sheffield United and 8-1 romp against Burnley. Five victories before New Year, including a double over title challengers Manchester City, brought rave reviews in the press, but our inconsistent form returned just before we embarked on another FA Cup campaign.

As a player, the FA Cup was the big one, but since my West Brom debut, we had not progressed past the fourth round. Every year I looked forward to the third round draw and gathered around a radio with the lads after training for the Monday lunchtime draw. On this occasion, we were very satisfied with a trip to Colchester United from Division Four.

The competition was full of history. The first final I recall was in 1957 when Peter McParland knocked over Manchester United keeper Ray Wood on the way to winning the Cup for Aston Villa. I was upset because the Busby Babes would have clinched the double. Our League Cup final defeat to QPR had a massive impact on the players. We were determined to have a good FA Cup run. Graham Williams, our skipper, predicted that we would win the FA Cup. We had let the fans down big time; Graham was convinced we would redeem ourselves.

Everyone says you need luck to win the FA Cup and we had our share at Colchester. On paper, we should have won comfortably, but we knew it would be a tough game, especially on a compact ground. Before kick off Alan reminded us of the QPR final and told us to get at them from the start. He said, "it's their cup final, they won't allow you to play." Lower league teams don't have the same skill level so try to put you out of the game. We were prepared, but it's hard to combat a player coming in from all angles. In the 1960s, defenders got away with horrendous challenges that you'd get a straight red for nowadays.

The main thing was to get a draw at worst, but we went a goal down before I equalised from a penalty. It was a relief, but Colchester scored a minute from time through Mickey Bullock. We walked back to the centre circle feeling thoroughly dejected because it appeared we were going out of the Cup when the referee signalled a free kick to us. He'd disallowed the goal, but we had no idea why. We had survived. In the replay, we knew that Colchester could not play at the same intensity. They would defend more, which suited us. We got an early goal and easily won 4-0. Jeff scored two goals, John Kaye and Clive Clark grabbed a goal apiece.

The fourth round paired us at home with Southampton, who had beaten us 4-0 at the Dell earlier in the season, prior to a 0-0 draw at our place just before Christmas. We went behind to a Frank Saul goal, but as in the previous round enjoyed good fortune when I tried a speculative shot. Saints keeper Eric Martin went down to collect it, but the ball hit a divot, bounced over his shoulder and into the net. I was delighted, but I knew that luck had saved us once again.

A packed house at the Dell expected Southampton to win and they must have felt confident when Saul, who'd struck the winning goal for Tottenham in the '67 final against Chelsea, opened the scoring. Steeling ourselves, Jeff equalised, then I edged us ahead, but just before half time, John Osborne got clattered. After treatment, John carried on, but with our trainer telling him from behind the goal when the ball was coming towards him. It was obvious John could not carry on like that and, with no substitute keepers allowed, we had to reshuffle at the break. Graham Williams was our smallest player, but fancied himself in goal. Saints forwards were laughing when they saw him between the posts and appeared favourites to win when Hugh Fisher equalised.

We had to defend for long periods as Southampton launched the ball into our penalty area, but Graham looked assured and our centre-half's were brilliant. Just when it looked like extra time, in the last minute Jeff scored the winner. We'd pulled off a brilliant 3-2 win and it was a happy journey home. I couldn't help but think that, after all our good fortune, this might be our year.

Our win coincided with improved league form as we travelled down to the South coast to play Portsmouth in the fifth round. Jeff pummelled in a header before 'Chippy' Clark tapped one home on the line. Portsmouth threw everything at us after getting a late goal to make it 2-1, but we held firm. John was brilliant in goal and pulled off some great saves. Portsmouth boss George Smith said afterwards that if West Brom won the Cup he'd eat his hat! Whether it was sour grapes I don't know, but we were through to the quarter-finals and received a home draw against Liverpool. Bill Shankly's team had won the League twice and the FA Cup in recent years, so were a formidable team. I thought, "now the real stuff starts." FA Cup fever was gripping the club.

The clash was the tie of the round, as Leicester City entertained Everton; Leeds faced Sheffield United, while Birmingham City took on Chelsea. It was a cracking tie, but we were happy it was at home, which is all you can hope for at the quarter-final stage. We were not pundits' favourites, but fancied our chances. We warmed up by defeating Stoke 3-0, before suffering a heavy 6-2 defeat to Everton, which must have pleased Liverpool. We responded positively, however, with a 3-2 win at Leicester.

The atmosphere was electric when we ran out to take on Liverpool, but it wasn't the best of games. Liverpool came to give nothing away and kept us at bay. It finished goalless and we now faced a huge task in the replay at Anfield, which was one of my favourite grounds alongside Old Trafford and White Hart Lane. Liverpool took the lead through Tony Hateley then Jeff equalised. We held out through extra time to get a draw, which was a great result. There was a lot of pressure on us, but we had defended well, so felt confident going into the third match at Maine Road.

We were forced into making one change for that match because right back Eddie Colquhoun broke a leg in a 2-2 draw at Newcastle, which put him out for the season. The clash at St. James' Park was the start of four games in eight days over Easter. The gaffer took a risk by moving John Kaye back to defence to cover for Eddie as another capacity crowd generated a terrific atmosphere.

Playing out of position, John, in spite of a nasty head wound that needed 12 stitches, battled away and Jeff opened the scoring when he beat Tommy Lawrence at the near post. Tony Hateley equalised, but we got our noses in front again when I combined with Jeff before slipping the ball to Clive Clark who scraped the ball home. We had to defend well and John Osborne was superb. When the whistle went, the elation was unbelievable; we'd beaten the mighty Liverpool. To a man, we knew this was our turn to win the FA Cup.

The result pleased local journalists because a Midlands team was now guaranteed a place in the final as we faced Birmingham in the semi-finals, who'd caused a surprise by defeating Chelsea in their quarter-final clash. Even though at the time of the draw we had not overcome Liverpool, we hoped for Birmingham as it would mean a derby clash and they were not a Division One side. When we got our wish, the roof went off because we'd missed the big guns. In the other semi-final, Leeds took on Everton.

Only one league game took place before the semi-final and perhaps not too surprisingly, the manager rested players carrying knocks. We lost at Leeds, but our focus was on Birmingham, who stood in our way of a place in the FA Cup final. We were clear favourites and the gaffer to his credit, as in all the cup games, prepared us at the Prince of Wales Hotel in Southport. The season had been a struggle in the league, so the chairman decided the lads could get away for a break before cup-ties. It had started the previous season and we'd had that great run to the League Cup final. We trained on the beach and the fresh air helped. We bonded and it became part of our routine.

As usual, I room-shared with Jeff Astle. He liked his sleep, so there was no messing about. In the morning, I was his butler. I'd make a cup of tea and collect the *Racing Times* for him. It was our ritual over ten years. The nerves got worse as the game approached. The atmosphere at Villa Park was terrific. The gaffer simply said we were so near, don't let it slip. Alan was very different to Jimmy Hagan. He was always the gentleman and asked our opinions, but there was only so far you could push him. Everyone responded to Alan, probably because with Jimmy you didn't really have a say. You did it his way.

On the day, Birmingham played well. Fred Pickering missed early chances and that was our luck because after around 20 minutes we got a free kick just outside the box. Bobby Hope tapped it to me; I struck a shot, which the keeper could not hold. Jeff ran in to side foot it home. It was against the run of play, but we were ahead. Birmingham came at us and had more chances, but didn't take them, so we were satisfied at be 1-0 up at half time. Alan said, "you're halfway to Wembley, it's your big chance to play in an FA Cup final, give it everything."

We knew Birmingham would put us under severe pressure. They threw everything at us, so we had to rely on breakaways, but had the players to do it. Suddenly, Bobby Hope picked up the ball in midfield. I went on a run and Bobby spotted me on the right hand side of the penalty area. I took the ball into the box at an acute angle and hit a right foot shot across the keeper into the far corner of the net. I jumped up in elation; it's unbelievable the height I reached! There was no better feeling as the players congratulated me. I knew that was it, we were back at Wembley.

From being a schoolboy I'd dreamt of playing in an FA Cup final at Wembley, so to score the goal that clinched the opportunity for West Brom was a special moment. In the dressing room, there were wild, wild scenes of celebration as we all drank pop. Birmingham had created far more chances than us. They had 12 strikes at goal; we had four, but put two away. The media came in for interviews and took pictures of Jeff and me. I posed for photographers kissing my right boot. It was a great feeling despite being knackered, but the adrenaline carried you through.

A few of the lads went out celebrating and the next morning it was great seeing the Sunday papers. You think, "wow!" We were pleased to be playing Everton in the final because we didn't have the best of records against Leeds. Don Revie's side were probably the best side I ever faced, certainly the hardest. Everton was a footballing side, so it promised to be a great occasion.

Due to fixture congestion, we had three league games to fulfil. We thumped Manchester United 6-3, which was some achievement as they had reached the European Cup final and were chasing the Division One title. It was a cracking game. Jeff scored a hat-trick, Denis Law missed a penalty, while I slotted a spot-kick home. Supporters still talk about that match as one of the great games. We murdered United, but I picked up a thigh injury, so missed a win against West Ham and draw at Sunderland. I was fit enough to test it out in the final game at Arsenal. We lost, so ended up finishing in eighth place, but more important for me, I came through and was fit for Wembley.

We had a relaxing week in Southport to prepare for the final. We'd been through the routine before, so it wasn't too intense as the gaffer tried to keep everything normal. There was great camaraderie. There were no injuries and the lads more or less knew the team, except who would play outside right, which was between Dennis Clarke, Graham Lovett and Kenny Stevens, who had all played in the cup run. Graham was so pleased to get the nod because he had got back into the team after horrendous injuries from a car crash. Dennis was substitute. Alan told me later that he played Graham on the right wing to combat Ray Wilson. It was extremely disappointing for Kenny, but there are only 11 places and balance was essential.

John Osborne was a superb keeper. He commanded the penalty area, came out for crosses and was a terrific shot stopper. I rated him very highly. John was brilliant in every round of the cup run. At times, he could be unbelievable; he was the main man.

Dougie Fraser was right-back and a craggy Scot. Dougie was hard as nails, took no prisoners and screamed at anyone not doing their job. Graham Williams played left-back and was an inspirational leader. Like Dougie, Graham took no prisoners and kicked anything that moved. As captain, he was the best I played with and looked after the lads. John Kaye and John Talbot were our stoppers; nothing passed them. Both were good in the air and could play on the ground. They didn't venture up field often, they were defenders and stuck to their duties.

We called Bobby Hope 'The General'. Everything went through Bobby. He was a superb passer of the ball, had great vision and was an old style ball-playing midfielder. Bobby was great to have in your side and made goals for everyone. Ian Collard was one of the younger lads, who'd just got in the team and had a terrific engine. He was up and down the pitch and had a great left-foot. Ian didn't score many goals, but made loads and added balance to the side.

Graham Lovett played right midfield and was a terrific player, a Duncan Edwards type, which is saying something. Bar injuries, he'd have played for England many times. As a young lad, Graham was one of the best I've seen. Clive Clark was an orthodox left-winger, but cut in to score many goals. Clive was great getting into the box; he'd be worth a fortune today and probably be an England regular given that we can't find anyone to play on the left side of midfield.

Jeff was our main striker and an old-fashioned style centre-forward. We'd pump balls into the box and Jeff would get onto everything. He was a power header, without doubt the greatest header of a ball I have seen. He was good on the floor and led the line superbly. Jeff was a brilliant goalscorer, capable of 30 goals a season. He was also the big Mickey taker. Everything revolved around him in the dressing room. If you came in with new clothes, Jeff would pull your leg and on a journey to a game, he would tell jokes all the way. He was part of a card school that included Bobby, Graham, Dougie and myself. Jeff always won, he'd out psyche you! Jeff was the life and soul of the team in good and bad times; he kept spirits up. Jeff was my best mate; he was the king and the big favourite with supporters.

As for myself, Ian and Bobby enabled me to go on forward runs and strike from midfield. A midfielder generally stayed in their position back then, but I broke forward whenever I saw gaps to join Jeff and Clive. Coming late from deep meant that I was hard to pick up, which caused opponents problems. My goals gave us three regular scorers. Not many played my style at the time and it worked well.

We travelled to London the day before the game. We'd done all our preparation and the gaffer kept media interviews to a minimum. Also, there were no gimmicky photographs, but the occasion was far bigger for the FA Cup than with the League Cup. Local press always came with us. We used to joke that reporter Ray Matts was assistant manager! There was much more hype, the FA Cup has that magic about it.

In London, Jeff and I bought new suits. The night before the game, I had trouble sleeping. I did not want to slip up, so went through my mind what I would do in certain situations. After breakfast and a light lunch, we were on our way to Wembley. Jeff was boisterous as ever, telling jokes, easing the tension. We walked around the pitch, soaked in the atmosphere and gave a few interviews before the nerves kicked in as we changed.

Because of a colour clash, we wore all white with red socks. Most of the players had the odd superstition, the order they came out and so on. Clive Clark would always put his kit on a number of times. John Osborne used to go missing for a quick fag. John was the only man I came across in football who actually hated playing. He used to say, if it was a Monday to Friday job, that it would be the best job in the world, but Saturday spoilt being a footballer! In the dressing room, John was always a bundle of nerves. He'd throw the ball against the wall and drop it. We'd say, "here we go again!" But that was John. Once on the pitch, he was brilliant.

We'd had our final instructions from Alan when there was a knock on the door and it was time to go. Waiting in the tunnel was a quiet time as the nerves kicked in again; you just wanted to get on with it. Then the signal to walk up the tunnel and you can hear the buzz of the crowd, which gets louder and louder and louder, then that crescendo as you come out. I'll never forget the moment, it's incredible as the noise of 100,000 fans hits you. I looked for family and saw my Ilene with the players' wives. Then we lined up and Princess Alexandra wished us luck. It's a nervous time, then finally we could limber up for the kick off.

Pundits predicted a classic because both teams had a reputation for attacking football, but right from early on, it was not a great spectacle as defences dominated. Johnny Morrissey and Graham Lovett had half chances, but neither could take the opportunity. Slowly, both sides began to settle, though, and Morrissey tested our defence with a deep cross that John Osborne failed to hold, but Jimmy Husband failed to take advantage of the loose ball.

I had a half chance. Dougie Fraser clipped a ball in, I made a run into the box, it was going away from me and I could not get a good connection, so spooned it just over the bar. Alan Ball was in the thick of the action and set up Howard Kendall. We were relieved to see his dipping shot clear the bar. Ossy took time to settle, but showed his form when turning a Morrissey strike bound for the top corner over the bar. It was 0-0 at half time.

The gaffer said we were doing all right and to make sure we kept a clean sheet because opportunities would come. We had the opening chance of the second half when Jeff headed just wide from a Bobby Hope cross, but Everton went closer on the hour after Morrissey, fouled by Dougie, swung over a free kick, Joe Royle met it and would have opened the scoring, but for a goal line clearance by John Kaye.

Both teams continued to probe, but Brian Labone and John Hurst snuffed out potential problems for Everton, while John Talbut and Kaye were just as unruffled in our defence. Everton had great players in Colin Harvey, Ball, Royle and Husband but despite plenty of possession, we stood firm. As an attacking force we were struggling, but Ian Collard was just high with a shot before Ball had a shot smartly saved. At times, there were niggling fouls and Ball was fortunate just to get a ticking off for one challenge on Dougie.

Fortunately for us, Jimmy Husband continued to waste Everton's best chances. Firstly, a cross was going straight to Ball's head six yards out when Jimmy headed wide when he should have left it. Alan went berserk. Then with only a few minutes remaining, Jimmy headed Morrissey's pin-point cross over the top from close range. It was a terrible miss and a huge let off for us. There were tired legs towards the end as both sides settled for extra-time.

The gaffer told us to keep battling away. I had a touch of cramp, so had a massage, but we had a blow because John Kaye was struggling with an ankle injury and could not carry on. Dennis Clarke made history, as he became the first substitute to play in an FA Cup final. Denis moved to full back; Dougie went to centre-half alongside John Talbot.

We swapped ends and inside the first couple of minutes came the all-important goal. Jeff picked the ball up from Dougie, ghosted past the first tackle and tried a shot with his lethal right foot from just outside the box. The ball ricocheted back to him off Colin Harvey's knees, though Graham Lovett always claims he had an assist. Jeff caught it perfect on his 'weaker' left foot and the ball flew across Gordon West and into the top corner. From the moment it left his boot, the ball was in the net. Jeff had scored in every round. I was the third to him and jumped on his back, it was the crucial goal. "Brilliant," I thought. "That's it, we've won the cup."

Everton pushed forward looking for an equaliser and chances came as we dropped back. Both Royle and Hurst went close, but we held firm and should have settled it just before the end. Our opportunity came when Everton won a free kick and threw everybody forward, leaving just Ray Wilson as the last man. Wilson pumped the ball into our box. John came out, collected and threw the ball to me instantly. I'd already started running into the Everton half and only Ray was in front of me. Taking it forward, all of a sudden, I hear Graham Lovett running alongside me on my right, and, looking over, Dennis Clarke was on my left. We had a three against one situation. I thought, "knock it to Graham; he will make it 2-0." As Ray closed me down, I passed to Graham, but he hit it high and wide. We laugh about it now; he says that when I passed it to him he closed his eyes and waited for the roar of the crowd, but all he heard was a groan. He did waste a few precious seconds though!

Shortly afterwards the final whistle went and everyone was hugging each other. We'd done it. We'd won the FA Cup. I'd dreamt about this moment as a schoolboy and now it had come true. It was an amazing feeling. We shook hands with the Everton players and you could not help but feel sorry for them, it had been an energy-sapping game.

Suddenly, we got the signal to collect the Cup. I remember walking up; I was around sixth in line. I looked along the front and saw Graham receive the Cup, turn and lift it towards our supporters.

There was a feeling of jubilation, relief and tiredness all rolled in together. I then received my medal and immediately looked at it, which was a great feeling. Then came the team picture and I was one of the first players to grab hold of the Cup to run around the stadium during the lap of honour with Ian Collard. We went halfway around the stadium before letting anyone else have it. I jumped over a little fence and gave a few women in the crowd a kiss to celebrate. Back in the dressing room, champagne was flowing, not pop as in the semi-finals. We all had a drink out of the Cup. Losing against QPR the year before made us appreciate winning even more.

We had a banquet at the Park Royal Hotel where comedian Bob Monkhouse was incredible. The chairman quipped that he was fed up coming to Wembley. "It's the title I want," he said. Fed up of coming to Wembley, how can anyone be fed up of coming to Wembley!? We knew what he meant; he wanted improved form in the league, but his comment was surprising.

The gaffer wouldn't let the trophy go, it was in his compartment when we travelled back to Birmingham by train and there were incredible scenes at the station. Around 250,000 fans packed the route. It was an amazing sight. When we got back to West Bromwich it was chaotic, we could hardly get through to the Town Hall.

All the lads borrowed the Cup and took it to show family and friends. We'd say, "who's having it today? Nobody? OK I'll have it then." I took it to Manchester to show my family. Graham Williams was playing hell, "who's got the cup?" he'd say. "Oh, I've got it in the boot," I replied on my return. We took it the local pubs and clubs so supporters could see it as well. It was an incredible summer.

In our defence the next season, I scored against Arsenal and Chelsea as we reached the semi-finals, but we lost to Leicester. It was a huge disappointment. Graham Lovett was so sure we'd retain the Cup, he ordered a Rover car assuming we'd get a bonus. All our hopes disappeared when Allan Clarke scored late on. On the Monday morning,

Graham cancelled his order. To cap a frustrating campaign we finished tenth in the league and lost in the European Cup Winners' Cup quarter-finals to Dunfermline Athletic.

We did make it back to Wembley in 1970, knocking Leicester out on route to the League Cup final, but lost to Manchester City after Jeff gave us an early lead. The coming years would see us slip down the league as the Cup-winning team broke up. Following relegation in 1972/73, we won promotion in 1975/76 and I scored the crucial goal at Oldham Athletic that saw us promoted.

Johnny Giles was manager then and developed a cracking team as Len Cantello, Alistair Robertson, John Wile, Bryan Robson, Ally Brown and Willie Johnston came in. As for getting back to Wembley, the closest we came was in 1977/78 when Cyrille Regis was leading the line. Ron Atkinson had taken the helm, but we lost to Ipswich Town in the semi-finals. For me it would have been the perfect end to my career, but it ended as one of the biggest disappointments. We were favourites, but on the day, Ipswich were the better team.

The following season we came third, which was Albion's best league placing since finishing runners-up in 1953/54. I found the target in brilliant displays as we defeated Manchester United 5-3 at Old Trafford and Coventry 7-1 at the Hawthorns. I also broke Ronnie Allen's club record of 208 League goals at Elland Road, which was a personal highpoint. I played my final game for the club in 1979/80, before ending my career in the NASL. For some time I have worked on local radio, which enables me to see all Albion's games, which is great.

I don't have any regrets, I had a great career and achieved the things I wanted. I became a professional footballer, won an FA Cup winner's medal and played for England, even though it was just once against Wales. Just to get in the squad was an achievement; there were so many good players. To have made more appearances and scored more goals than anyone at West Brom are records I am proud to have set.

Winning the FA Cup was everything I imagined and our triumph is the last major honour West Brom have won. The thing that always sticks in my mind will always be the disallowed goal at Colchester United. To this day, I still don't know why the goal was disallowed. Fans always bring up our FA Cup triumph when we attend Supporters' Club meetings. Winning the FA Cup and going up for my medal are the highlights of my career, no doubt about it.

NEIL YOUNG

1969

STRIKER 1961-1974

BORN   17 February 1944, Manchester
SIGNED February 1961 from apprentice
MAN CITY CAREER   416 games, 108 goals
HONOURS   1 FA Cup, 1 Division One Championship, 1 Second
Division Championship, 1 European Cup Winners Cup
LEFT Transferred to Preston North End, January 1972

Neil Young started out as an apprentice professional at Maine Road before signing full time in February 1961. He is best remembered for his excellent ball control and shooting power. Top scorer in both City's Championship seasons of the '60s, besides First and Second Division Championship medals, Neil won FA Cup and European Cup Winners' Cup winners medals. A City legend, Young scored a century of club goals, but none more memorable than his left-footed winner against Leicester City in the 1969 FA Cup final.

Manchester City 1 v Leicester City 0

FA Cup final
Saturday 26 April 1969

Wembley Stadium
Attendance 100,000
Gate Receipts £128,238

*Neil Young strikes the winning goal as Manchester City win their
first FA Cup for 13 years*

Teams

Joe Mercer	**Managers**	Frank O'Farrell
Harry Dowd	1	Peter Shilton
Tony Book (capt.)	2	Peter Rodrigues
Glyn Pardoe	3	David Nish (capt.)
Mike Doyle	4	Bobby Roberts
Tommy Booth	5	Alan Woollett
Alan Oakes	6	Graham Cross
Mike Summerbee	7	Rodney Fern
Colin Bell	8	David Gibson
Francis Lee	9	Andy Lochhead
Neil Young	10	Allan Clarke
Tony Coleman	11	Len Glover
		(Sub. Malcolm Manley)
Young 24	**Scorer**	

Referee: G McCabe

DURING THE LATE 60s and early 70s, Manchester City had an attack that rivalled the best sides around. Opponents never enjoyed having to face Mike Summerbee, Francis Lee, Colin Bell, Tony Coleman and myself because we destroyed defences that included the likes of Bobby Moore, Norman Hunter, Ron Harris, Brian Labone, Dave Mackay, Ron Yeats and Tommy Smith. We won four major honours in a three-year period and among many highlights, I will never forget the day my goal won the FA Cup at Wembley in 1969.

I've always been a Blue and was born five minutes from Maine Road. I could see the Kippax stand from my bedroom window. My brother Chris taught me to play football and took me to my first game in September 1954 when City defeated Arsenal 2-1. I soon got used to the routine. Around 20 minutes from full time, as stewards opened the gates for home fans to leave, we walked in and stood at the back of the Kippax until the final whistle. My heroes were Don Revie, Bert Trautmann, Ken Barnes, little Joe Hayes and Bobby Johnstone.

One of my idols was Newcastle United striker Jackie Milburn, but I was devastated when he scored against City to win the FA Cup in 1955. Our captain Roy Paul said, "we'll win it next year," and he was right. It was a forgone conclusion; we were bound to win. I was 12 when City fans crammed around a neighbour's television to see us defeat Birmingham.

As a kid, all I wanted to do was play football. The first step was making my school team, which I did at Heald Place School. If you were good enough, you represented Manchester Boys U15. Chris did, but professional footballers weren't paid a lot and at the *Daily Express*, he earned more working two nights than at football. Chris decided to carry on working, but I am sure he could have made it as a footballer.

I played as a centre half at school and used to score more goals than the forwards. When I was 10, I played with my brother and his mates. They were 15 and big lads, but I got used to it. Without being big-headed, I was one of the best players at controlling the ball quickly, and needed to be. I grew up quickly. Playing with 15 year-olds every week then facing my own age group made it easier for me to progress.

I was soon playing for Manchester Boys and switched to inside left. In May 1959, I came home after a game one Sunday when there was a knock at the door. It was Manchester City chief scout Harry Godwin. City wanted to sign me. I thought, "give me the forms quick!" United also came in for me, but there was no chance, I wanted to play for City.

Les McDowall was manager and they had five left-sided forwards. Dave Wagstaffe, Clive Caldridge, Ray Sanding, David Fidler and myself. I thought, "blimey, I'm never going to get in the first team," but City sold Clive and Ray, then David got injured, Waggy played on the left wing, so I made my first team debut at 16 on the right wing at Aston Villa in November 1961.

Being told I was playing was a tremendous feeling. I did not sleep before the game. Travelling to Villa Park was fantastic, though I was shaking like a leaf, but the players were brilliant. When I put the shirt on there was no way that I was not going to make it. My first goal came at home against Ipswich Town. I also hit a hat-trick against Arsenal. It was a night game and pouring down with rain. It was a tremendous feeling.

City supporters were great. I was still living at home, so used to walk to the ground with them chatting about the game we were about to play. We had a bond as I had used to stand on the Kippax. I quickly became a crowd favourite - not only because I was Blue, but also because I scored goals. Supporters love goalscorers. Whenever I ran down the left wing past the Kippax stand, I could hear them screaming, "come on Youngie; give us another goal." I signed professional forms and after 12 games received a club blazer, which was a proud moment. Two goals on the final day of the season against Blackburn took my total to ten.

The more experienced players were great. I knew them all because the first team played against the reserves every week. We had Dave Ewing, Bert Trautmann, Bill Leivers, Ken Barnes and Jimmy Meadows and we played five-a-side in the gym. They bounced me off the wall. The dressing room banter was great. The Mickey takers were Barnsey, Jimmy and big Bill Leivers. Bert gave me my first pair of boots. He had them sent over from Germany. They were like slippers. When they began to fall apart, I used plasters to hold them together, I loved those boots so much; they were fantastic.

City were struggling in Division One and suffered relegation in 1962/63. Among a number of heavy defeats, Wolves thumped us 8-1 in the opening game, while West Ham hammered us 6-1 home and away, the latter on the final day of the season. Six defeats in our final eight games summed up the campaign. I did experience my first derby win, however, as we beat United 3-2 at Old Trafford, but relegation was confirmed when we drew against United in our final home game. To complete our misery, United won the FA Cup.

George Poyser replaced Les as manager, but we failed to mount a decent promotion charge despite some great displays - as Scunthorpe found out on Boxing Day 1963 when we won 8-1. Supporters were frustrated and made their feelings known the following season after a match against Swindon Town when a record low attendance of only 8,000 watched us lose 2-1. We had to leave via the back of the Kippax stand rather than the Players' Entrance in the Main Stand.

Training during this era was mainly stamina-based and there was no 'tactical' team talk as such. The team line up was changing as Dave Bacuzzi, Harry Dowd, Alan Oakes, Mick Doyle, Glynn Pardoe and Dave Connor replaced older players. Johnny Crossan was captain. We did reach the League Cup semi-finals before Stoke City knocked us out, but the bigger sides didn't enter the competition at the time. Two seasons of mediocrity saw Aston Villa manager Joe Mercer replace George in July 1965. Joe's assistant was Malcolm Allison.

The mentality at City changed overnight. It was unbelievable. I quickly realised we were going places. Joe was like the father figure and looked after us. When I first signed for City, I was on a one-year contract with a one-year option. Joe gave me a pay rise from £20 to £27. When he gave me £40 a week, I was so grateful. As I walked out, Joe stopped me and said what about a signing on bonus. I felt like a millionaire. It had not even crossed my mind; all I wanted was to play for City. Joe was a terrific man-manager.

To be a great footballer it is born in you, you have to have certain skills. Often, you hear pundits say that a player has quick feet, they don't, the player has a quick brain. Joe said to me early on that he believed there is hardly any difference between a Division One and Division Two player. The difference is speed of thought. When a Division Two player gets the ball, he controls it, looks round and passes it. When a Division One player gets the ball, he knows what he is going to do before he gets the ball, as he has already looked round. Three seconds seems a lot, but when you have opponents charging in, it is no time at all. Awareness is crucial; you must know where everyone is on a pitch; you then have options.

Malcolm would put Joe's ideas together on the pitch; tactically, most came from Malcolm. He studied Ajax, who were a forward-thinking club. In training, we played a lot of attack against defence; five forwards against three defenders then five forwards against six defenders and we had to keep the ball. Everybody learned new skills. Our movement off the ball was really fantastic.

Our fitness levels also improved because world miler Derek Ibbotson came in to train us. We became astute in every aspect of the game. We had the widest pitch in the league and had it flooded with a fire engine on a Saturday morning. On a greasy surface, as a forward, it was great running at defenders struggling to turn sharply. At first, we were not great defensively, but we could attack. But Malcolm gave us so much confidence and belief in ourselves.

Unbeknown to us the club's glory years were about to begin. We had a solid start in 1965/66 and got among the pacesetters for promotion. I scored at Southampton and Preston North End before hitting a hat-trick in a 5-0 win over Leyton Orient. The victory was the start of a 22-match run that would bring one defeat and clinch the title. With the title and promotion issues settled, we entertained runners-up Southampton for a party; the match ended 0-0.

George Heslop and Mike Summerbee made a terrific impact and in the second half of the campaign, Colin Bell made his mark. To cap a memorable season, I scored 14 goals, just edging out Johnny Crossan in the goalscoring stakes.

Away from the league, we enjoyed a great FA Cup run. Whenever we had a big cup match, there was always a different atmosphere and you get a taste for that kind of day. We reached the quarter-finals and played three games against Everton, who went on to lift the Cup. Malcolm said to us afterwards, "you have almost beaten one of the best teams in England. That is how good you are going to be." He was right. Everything stemmed from these games; we gained confidence and went from strength to strength.

Back in Division One, Tony Book joined the club, replacing Johnny Crossan as skipper. We found our feet, finishing just below mid-table and reached the FA Cup quarter-finals again. Leeds United knocked us out. I first played against them in 1963/64 when they won promotion. They were now a real force in the game. Big Jack Charlton scored the winner, but we thought there was a foul on Harry Dowd.

I used to have great battles against Leeds' right-back Paul Reaney. Paul had pace and could turn quickly. Malcolm would sit next to me in the dressing room before the match, put an arm around me and say, I've just seen that Reaney and he looks worried. I'd say, "never," and he'd say, "I'll prove it to you. When Leeds run out, Reaney will be looking at you trying to psyche you out." So we ran out, began kicking the ball around and yep, Paul's looking at me; I thought, "you're right, Malcolm."

There were some hard players around in my era and none more so than Norman Hunter. Leeds had a number of players who could mix it. They used to quip that Norman would break your legs, but I always found him hard and fair. I bumped into Norman on holiday recently and he yelled, "Youngie, how you doing?" There is still a lot of camaraderie.

I was a confidence player. Malcolm Allison used to say before a game, "the first ball you get, control it and just pass it three or four yards. Don't try and do anything fancy, control it and pass it 20 yards, build your confidence." After ten minutes, I was flying. That season, I played against George Cohen of Fulham, who'd been in England's World Cup winning side, and murdered him. I went inside and outside George, leaving him for dead. Malcolm afterwards said, "you've just pulverised England's right back." It hadn't crossed my mind as I was playing, it was just another match. Reputations never bothered me at all. I always fancied my chances against any full back.

We found at most grounds that you got your share of decisions, but not at Anfield or Elland Road. The referees always seemed intimidated. They were fantastic games though and for spectators it was brilliant to watch the likes of Geoff Hurst, Roger Hunt, Alan Ball, Billy Bremner, Jimmy Greaves, George Best, Denis Law and Bobby Charlton every week. For players also, it was marvellous pitting your wits against top stars.

We began the 1967/68 campaign poorly, but five consecutive victories demonstrated our potential. Ken Mulhearn was now in goal because Harry Dowd picked up an injury, but it was not until the arrival of forward Francis Lee from Bolton that we had the balance to compete with the best sides consistently. We had a good team, but didn't score regularly. Frannie gave us a cutting edge and was the last piece in the jigsaw for Joe and Malcolm. We didn't kick long, which was unusual because fans liked the ball played quickly to big strikers like Joe Royle, Ron Davies, Jeff Astle and Mick Jones. We played two-touch football on the floor. You had to move and we had players to do it.

We lost just two matches in a 20-game spell and that put us in the title race. Our team talk on a Friday became something of a standing joke because we were playing so consistently. Malcolm would gather us, then Joe would walk in, "same as last week lads, see you 3pm tomorrow."

Among a number of victories, we defeated Leeds United with a Colin Bell goal, hammered Leicester City 6-0 and overcame Tottenham Hotspur 4-1 in a classic match televised on *Match of the Day* dubbed 'ballet on ice'. Before the Tottenham game, ten of the City first team squad were sweeping snow off the pitch to get it playable; can you imagine some of today's top stars sweeping snow of the pitch before a game today?

Some of the pitches we played on you would never play on today. In the '60s they kept frost off with straw. Every week a pitch was different. One week it could be bone hard, then sandy, muddy or perfect, but that is where control came in. Derby County's Baseball Ground was a nightmare. Now surfaces are superb. When I see players mis-control a ball today, it's unforgivable.

Following a vital 3-1 win over United at Old Trafford, over Easter we won home matches against Chelsea and West Ham. We clinched the title with victories in our final four matches against Sheffield Wednesday, Everton, Tottenham and Newcastle United. For supporters it must have been some experience. Coming out of the tunnel at Newcastle, we looked around and all you could see was blue and white. How they got there, I'll never know.

We knew we'd win the title when we beat Tottenham 3-1. We were on fire. United played Sunderland, who were already relegated, on the final day, so were bound to win, and that meant we had to make sure at Newcastle. Because of crowd congestion, we kicked off late, so knew we were champions before the end. There were 25,000 supporters with pocket radio's screaming, "Youngie, United have got beat." I could not believe it. We didn't need to beat Newcastle, but we could not rely on United's result. In any case, we wanted to win it in style.

On an unforgettable day, I scored twice in a 4-3 victory at St. James's Park. Both were special, but one was particularly sweet and one of my best goals because I had my back to goal when the ball came over. I swivelled, caught it and it flew in. I top-scored with 19 goals. United finished second; followed by Liverpool and Leeds United.

It's such an amazing feeling winning the title because you have worked ten solid months for it. After 42 games you think, "we are the best team in England." Decisions go against you, but they even out over a season.

It took an hour to get from the dressing room to the coach and the coach was only 100 yards away. Supporters were lying down in front of the coach. They would not let the coach move; they were cheering, they were drunk. It was incredible.

United had star players, but we deserved the title. We had great players and knitted together. Yet, when we claimed the title, United went and won the European Cup. We could not believe it. It was a great achievement, but there were 15 of us in a hotel lounge in America watching and did not speak for 20 minutes. It didn't take the gloss away from the title as such, but we would have really taken over in Manchester as they were on the slide.

Before the 1968/69 campaign, we beat West Brom 6-1 in the Charity Shield and thought, "we'll murder them all this year," but we got off to a terrible start in the league and were out of the title race. The more we tried, the harder it became. Teams also got wary of how to play us, especially away, so it took time to adapt. At home, it was fine and we enjoyed a great win over champions-to-be Leeds United. We also thumped West Brom 5-1, Burnley 7-0 and Coventry City 4-2.

I scored in all four games and felt confident of hitting the target regularly. On our day we could beat anyone, the only disappointment was going out of the European Cup in the first round to Fenerbahce. We were also out of the League Cup, so now had just the FA Cup to aim for. We knew this was our chance of glory, but it depended on the draw, form, a bit of luck and so on. Malcolm believed we'd win the FA Cup. We'd watched the 1968 final when West Brom defeated Everton before flying off to America on a post-season tour. During the game Malcolm said, "we'll win this next year." There was a feeling that we would and it was a massive target for every player.

We didn't play particularly well in the third round, but we won 1-0 against Luton at Maine Road thanks to a Frannie Lee strike. Next up was a tough tie at Newcastle United. They had fanatical supporters, so we knew the atmosphere would be electric. We came into the match in fine form, as we had defeated Chelsea 4-1 and drawn at Sheffield Wednesday, who'd knocked pre-tournament favourites Leeds United out in the third round. Fans packed St. James's Park. We drew 0-0, which was a great result. We progressed in the replay with a 2-0 win. I scored our second goal and struck the ball really well.

We all worked on different areas of our game and striking a ball was something I practiced continually. I went into the gym and placed a skittle at the end. I would not leave until I'd hit the skittle ten times running, really belting it. It developed accuracy and I was able to put the ball on a sixpence for team-mates. I became one of City's best passers. Malcolm said I could play wherever I wanted, even though I was down as inside-left. He knew I would not give the ball away. I waited for Bellie to make 30, 40 or 50-yard runs and could pick him out every time. I was not the only one, though, we could pulverise teams with our passing ability.

We were beginning to fancy our chances. Blackburn Rovers away was next out of the hat for us in the fifth round. Blackburn were a Division Two side. Having home advantage would help them, but we played really well and won comfortably 4-1. Frannie Lee and Tony Coleman grabbed two goals apiece.

Our luck with the draw finally ran out. After facing only one top-flight team, we drew Tottenham Hotspur in the quarter-finals. It was at home, though, so we fancied our chances. In the other ties, Chelsea took on Cup holders West Brom, Manchester United entertained Everton, while Leicester City had the easiest looking task at Mansfield Town.

With the two top clashes taking place in Manchester, all talk in the city surrounded the cup-ties in the days leading to the games. We had thumped Tottenham 4-0 earlier in the season at Maine Road and drawn 1-1 at White Hart Lane just before Christmas, but this was a one-off. We had a tough task on our hands because Tottenham had great players in the likes of Pat Jennings, Cyril Knowles, Mike England, Alan Mullery, Terry Venables, Jimmy Greaves and Alan Gilzean. We always had entertaining matches against Tottenham; they played attractive football and had won the FA Cup three times during the '60s, most recently in 1967.

Their danger man in particular was Jimmy Greaves. I remember one match against them. Tottenham had a free kick and Jimmy stood on the end of the wall. Most teams would have had a shot, but they passed it to Jimmy with four players around him. His skill factor was unbelievable; bang, straight in the net. I'd seen him on television, but when you are close up and see the balance and skill factor Jimmy possessed, it was tremendous, you could not get near him. The match was a tremendous battle and we came through with a Frannie Lee goal.

In the semi-finals, we drew 1966 winners Everton; the other tie was between West Brom and Leicester City. Everyone tipped Cup holders West Brom to make it through to Wembley, but that was not our concern. Everton was, and it would not be easy, as they had done the double over us during the season, winning 2-0 at Goodison and 3-1 on Boxing Day at Maine Road. With the likes of Gordon West, Brian Labone, Alan Ball, Colin Harvey, Joe Royle and Johnny Morrissey against us, it would be tough.

Any FA Cup semi-final is a huge match, which is why they are normally not great games to watch. Its real cut and thrust stuff because it's winner takes all. We stayed at a hotel and the night before the game spoke about the challenge. It was very intense; we knew that so much was at stake. Malcolm made it clear we were playing one of the top teams in Europe, so had to play well. Everton had numerous internationals, but he was convinced that if we played well, we'd win.

It was a tense game and both teams had chances to win. It looked like it could go to a replay. Late on I played a one-two with Bellie, which got me near to the halfway line, another one-two with Frannie put me through, then I blasted it. I thought it was a goal all the way, but it hit West on the elbow and went out for a corner. The ball came over and Tommy Booth, who'd broken into the side earlier in the season, crashed it in. No way were Everton coming back from that.

We'd won the Division One and Two titles, but this was a different feeling. There was pandemonium in the dressing room, champagne came out. After about 15 minutes, I sat down and it slowly began to sink in, I was at Wembley. For me, this was my first semi-final and it was a fantastic feeling, pure relief to have won because I might never get another chance.

For us all, this was our first cup final and for most, our first game at Wembley. This is where Joe came into his own because he was so calm and it passed on to the players. Yes, we were in the FA Cup final, but we were at Wembley to win. There was no, do this and do that. Joe was so calm.

As a kid, I always looked forward to the FA Cup final and when I became a City player, it was no different. The final was televised around the world and I was playing for my club. We were clear favourites because Leicester, who'd surprisingly beaten West Brom, were relegation-bound. During the season, we lost 3-0 at Filbert Street, but had defeated them 2-0 earlier in the month. More significant, we had proved a bogey team to them in cup games because we had played Leicester in the FA Cup for the past three seasons and won twice. We had also won two League Cup ties in the same period.

I scored the winner in an FA Cup tie in '66. Gordon Banks was not happy! He knew where the ball was going and dived, but my scuffed shot went under his body. I did mis-hit the ball and sometimes that is the only way you can beat great keepers, and Banksy was the best around. Four wins in five cup-ties gave us all the confidence we needed. Leicester had dangerous players in Andy Lochhead, Mike Stringfellow and Allan Clarke, but we had a much stronger side.

Harry Dowd had regained his place in the side after recovering from injury. Dowdy was a solid keeper, who did nothing spectacular, but he was always reliable. Dowdy was also one of the jokers. Tony Book made his top-flight debut at 31 and became a great full back. He was an inspirational skipper, solid as a rock, hard, quick and reliable. He picked up the Footballer of the Year award during the season, which showed how far he had come. Glyn Pardoe started as a forward, but Malcolm converted him to full back. I don't know why, but it worked really well because he was solid. Very few players got the better of Glyn, who was on many occasions a utility player, playing everywhere except goalkeeper.

Mike Doyle started out as a centre-forward, but made his name as a determined defender, who was eventually appointed club captain. Mike was very hard, good in the air, did not score many goals, but was a great tackler and a solid player. Alan Oakes was dependable and had a great left foot. Oakey was a typical City player; he would run all day. There were more flamboyant players, but none as consistent. Tommy Booth was one of the best centre-halves around when it came to ball control and distribution. Boothy lacked a bit of speed, but made up for it with his positional sense.

Mike Summerbee was a very direct winger and hard to knock off the ball. Mike was a great crosser of the ball, caused havoc for defences and made loads of goals. Colin Bell was a hell of a player. If he had my left foot, he would have been one of the best three players in the world. Bellie was brilliant in the air; his control was great, had pace and would never stop running. Bellie had tremendous stamina; he was a terrific player and an out and out goal scorer. Over 10 or 15 yards, he was devastating.

Frannie Lee led the line and gave us a cutting edge in attack as he was hard to knock off the ball. An expert penalty taker, his powerful strike brought loads of goals. I had a good left foot and brought balance to the side. I was never the best header or tackler, but made up for that with my distribution skills and scored a number of goals. Tony Coleman was next to me on the left wing. Tony was a very reliable and an underrated player. Whenever I got into difficulty, I always knew that I could lay it off to Tony to get us out of difficulty.

The journey to Wembley was lively; we were up for the game. Seeing all the fans was great. After walking around the pitch, back in the dressing room, I got a sense that it was our day. Confidence was sky high. Also, with Leicester wearing blue and white, we wore the lucky striped shirts just as the '56 team did.

We'd had our main team talk on the Friday when Joe and Malcolm went through our opponents' strengths and weaknesses. Before we went out, Joe said, there would be a lot of emotion out on the pitch, leave it to the City supporters to get worked up. We had to play our natural game.

We all had our own individual routines. Bellie wouldn't put his shirt on until just before we went out and a few of us had a crafty smoke. Walking up the tunnel, the nearer we got to the pitch the louder the noise became. Then, when you walked across the sandy part of the ground, the noise was tremendous. Despite the nerves, it was a fantastic feeling.

We made a bright start and should have taken an early lead through Tony Coleman. If Tony had hit the target, we could have gone on to score four or five. Mike Summerbee was giving Leicester skipper David Nish a torrid time, while Frannie Lee troubled Alan Woolett every time he was in possession. Our forward line was finding space on Wembley's wide pitch and chances were beginning to come our way.

Colin Bell was finding space and I had two openings in quick succession from a similar position. The first opportunity happened quickly and I hit the ball a foot over the bar. A few minutes later, as we broke forward, I could sense a chance was coming. Mike Summerbee picked up the ball on the right wing, took on Woolett, cut in along the goal line and rolled the ball across the penalty area as I ran in unmarked. I thought, "I've waited 24 years for this moment, this ball is going in. No way it's not going in," and I banged it past Peter Shilton.

You don't always have time to aim for a particular spot. You just sense the chance, hit it and hope for the best. My initial thought was, "catch me if you can!" I didn't know if it would be the winning goal as it was so early in the game, but all I'd ever wanted to do since the age of five or six was score in an FA Cup final. I had dreamt about it, it was Roy of the Rovers stuff and I had done it.

Slowly, Leicester gained confidence. They may have been favourites for relegation, but were not overawed by the occasion as many pundits predicted. Allan Clarke went close with a shot, but Harry Dowd made a great save to turn the ball round the post for a corner, which came to nothing. A few minutes later Peter Rodrigues missed a glorious opportunity from close range, but somehow failed to connect with the ball. A goal ahead at half time, Joe and Malcolm told us to keep it up; I felt that this was our year.

In the second half, both teams created more chances. Andy Lochhead missed a sitter from just a few yards out, just as Rodrigues had earlier in the game, from Rodney Fern's cross that Clarke knocked down into his path. Leicester brought their substitute Len Glover on 20 minutes from time. Almost immediately, Lochhead burst through dangerously before being bustled off the ball.

Clarke, who would join Leeds United in the close season for a British-record transfer fee of £165,000, was causing us problems from midfield with his distribution, but his efforts were in vain as Mike Doyle, Tommy Booth and Alan Oakes were giving nothing away in defence. Both goal-keepers had an equal amount of shots to save, but we got the all-important goal. At the end, it was sheer relief that we had actually done it.

We all congratulated each other. Joe and Malcolm came on the pitch; we were all so thrilled. Going up the Royal Box to collect my medal and the lap of honour were both magical moments and then we had a fantastic party at the Café Royal. Malcolm had a big glass of champagne and his trademark cigar. Joe sat conservatively, taking it all in, he was used to all the excitement and was a proud man. The day after, there was a brilliant reception back in Manchester when we went through the city centre with the trophy.

Going into the 1969/70 season, we were full of confidence, but, after losing to Leeds United in the Charity Shield, inconsistency brought a tenth place finish. Joe Corrigan was now first choice keeper, and on our day, we took teams apart. It was brilliant claiming a double over United. I scored in a 4-0 win at Maine Road before a 2-1 victory at Old Trafford. United gained revenge in our FA Cup defence, but in the League Cup, a last minute winner in the semi-finals by Mike Summerbee saw us through to the final on aggregate. I loved derby clashes and we had the Midas touch that season. We were underdogs to United until Joe and Malcolm arrived. Malcolm knew the rivalry and said we'd be the top team in Manchester. He was right.

Away from the domestic scene, a European Cup Winners' Cup quarter-final clash with Academia Coimbra of Portugal took place either side of the League Cup final. Unfortunately for me, after a hard-earned 0-0 draw over there, I missed the final against West Brom, which we won 2-1. I was back for the second leg against Coimbra, which we won with a last-minute Tony Towers goal. After beating Schalke 04 in the semi-finals, in torrential rain we defeated Gornik Zabrze 2-1 in the final. I grabbed our first goal before Frannie Lee stuck away a penalty after I had been fouled.

Four major trophies in three seasons; it was a truly amazing period for the club.

Inconsistency however ruined an assault on the league title in 1970/71 and Chelsea ended our defence of the European Cup Winners' Cup at the semi-final stage. By the new campaign, I was out of favour and joined Preston in a £48,000 transfer in January 1972, before ending my playing days at Rochdale.

It broke my heart to leave City; it was like a second home to me. Malcolm wanted Rodney Marsh and he was a terrific ball player, but Marshy did not fit into the team. If we had not bought Marshy, City would have won the league again and could have gone on from there for a few more years because confidence was sky high.

When I look back, winning the FA Cup was so special. Most of our Cup final squad were local lads and all of us were English, so had been inspired by the competition as youngsters. I doubt you will ever get that again these days. Nowadays, foreign imports want to win it, but they don't have the same feeling for the FA Cup's history. Pride and playing for the shirt was what it was all about during my era. After making my debut at just 16, they had to rip the shirt off my back to get it back off me. The City result is still the first I look for and I would love to see them win the FA Cup again at the new Wembley.

I was fortunate because I scored crucial goals in three of the biggest games in City's history, the win against Newcastle when we clinched the Division One title, the FA Cup final and European Cup Winners' Cup final. Although it may not have been the best goal I scored, my winner against Leicester City was the most memorable. The day goes far too quickly and it's not till later that you think, "I was there and City have won the Cup." You don't take everything in and watching finals now I can't help but recall moments that occurred in the 1969 final, especially the spot where I scored the winning goal. They are wonderful memories and ones I will never forget.